National Rhythms, African Roots

A series of course adoption books on Latin America:

Independence in Spanish America: Civil Wars, Revolutions, and Underdevelopment (revised edition)—Jay Kinsbruner, Queens College

Heroes on Horseback: A Life and Times of the Last Gaucho Caudillos—John Charles Chasteen, University of North Carolina at Chapel Hill

The Life and Death of Carolina Maria de Jesus—Robert M. Levine, University of Miami, and José Carlos Sebe Bom Meihy, University of São Paulo

The Countryside in Colonial Latin America—edited by Louisa Schell Hoberman, University of Texas at Austin, and Susan Migden Socolow, Emory University

The Faces of Honor: Sex, Shame, and Violence in Colonial Latin America—edited by Lyman L. Johnson, University of North Carolina at Charlotte, and Sonya Lipsett-Rivera, Carleton University

The Century of U.S. Capitalism in Latin America—Thomas F. O'Brien, University of Houston

Tangled Destinies: Latin America and the United States—Don Coerver, Texas Christian University, and Linda Hall, University of New Mexico

Everyday Life and Politics in Nineteenth Century Mexico: Men, Women, and War—Mark Wasserman, Rutgers, The State University of New Jersey

Lives of the Bigamists: Marriage, Family, and Community in Colonial Mexico—Richard Boyer, Simon Fraser University

Andean Worlds: Indigenous History, Culture, and Consciousness Under Spanish Rule, 1532–1825—Kenneth J. Andrien, Ohio State University

The Mexican Revolution, 1910–1940—Michael J. Gonzales, Northern Illinois University

Quito 1599: City and Colony in Transition—Kris Lane, College of William and Mary

Argentina on the Couch: Psychiatry, State, and Society, 1880 to the Present—ed. by Mariano Plotkin, CONICET (National Council of Scientific Research, Argentina), and Universidad Nacional de Tres de Febrero, Buenos Aires, Argentina

A Pest in the Land: New World Epidemics in a Global Perspective—by Suzanne Austin Alchon, University of Delaware

The Silver King: The Remarkable Life of the Count of Regla in Colonial Mexico—by Edith Boorstein Couturier, Ph.D., Professor Emerita

Series Advisory Editor: Lyman L. Johnson, University of North Carolina at Charlotte

National Rhythms, African Roots

The Deep History of Latin American Popular Dance

John Charles Chasteen

University of New Mexico Press
Albuquerque

First edition

Library of Congress Cataloging-in-Publication Data

Chasteen, John Charles, 1955–
National rhythms, African roots : the deep history of Latin American dance/
John Charles Chasteen.—1st ed.
p. cm.—(Dialogos)
ISBN 0-8263-2940-3 (cloth : alk. paper)—
ISBN 0-8263-2941-1 (pbk. : alk. paper)
1. Dance—Latin America—History. 2. Dance—Social aspects—Latin
America. 3. Dance—Political aspects—Latin America.
I. Title: the deep history of Latin American dance. II. Title.
III. Diálogos (Albuquerque, N.M.)
GV1626 .C47 2004
792.8′098—dc22
2003019742

Printed in the USA by Thomson-Shore, Inc.
Typeset in Bembo 11.5/13.5
Display type set in Stone Informal
Design and Composition: Maya Allen-Gallegos

Table of Contents

Preface and Acknowledgments

Just out of college in the late 1970s, I spent several years teaching English in Cali, Colombia, a city famous for its enthusiasm for dance. Like a lot of U.S. males, I feared and loathed the dance floor. In Cali, however, refusing to dance was not a socially acceptable option. Perhaps a bit relieved to be compelled, I finally enjoyed myself. Then I went to graduate school to study Latin American history and wrote books and articles about machismo, gaucho knife fights, and the charismatic leadership of nineteenth-century generals on horseback. Many historical tough guys, it turns out, were avid dancers. I read that Simón Bolívar, the Liberator, one of the great military heroes of his age, spontaneously climbed on a banquet table and danced to celebrate the final patriot victory over Spain in 1824. It was that image, in fact, that spurred me to begin research for this book in 1994. How, I wondered, did Bolívar dance up there on the table? Did he bounce, stiff-backed, in his dress uniform? Or did his body undulate gracefully from the hips, his center of gravity low, his knees slightly bent? In a word, did Bolívar dance like a modern Caribbean man, with African influence? A yawning social gap separated Simón Bolívar, an elite plantation owner conversant with the European classics, from African influences. But my research demonstrates that popular culture bridged the gap. African musical and dance traditions had begun to influence Latin American societies at all levels long before Bolívar's day.

Many, many thanks to the U.S. National Endowment for the Humanities for providing a wonderful fellowship year 2000–2001 in which to reach these conclusions. Earlier, in smaller increments, but even more crucially, support from UNC Chapel Hill's University Research Council and its Institute of Latin American Studies enabled me to do research for this book in Rio, Havana, and Buenos Aires. Chapel Hill is so many things to me: my birthplace, my alma mater, my professional home. This book could never have been written without the encouragement (and practice) provided by my friends in Chapel Hill. The spontaneous interest with which people respond to the topic of dance history, despite its unconventionality in the historical academy, always indicated that I was on the right track.

Most essential of all was the love and enthusiasm of the woman I met in Cali, all those years ago, my definitive dancing master. To her I dedicate this book.

For (and because of) Carmen

A Word on Language

Words matter little in dance, but much in dance history. Few readers of this book will know both Spanish and Portuguese, and many will know neither. Yet Spanish and Portuguese words—names, titles, untranslatable terms—must appear frequently in these pages. Sometimes, it is even necessary to use Spanish and Portuguese forms of the same word.

Readers who know little Spanish and less Portuguese, do not despair! Those who read Spanish will find extra pleasure here, and those who know some Portuguese, too, will enjoy themselves even more. But the meaning of every sentence will be plain to readers who understand only the Spanish and Portuguese that this book itself teaches. Frequently, a symbol (* or †) will be used in these pages to signal a convenient translation at the foot of the page, where it will not interrupt the flow of a quotation. When Spanish or Portuguese words first occur, they appear in italics with a definition or explanation of their meaning. Sometimes, though, readers will naturally have forgotten the meanings of these words when they reappear. Therefore, a glossary is provided at the end.

In Spanish people always say *el tango* and *la salsa,* in Portuguese *o samba* and *a valsa*—using definite articles. In English, I have left definite articles off for the sake of consistency. Speakers of contemporary English don't say "the salsa" or "the samba," though we do say "the tango" and "the waltz." In contemporary English, *the* makes dance names sound exotic or old-fashioned. It also makes them sound, well, too definite, which is unsurprising for a definite article, but also undesirable for dance history. The history of Latin American popular dance is all about fluidity and transformation. So, in this book, I speak of salsa and samba, of tango and waltz, and of all other dance forms—uniformly without definite articles.

Finally, a word on the word *popular,* as in "popular dance." While popular generally means "widely liked" in current English usage, this book uses it in an older sense (still quite common in Spanish and Portuguese), in which popular relates more specifically to "the common people"—as opposed to the elite or the middle class.

Chapter One

Transgressive National Dances?

On a March evening in 1854, an avid crowd in formal dress gathered for the first Havana performance of an international star. The performer was Louis Moreau Gottschalk, the most famous U.S. piano virtuoso of the nineteenth century. Havana's relentlessly stylish elite society liked Gottschalk's nimble variations on Stephen Foster songs like "Old Folks at Home," and they were positively delighted by his improvisations on that season's local dance sensation, "El Cocoyé." In future concerts, such as his first in the city's most prestigious theater, the Tacón, Gottschalk closed with "El Cocoyé," a medley of other Cuban dance tunes, and "María de la O," a hit from the preceding year's carnival festivities. Eventually, the Paris-trained pianist would introduce Cuban rhythms and themes to the international classical music repertory.[1]

Gottschalk's concerts were often followed by social dancing, and so, as the pianist lingered in Cuba for half a year, he steeped himself in the sophisticated rhythms of *danza cubana*, and learned to compose in that idiom. He made a point of visiting the distant city of Santiago, home of "El Cocoyé" and "María de la O," in eastern Cuba, where, far more than in Havana, popular music pulsed with the enlivening influence of nearby Haiti. Gottschalk had a family connection to Haiti, as we shall see. Gottschalk's various dalliances in Santiago led both to a brief romance and a longer infatuation with the drumming of Haitian blacks. On a later visit to Cuba, Gottschalk organized a remarkable Havana concert, putting a battery of French-speaking drummers brought from Santiago (a Tumba Francesa, such a group was called) on stage with forty pianists. Out in front stood the group's "king" playing a large drum that must have seemed, to the eyes of elite Havana, as purely African as the king himself. Nothing else about Gottschalk's symphonic composition, "La Nuit des Tropiques," premiered that night, was nearly so notable as the presence of the Tumba Francesa on Havana's concert stage.[2]

Gottschalk's presentation of the Tumba Francesa represents the gradual embrace of African-influenced dances as national symbols in many parts of Latin America—an embrace often stimulated by prestigious outsiders. Conventionally, official embrace of African-influenced national rhythms is a twentieth-century story in Latin America, yet it has powerful antecedents in the nineteenth century and before. Gottschalk exemplifies those antecedents. His family was Haitian on his mother's side, having arrived in New Orleans in the 1790s, amid the exodus of Haitian whites fleeing the French colony's great slave rebellion and successful war of independence. The nurse who raised the boy was a Haitian slave, and all his life he spoke English with a French accent. During the U.S. civil war, Gottschalk became an outspoken supporter of the Union war effort, and gave patriotic concerts all over the northern states, never returning to New Orleans. The Creole pianist spent years in Spain and Latin America and learned to speak Spanish fluently. He gave concerts in Buenos Aires and Rio de Janeiro, as well as Havana—the trio of Atlantic ports most famous for their national rhythms in the twentieth century, the very trio whose nineteenth-century antecedents we aim to explore. Therefore, we can use incidents from Gottschalk's journey to signal matters of interest.[3]

Gottschalk believed that his music, like that of his contemporaries Chopin and Lizst, could express an authentic national spirit. Everywhere he traveled in Latin America—in Peru and Chile as well as Cuba, Puerto Rico, Argentina, and Brazil—he organized enormous concerts that endorsed popular cultural nationalism. One of his standard procedures was to devise virtuosic variations on the national anthem of countries where he performed, an effort always enthusiastically rewarded by his audiences. More than national anthems, though, Gottschalk liked Latin America's national *rhythms*, local dance music styles of infinite variety, normally characterized by their basic rhythmic groove and their regional connections. Today, these musical styles, and the dances that go with them, are among the most esteemed expressions of Latin American culture.

Once this music and dance belonged almost exclusively to poor and despised people who lacked, in the colonial Spanish phrase, *limpieza de sangre,* clean blood, because theirs was partly African or indigenous American. The folk materials that Gottschalk used in his compositions, whether from the Caribbean and South America, or those he remembered from his New Orleans childhood, always had African roots. Latin America, after all, was the primary destination of the African diaspora. Latin Americans often claim African roots, not just for people of African descent, but culturally for entire national populations. More than in the United States, the idea of African roots has been linked to the "official" national identities of Brazil, Cuba, Colombia, Venezuela, and many other countries. In Argentina, Uruguay, and the Dominican Republic people downplay African roots despite their undeniable historical presence, but de-emphasis is not typical of Latin America as a whole. Whether main-streamed or downplayed, African roots are frequently at issue when defining Latin American national identities. (So are indigenous roots, but they have been much less influential in the history of Latin American popular dance.)[4]

African roots are sometimes imagined to be a timeless essence, but nothing could be further from the truth. African culture in the diaspora was a living, changing entity that involved intense interaction among diverse populations, enslaved and free, African-born, European-born, and American-born. Gottschalk's tour, again, makes the point. He visited Rio, Havana, and Buenos Aires, precisely because each was a cosmopolitan port, open to the winds of a wider Atlantic world. The music that influenced him was not the music of slaves but the music of free people of mixed race, with rhythms that sounded African but melodies and lyrics that sounded European. The idea of give-and-take cultural mixture, *transculturation* that produces something new, is another matter for readers to consider in what lies ahead. Local black/white encounters are key, but so is the cultural influence of Europe and the United States. A bit before Gottschalk's time in Rio, a journalist lamented that the capital of the Brazilian Empire boasted four theaters but no local company of actors. Instead, French and Italian companies modeled musical and choreographical styles, even the ones on display in Rio's carnival dances. Meanwhile, in Buenos Aires, a U.S. minstrel company presented its blackface version of *Uncle Tom's Cabin*. By the 1870s, blackface performances had become a mainstay of Buenos Aires carnival celebrations, an arena in which white and black parade groups (some of the black ones, too, in blackface) competed for tango glory.[5] Consequently, change and mixture are recurring themes in these pages.

Carnival is another recurring theme. The three-day period preceding Lent on the Catholic calendar has played a fascinating and little-understood role in the history of Latin America's national rhythms. In a nutshell, carnival's "anything goes" ethos facilitated white experimentation with dance styles that originated among the poor, mixed-race populace. Samba and carnival famously go together today in Rio. Havana and Buenos Aires had similar experiences in the nineteenth century. For example, Gottschalk's variations on "María de la O" made a hit among Havana concert-goers, apparently, because of its recent vogue during Havana's 1853 carnival dance season. The real María de la O was a black singer from Santiago, and a tune with her name is credited with introducing a particularly catchy Afro-Cuban rhythm to Havana's upscale social dance scene.[6]

Next, there is the matter of illicit sex. The worldly Gottschalk who had met Victor Hugo and rubbed elbows with European royalty, Gottschalk of the expressive eyes, the French accent, and the white gloves that he took off slowly on stage before each performance, was a famous ladies' man. In fact, he abruptly launched his South American tour of several years beginning in 1865 partly to duck out of a sex scandal in San Francisco. Gottschalk discussed few romantic encounters in letters to his family or in his intended-for-publication travel diary. He probably had ephemeral sexual relationships with young women not of the respectable middle class. To do so would have been quite typical, in the nineteenth century, for unmarried men of his status. In many parts of Latin America, it was typical for married men as well. A local Cuban account describes Gottschalk, between performances there, on a stroll through a black neighborhood, ogling the pretty women with an experienced eye. The memoir laments this "irresistible inclination of white men born in slave-holding lands."[7] Such liaisons were strongly associated with the popular dance venues where Gottschalk encountered ideas for his compositions—from brothels, to carnival balls, to cheap dance halls.

These "venues" bring us to the main point. Latin America's national rhythms were often *transgressive.* They somehow *crossed a line,* usually several lines at once. Transgressive dances often crossed a "color line." Because they mixed African and European styles, they introduced black culture into white society. Also, with an astounding frequency that will become plain by dint of repetition in the coming pages, the national rhythms were at the center of cross-racial sexual encounters of the kind Gottschalk seems to have had on occasion. These were generally, in addition, cross-*class* encounters between poor women and men of means—another transgression associated with this dancing. In the early days, national rhythms commonly violated the law, too. The dancing of slaves was frequently illegal without special permission. Furthermore, transgressive dances by their very character seemed to flaunt Catholic sexual propriety, liberating the lower body (more on this later) and facilitating physical contact between the dancers. To quote Gottschalk's diary, in reference to Peru's emerging national rhythm "although very picturesque [this dance was] not such as prudent mothers permit their daughters to indulge in."[8] Exuberantly lascivious lyrics frequently displayed an "in your face," nose-thumbing attitude toward Catholic morality. In colonial Latin America, this alone was enough to get transgressive dancing banned. Later, popular dance in Buenos Aires became particularly notorious for its association with prostitution—a link evidenced in many early tango lyrics—but the same association existed in Rio and Havana, not to mention the parallels in Gottschalk's hometown of New Orleans, with its "quadroon balls" and its Storyville red-light district, the cradle of Jazz. Latin America's national rhythms almost all started out as "dirty dancing."[9]

The whole notion of transgressive *national* dances seems puzzling. By violating proprieties, crossing lines, and breaking laws, transgressive cultural forms challenge social controls. Social controls, in turn, hold political structures in place. Why are transgressive dances countenanced at all, much less encouraged and imitated by the masters of that structure? And how did transgressive dances become official national rhythms? These are the main questions that this book seeks to answer. Most readers will be wondering, first, how these national rhythms are danced today. A description of modern tango, samba, and salsa follows. Before proceeding, however, a farewell to Mr. Gottschalk, with whom readers are about to part company. Gottschalk might be offended by my discussion, I suppose. But a book about dancing has to include gossip. Furthermore, Gottschalk or any of the other once-famous people in this book ought to appreciate a published reminder of their achievements. Here is a good one for our tireless touring virtuoso: Certain rhythms, melodic devices, and bass lines that Gottschalk picked up in Cuba make some of his compositions reminiscent of ragtime piano, a major genre of U.S. popular music around 1900. Since Gottschalk's sheet music was among the most widely circulated in the nineteenth-century United States, his rag-like pieces were no doubt familiar to the pianists who created ragtime. So ragtime is really reminiscent of Gottschalk, rather than the other way around.[10] (How's that for the record, Mr. Gottschalk?)

Dances are forever changing, and they are forever changing names, too. In 1830, *tango* meant something entirely different from what the word means today. It was not a specific dance at all, but rather, an event (as in, an "all-night tango") involving any kind of dancing that black people did to drums. *Samba* had a similar meaning in the 1800s. The name *salsa* dates only from the 1960s, but salsa's dance moves draw on a centuries-old tradition. The place to start making sense of change is current dance practice, the image readers already attach to the terms tango, samba, or salsa.

Today, tango has become a highly international dance genre. Its internationalization dates from the eve of World War One, when tango became a vogue in Paris. By 1913, there were reportedly a hundred Argentines giving tango lessons in Paris. But dance instructors from elsewhere, notably from Britain, learned tango in Paris and then propagated it as an international ballroom style. This was tango "by the numbers," with manuals and diagrams of the steps, eight to ten "basic movements," and a repertoire of seventy-two specific "attitudes." The international tango's choreography was "stylized into glamorous, almost balletic postures (extended arms, stretched torsos and necks, light feet)" very unlike the funkier, early tango that gestated so famously in the brothels and cheap dance halls of Buenos Aires. The international ballroom tango signaled its transgressive origins with menacing dips and bends of the woman's body. As a result, the tango envisioned by people outside of Argentina (or Uruguay) is quite exoticized and theatrical.[11]

The image is remote from tango as danced socially. But then, tango danced socially is something few see, even in Buenos Aires. The golden age of tango as a popular social dance was the 1930s and 1940s. By the 1960s, it was no longer what most Argentines danced, nor has it ever been since, despite a revival that brought interest in the dance to a new generation during the 1990s. As a modern social dance, tango is not particularly flamboyant or daring. At least in the United States, people who dance it are serious dancers whose get-togethers are really about dancing. But the tango is difficult as a social dance, especially for the man, who invariably leads.[12] The leader's part is more difficult because leaders and followers do not make the same moves. The leader must know what moves his partner can and cannot make. He must know at all times, without looking down or even thinking too hard, on what foot his partner has her weight. The couple communicates through small shifts of balance and, if things go well, they create an intimate and flowing dialogue without extravagant gestures or rose-in-the-teeth theatrics. The socially danced tango retains a bit of its old transgressive allure only in the close-embrace style of the dance, in which the dancers maintain upper-body contact all the time. The close embrace does not permit much fancy footwork, and there would there be no room for it anyway on the crowded dance floors where the style generally occurs.

Current interest in tango dancing has a clear "retro" orientation. Today dancers still dance tangos recorded half a century ago. The great tango orchestras were those formed in the 1930s and 1940s. Fortunately, that musical legacy was well recorded on phonograph discs, and these "oldies" still dominate the playlists of most tango dance venues. The greatest tango singer ever, according to almost everybody, died in 1935. Given Carlos Gardel's good looks, indubitable talent, and tragic death at the height of his career, it is perhaps no surprise that his reputation has never been eclipsed. More strikingly, though, Gardel is still *the most listened to* tango singer. Overall, the tango compositions of the late twentieth century, decisively influenced by Astor Piazzola's quasi-classical tango chamber music, have never been as popular as the tangos of Gardel's day. Piazzola and his followers used a small ensemble of violins, an occasional piano, cello, or flute, and the tango's signature *bandoneon* button accordions to create an experimental musical language rich in extravagant gestures but poor in danceable rhythms. A bit like late twentieth-century jazz bands, today's tango orchestras play to a dedicated following of aficionados but not a mass audience.[13]

Samba has seen a similar ebbing of its popularity in Brazil, and, compared to tango, it was never as much an international style. But samba returns to Brazilian streets and dance floors in full force each year during the pre-Lenten carnival, which blossomed in the 1930s and 1940s into Brazil's premiere national festival with samba as its centerpiece. At carnival time, parade groups called *escolas de samba* (literally, "samba schools") strut their stuff in Rio de Janeiro's specially constructed "sambadrome" (something like a stadium eight blocks long and one street wide) and get around-the-clock coverage by sophisticated telemedia. Free-form street dancing still occurs in the northern part of the country, however, and all across Brazil, people congregate at carnival balls. The sound track for this national event is not exclusively Rio-style samba, since various other sorts of Brazilian carnival music dominate here and there. But the national telemedia coverage of the festival insures that all Brazilians remain familiar with Rio-style samba and know how to move when they hear it.[14]

Whether in a parade, on the street, or at a club, samba is rarely a couple dance. (The main exceptions are a Brazilian nightclub style called *gafieira* and an international ballroom samba that bears very little resemblance to anything called samba in Brazil.) For the most part, Brazilians dance samba in crowds as a sort of synchronous march, a vibration that flows through everyone for hours, transcending fatigue. Most people who dance samba during carnival celebrations might seem, from the footwork point of view, to be jogging in place. This is true even of the thousands of costumed paraders who fill the sambadrome. There is another form of samba performed generally by women, especially the glamorous "standouts" who ride on

Rio's carnival floats instead of dancing between them. This samba has lightening fast, whirling steps that give the impression, when successfully done, of a mechanical eggbeater. Most people cannot keep this up for more than a few seconds, if they attempt it at all.

In Rio's carnival samba parades, featured female dancers maintain samba's risqué reputation. The rolling movement of their buttocks, the celebrated or dreaded *reboleio,* seems intended to express an unleashed, uninhibited sexuality—unleashed because of the movement's explosive energy and uninhibited because of the dancers' near total nudity. As the television cameras pan the parade, they linger occasionally on the fancy footwork, but use their low angles more often to zoom in unabashedly on the reboleio. The dancers most distinguished for their footwork and reboleio tend to be black, although not very black—*mulatas,* in the Brazilian racial scheme.

Samba as an accompaniment for carnival parading today means massed percussion batteries, literally hundreds of drummers. In addition, parade sambas tell a story for the paraders to dramatize. The name samba also refers to a romantic genre characterized by strings, light percussion, and occasional wind instruments that had its golden age in the 1930s and 1940s. Most readers of English will associate this style with Carmen Miranda because of her U.S.-made movies. Samba as a musical genre is much more up-beat than tango with generally romantic, often tongue-in-cheek, lyrics. Only occasionally does one hear in samba the embittered denunciations of faithless love so characteristic of tango lyrics. The samba repertory of the 1930s and 1940s is rarely heard today.[15] Samba's post–golden-age departure, called *bossa nova,* achieved wider popularity than did Piazzolla's new version of the tango, but it led in a similar direction. In some ways, this new form of samba was a bigger success internationally than it was inside Brazil. Sophisticated and innovative, bossa nova was not dance music.[16] Overall, fervor for social dancing to any sort of music has declined since the mid-twentieth century in both Rio de Janeiro and Buenos Aires.

Havana is another matter. If people enjoy social dancing less now, then the past must have been awesome to behold. These days the people of Havana are dancing mostly salsa, and there was no such genre in the 1930s and 1940s. But salsa, in its basic rhythmic, melodic, and harmonic structures, is descended directly from *son* (sounds like "sawn"). The name *salsa* has been applied since the late 1960s to a musical genre that first emerged in New York among Latino musicians (many of them Puerto Rican) who were innovating within the *son* tradition introduced years before from Cuba. The new music tended to abandon guitars (except for bass) and add an electric keyboard. Gritty urban themes, the life of the barrio, replaced the *son*'s nostalgic evocations of rural Cuba. During the 1970s, salsa colonized the popular dance culture of the Caribbean basin, gaining rapid acceptance everywhere earlier Cuban musical genres had already warmed up the audience, including Havana. Today, variations in salsa dance and music abound in the wide area of its influence, which includes spots in Europe and the West African coast.[17]

Salsa dancing in Havana today has several different forms. One is a kind of "share the vibration" mass musical socializing like what Brazilians do at carnival. Imagine a cocktail party where everyone is dancing as they chat. Two or three hundred students might do this on any weekend evening (after midnight, when it is cool enough). The music that lends itself to this shared vibration is sort of Cuban rap to salsa rhythms—not at all hip hop musically, not built on sampling, but played by a salsa band in a continuous jam while the lead vocalist improvises, often speaking directly to the audience of local concerns. Another form of dancing salsa in Havana is called *casino* and is strictly for couples. One might see casino moves here and there amid the vibrating crowd, but it becomes the primary form at discotheques and other settings where the main point is dancing.[18]

Casino-style salsa is characterized by its non-stop turning figures. The woman turns most often, led by the man's raised arms. While the aspect of a male lead is similar to tango, casino figures are entirely different because casino dancers spin completely around in relation to each other (as tango dancers never do), always maintaining contact with one or both hands, sometimes lacing their arms into a complicated "pretzel" as a result. Such figures are also characteristic of Dominican merengue, and in both cases they descend—surprisingly enough, from English country dancing. Sometimes casino dancers form a circle of couples and synchronize their figures, which are made to flow periodically into a change of partners, men moving clockwise (for example) and women counter-clockwise. Casino-style salsa is not notably transgressive as a social dance, though it does seem that way when portrayed, as often in U.S. popular culture, through the "hot Latin" lens. Salsa dancers do not dance close together because turns require separation. Nor does salsa have the pelvic movements that make *rumba,* for example, so suggestive. The "heat" in salsa's "hot Latin" U.S. stereotype comes from sultry attitude and stylistic raciness.

Son from the 1930s and 1940s is still heard, but has lost importance as dance music. It certainly cannot compete with salsa in terms of popularity. But in the late twentieth century the Cuban government promoted folkloric rumba as the official national dance.[19] Never, or almost never, danced socially today, state cultivation of rumba is a bid to strengthen the legitimacy of the revolutionary government among Cubans of African descent by showcasing their cultural heritage. Something similar has been going on among Spanish- and Portuguese-speaking people since the 1400s. That, anyway, is the major argument of this book.

This is a study in dance history. Latin America's national rhythms are simultaneously music and dance. Most studies of them, however, concentrate on music. Music is an important but specialized activity within popular culture. Most people enjoy music, but few make it. Social dance, on the other hand, is much more broadly participatory. In nineteenth-century Rio, Havana, and Buenos Aires, almost everyone danced. Therefore, studying dance offers a look at the lives of ordinary people. The study of music leads one to explore discographies, to analyze lyrics and sheet music, and to think about the lives of musicians and composers. This historical study of dance, on the other hand, will describe few landmark compositions, few musicians' biographies. Instead, it will explore lowlife dives, fancy balls, and private parties, religious celebrations and street festivals, lingering always on descriptions of people dancing.[20]

Dance, even more than music, speaks to collective identities of various kinds. First, it plays a part in *generating* those identities. World historian William McNeill has shown that dance is a basic mechanism of group solidarity in human history. McNeill argues, moreover, that dancing in groups—any coordinated rhythmic movement, such as close-order infantry drill, too—physiologically generates feelings of affinity, something he calls "muscular bonding."[21] Many readers will have experienced how effectively coordinated physical work or sport "breaks the ice." Such bonding makes sense from the perspective of evolutionary psychology, too. If coordinated work makes us feel good, we will do a better job. Because in the contemporary West, dance is associated mostly with courtship, some readers may find the link between dance and work surprising. Yet, in premodern societies the world over, dance has been associated less with courtship than with group projects like hunting, planting, harvesting, and war.

If dance helps generate affinity and solidarity, perhaps that is why it often becomes a *sign* of group affiliation. Folk dance is frequently an aspect of ethnic identities, a stock element of nationalism. In Latin America few provinces or regions lack identifying dances, habitually staged on national holidays by school children. Latin America's national rhythms, then, are a high-energy, high-profile, high-stakes version of this phenomenon.[22]

Too bad, given what we can learn from dance history, that the sources are so limited. Once the dancers are still, dance leaves little direct physical evidence of itself, not even the antique instruments or written notation available to the historian of music. Before the twentieth century only descriptions or drawings give any idea of dancers' movements. Little evidence of dance appears in historical archives, and this is especially true of the dancing of the poor, our special concern here. The police who busted an illicit shindig rarely left helpful descriptions of the dancers' moves—except moves toward the door. Therefore, evidence for dance history appears less in archives than in memoirs, fiction, newspapers, magazines, and travel writing.

Fortunately, one kind of dance move, a kind particularly significant to us, is fairly easy to trace in Latin American history. This is lateral hip movement that "breaks" the body's vertical line and, rhythmically side to side, produces a sinuous, flowing motion of the dancer's torso. "Breaking" hip movement can be identified in historical Spanish and Portuguese sources because it took on considerable significance in societies where these languages were spoken, and so, unlike English, they have many names for it, usually involving some form of the verb *break* (*quebrar* or *requebrar*).[23] Often, this "break dancing," so to speak, included pelvic thrusting, rocking the lower body front to back, usually in fluid swiveling movements of hips and pelvis together. In historical European culture, these movements were associated almost exclusively with sexual intercourse, and their mere presence in dance was transgressive. Such dance seemed to empower the lower body, possibly the reason for its widespread practice during carnival, which also empowers the lower body.[24] In both Spanish and Portuguese, forms of the "break" word became synonymous with flirtation. In the 1700s, for example, a stylish young Portuguese-speaking gentlemen might direct verbal *requebros* to pretty women, left and right, as he moved through a crowded theater between acts. We are lucky to have the linguistic evidence of Spanish and Portuguese accounts, because in the descriptions of English and French-speaking travelers (one of the most abundant sources on Latin American popular dance in the 1800s), hip and pelvic movements are often indicated only by unhelpful expressions of horror and disgust.[25]

When Europeans and Africans encountered each other in the Americas, "break" movements were rare in European dance but common in African dance. Couple choreography, on the other hand, was rare in Africa but common in Europe. In the dominant historical pattern, associated with sowing and reaping and hunting and war, men danced, or women danced, or entire communities danced, but only occasionally did couples dance. Something new and powerful happened when couple dancing met the liberation of the lower body to create the *dance-of-two.*[26]

This dance-of-two, in which the couple danced face to face without touching, is the archetype or ancestral form of all Latin America's national rhythms. It emerged (probably in Mexico) during the 1500s and soon spread throughout Latin America. Over many generations, the dance-of-two evolved a hundred folk variations and underwent successive waves of influence from newer European dance fashions, such as contradance and polka. In the era of Latin America's wars of independence (the first quarter of the 1800s), somehow, despite their polifaceted transgressiveness, these folk dances were drafted to serve as national rhythms, symbols of native identity and cultural affiliation. They were cultivated particularly within patriot armies. To dance a *montonero* or a *jarabe* was to say (in an Argentine or Mexican accent) "I am American, not Spanish." The consecration of the national rhythms—their acceptance in schools, their full adoption by middle-class people—took another century.

By the 1930s, though, Latin Americans could name a string of national rhythms: Chilean *cueca* and Dominican *merengue,* Puerto Rican *plena* and Mexican *jarabe,* Venezuelan *joropo* and Peruvian *marinera,* all descended from the dance-of-two. In Colombia, one national rhythm, *cumbia,* gradually triumphed over another, *bambuco.* The national rhythms of Brazil, Argentina, and Cuba, our three case studies, were already strongly emergent around 1900.

We will begin our examination of those national rhythms in Part One, around 1900, when all were characterized by a transgressive close embrace between the dancers. Despite their similarity, the popular dances of Brazil, Argentina, and Cuba were responding in the early 1900s to contrasting national contexts. African roots were being gradually foregrounded in Brazil, whereas they were being gradually forgotten in Argentina. In practical terms, Brazilian carnival samba players *added* African percussion in the same years (the 1930s) that Argentine musicians and dancers made the tango more melancholy. Cuban musicians and dancers, meanwhile, neither foregrounded nor forgot their African roots. The distinctive evolution of these three national rhythms in the twentieth century is too complex to be summarized here. Fortunately, many books discuss the twentieth-century history of popular music and dance in Brazil, Argentina, and Cuba.

Part Two of this book, by analogy with an archeological excavation, unearths progressively deeper levels of dance history. Here we will encounter the tap root of African dance traditions in the Latin America: the black nations, diasporic social organizations with few parallels in U.S. history. We will also discuss some basics of dance history and examine such apparent oddities as dancing in church. We will observe that the political appropriation of Latin America's national rhythms has direct antecedents half a millennium old. And we will see that, continuously during all that time, transgressive dance has been closely associated with a salient fact of Latin American life. I refer to the gradual merger of cultures and genepools formerly separated by oceans, a process known especially by its Spanish name, *mestizaje.*[27] Finally, our archeology of African roots and national rhythms will take us right back to the dawn of the Atlantic world, where powerful creation myths hold sway. Perhaps this early period, when the dance-of-two began, can account for the stubborn audacity of all its progeny.

Perhaps. As is always the case in archeology, much depends on reasonable inference from scarce bits of evidence. Still, the resulting insights, however tentative, may change the way we understand society. Many have wondered, for example, why the lyrics of Latin American popular music sing almost always of the Dark Woman, the Morena, even though blondeness is more valued in advertising and marriage choices. That, too, is something we will attempt to explain. But enough introduction. Let us begin our archeology of Latin America's transgressive national rhythms with the forerunners of samba, tango, and salsa: Brazilian *maxixe,* Argentine *milonga,* and Cuban *danzón,* three notorious "dirty dances" that had triumphed nationally by 1900. Turn-of-the-century descriptions of couples dancing maxixe, milonga, and danzón are strikingly similar—so much so, that the three dances may seem merely versions of the same thing. And that is exactly the point.

The Transgressive Close Embrace and Popular Carnival, 1870–1910

Chapter Two

Maxixe, Milonga, Danzón

Rio de Janeiro, c. 1900

Brazilian *maxixe* (rhymes with "she she") impressed everyone, favorably or unfavorably, with its close embrace: "face against face, body against body." The phrase is from a journalistic description of 1905. It continues: "they sweat in sweet movement together," rocking back and forth in place, "swiveling their hips (*requebrando*) to the left, then to the right." The illustrations accompanying the Rio newspaper article just cited show the man's leg thrust forward between the woman's legs so that she straddles his thigh. The journalist calls this "the old way" of dancing maxixe and specifies that the less risqué "new way" involves more steps.[1] Here is a foreign visitor's account of maxixe at about the same time: "The couple enlace arms and legs and press their foreheads together." Three slow steps forward, three steps back. Then "quickly, they turn, keeping always the same embrace, and during that rapid movement, bend their bodies far forward and backward. . . . They turn again, bend again, while making three steps forward, three steps back, as if possessed." Descriptions vary, as the practice of the dance must also have varied, but the close, sustained contact between the dancers' bodies is a standard feature of maxixe descriptions. So are the swiveling hips. Lower body movement was maxixe's sine qua non. "Maxixe is a science/ Or maybe it's an art./To be good at maxixe,/You need move just one part," sang the dancers of a 1902 Rio musical review.[2]

Brazilian scholars agree that maxixe emerged as a new way of dancing conventional social dances, especially—believe it or not—polka. This new way of dancing was encouraged by Brazilian musicians. In an era before phonograph recordings, international styles necessarily passed through the hands of local musicians, who, in Brazil, were most often of African-descent. One of their favorite activities was adapting hit melodies from current musical theater productions, introducing rhythmic variations (syncopations and cross-rhythms)* to the "straight" version indicated by the sheet music. An indigenous rhythm instrument, the maraca-like *chocalho*—which accented syncopations, cross-rhythms, and backbeats—became the musical signature of maxixe. This rhythmic innovation did not depend on any particular instrumentation, however. Even military brass bands could put maxixe into a melody, as we can tell from the Brazilian Minister of War's 1907 order banning maxixe from official occasions.[3]

Buenos Aires (and Montevideo), c. 1900

Example number two: *milonga,* a dance of Buenos Aires (and Montevideo, Uruguay, the much smaller sister city of Buenos Aires on the other side of the Río de la Plata). Here is how milonga looked just before 1900 at a kerosene-lit, tin-roofed dancehall in Montevideo, the (in)famous San Felipe Academy, where women were paid by the dance. Envision it. The band—including flutes, violins, a harp, and a foot-pumped organ—strikes up a polka or perhaps a habanera, the great Cuban musical export of the period. The couples at San Felipe Academy embrace very closely: "their legs seemingly tangled, their heads . . . almost touching, when not actually doing so at the temples." Thus fastened together, "they move as if formed of one

* Syncopations are displacements of the main beat. Cross-rhythms complement the main beat, somewhat as harmony complements the melody line. Both syncopations and cross-rhythms abound when African musical traditions influence European ones.

piece, admirably obedient to the rhythm of the music, light and flexible."The couples sweep freely about the dance floor, their center of gravity low, their feet shuffling lightly, never far off the floor,"their course marked by sudden separations and turns" in which they reverse direction, now to the side, now toward him, now toward her. Sometimes they stop short, as if staggering, only to flow suddenly away again, so that "they give the impression of dancing on the deck of a ship in a rough sea." There is an extravagant quality to certain gestures. The woman sometimes straddles her partner's thigh; sometimes he bends her far backward.[4]

Milonga technique was called *corte y quebrada*. The *cortes* (or "cuts") were the stops and turns that cut the flow of the couple's movements across the floor. The *quebradas* were the now familiar swiveling or "breaking" of the hips executed, according to a 1906 Argentine description, with "the bodies of both dancers in full contact."[5]

While the quebradas are common to maxixe and milonga—and to danzón, as will shortly be apparent—the cortes are not. They give a distinctive profile to, and show the continuity between, milonga and tango. (A fast, early variant of tango is, in fact, still called milonga.) Here's the point. Before 1900, cortes were simply a Río de la Plata way of dancing any music from the international ballroom repertory. An elderly Argentine named Miguel Washington reminisced about the 1880s that "everything, even waltz, was danced with cortes."[6] A description of a public dance that appeared in a 1896 Buenos Aires newspaper corroborates Washington's recollections. It paints fearful scenes of delinquency and then asks of the dancing itself: "What do they dance? Habanera, milonga, polka, mazurka. How do they dance it? The criollo way." And the *criollo* way of dancing, according to the article, was defined by the technique of corte y quebrada.[7] In other words, milonga, like maxixe, started out as a new way of dancing the existing dance repertory.

Havana, c. 1900

Cuban *danzón,* had a reputation for delicate refinement, even stiffness, by the end of the twentieth century. It may seem an odd third example of dirty dancing. But in the late nineteenth century danzón had a different, highly transgressive, reputation. In his angry 1888 denunciation of *Prostitution in Havana,* a Cuban social reformer took special aim at danzón. He criticized especially contact between the dancing couples' bodies, "pushing their hips and thighs together, separated only by the wrinkled skirt," and, with explicit detail, evoked the dancers' lustful embrace, the woman's bust swaying against the man's chest, their groins and thighs in momentary, but frequent, contact. The reformer described the music as "pornographic." That is, at any rate, an accurate description of his own prose, that included reference, at one point, to the woman's "turgidly erect nipples." And he was not describing a house of prostitution in the quoted passage, but rather the manner in which a "perhaps honest and virginal" young woman might be led astray.[8]

Danzón prominently featured the lower body movements already described for maxixe and milonga. As early as 1878, a Havana newspaper inveighed against danzón precisely for its horrid *culebreo*—the snakelike movement of the body produced by "breaking" hips.[9] Worst of all was the "slippage" that occurred in the combination of close embrace and culebreo, when the dancers' bodies rubbed in the manner described above. The Havana paper called on the "patriotism" of Cuban youth to resist the scourge of "slippage."[10] "Watch it! Don't slip!" warned a different paper.[11]

Like maxixe and milonga, danzón began as a new way of dancing an older sort of music. The older sort of music, in this case, was Cuban *danza,* a mainstay of Havana ballrooms in the nineteenth-century. Like the 1853 hit El Cocoyé, that made an epoch in Havana carnival and inspired Gottschalk, the danzón rhythm was based on the regular pattern of syncopation called *cinquillo.* A syncopated rhythmic groove that rose with danzón to become the heart of Cuban dance music in the 1900s.[12] Danzón was slower and more Afro-Cuban than danza. By slowing danza melodies, danzón opened more room for cross rhythms between the main beats. A few Afro-Cuban percussion instruments, most notably the *güiro* (gourd scraper), were used to accent the cross rhythms.[13]

Dancers responded to the new rhythms by accentuating the movements that gave danzón its sinuosity, emphasizing movements of the hips and a lower center of gravity. They also simplified the multifigured choreography of danza and spent a lot more time dancing cheek to cheek. On the other hand, dancers also helped inspire the musicians to create these rhythms. The two-way interaction between dancers and musicians is, after all, what makes dancing to a live band special. Dancers encourage what they like by responding with special enthusiasm. Sometimes, too, they pull the rhythm in the direction of their own movements. This interaction is quite important in African-influenced music and dance traditions like Cuba's.[14]

Because they started spontaneously as new ways of dancing the existing dance repertory, maxixe, milonga, and danzon were eminently popular creations. Ordinary dancers and working musicians were taking the initiative, gradually creating something new. In each case, they tested and transgressed the limits of sanctioned social behavior, both by shucking off prudery and by adopting styles of body movement linked to African traditions. To understand the energies that animated this transgressive spirit, this testing of limits, we must consider that the dancers and musicians who invented maxixe, milonga, and danzón did not inhabit tidy, stable social spaces. Instead, they were encountering unfamiliar situations, meeting people different from themselves, receiving the impact of imported cultural forms.

Maxixe, for example, was closely identified with a particular part of Rio de Janeiro, the "new city," or Cidade Nova, so called because it was the first area of expansion beyond the old colonial limits of Rio. In the 1870s, when the population of Rio reached a quarter million people, the Cidade Nova was the fastest growing part. As the Cidade Nova attracted migrants from other parts of Brazil, including recently freed slaves—and poor Italian and Portuguese immigrants, too—the better-off white Brazilians began moving south into the beachfront neighborhoods like Botafogo and Copacabana that now dominate the international image of the city. Meanwhile, the Cidade Nova, with its sweaty quayside neighborhoods and train station, attracted poor Brazilians who were gradually being displaced from the city center. This predominantly black population moved north along the train tracks, toward where most of Rio's poor have lived ever since. Small manufacturing concerns followed them north out of the city center. By the 1890s, *favelas,* the famous high-rise slums that later proliferated in the city, began to be established on hills around the Cidade Nova.[15]

Some poor houses of Rio's Cidade Nova were not shanties but mansions overtaken by hard times, sold by their prosperous owners in flight to Botafogo or Copacabana. Such old mansions were usually divided up into many apartments. Closely-packed smaller dwellings filled in the mansions' formerly spacious grounds. These smaller dwellings were sometimes warrens of single rooms, *cortiços,* meaning "honeycombs," owned by a slumlord and inhabited by laundresses and day laborers. In the cortiços, Portuguese and Italian immigrants rubbed elbows with poor Brazilian whites and blacks. Recent arrivals from Bahia got to know recent arrivals from Milan or the Azores. Parties were inevitable. The music would have been an eclectic mix, much of what the rest of the city danced: quadrilles, mazurkas, and especially polkas. But the dancers of the Cidade Nova did something different with the standard repertoire, adopting a close embrace and incorporating requebros that would never have been allowed in Milan or the Azores. Who or what was to stop them? What social norms pertained in this new situation? If the dancers could forget what people might say "back in the old country" or in some Brazilian provincial town, no one in Rio's Cidade Nova reminded them.[16]

Milonga arose in a similar social milieu in Montevideo and Buenos Aires: the port districts, the areas where European immigrants clustered, the outskirts, and the neighborhoods around markets, army barracks, and slaughterhouses. A 1890 *Dictionary of Argentine Expressions* specified that milonga was "a dance found only among people of the lower orders."[17] Many of the people classed as belonging to "the lower orders" by the Argentine lexicographers of 1890 lived in *conventillos*—subdivided old mansions that were the exact Río de la Plata counterpart of Brazilian cortiços. A whole family, or half a dozen day laborers, might be crammed together in each room of the conventillo. Immigrants of the same nationality tended to share rooms, but conventillos brought everyone together. Neither Montevideo nor Buenos Aires was a city of ethnic enclaves. Both were even more heavily immigrant than Rio. In 1869, foreign-born men outnumbered native-born men in Buenos Aires by something like four to one. Half a century later, in 1914, day laborers (an important component of "the lower orders") were almost ten to one foreign-born in the city.[18] In addition, both Río de la Plata ports were like Rio de Janeiro in attracting many migrants from the countryside in the late nineteenth century. And, as is often true among populations of migrants, men outnumbered women by a wide margin.[19]

Perhaps that is why prostitution thrived. At any rate, houses of prostitution, where transgressive dancing was a prelude to commercial sex, figure insistently in all accounts of the development of milonga. (This makes a lot of sense when one considers that brothels are themselves a kind of institutionalized transgression.) The brothels of the Río de la Plata brought together diverse assortments of people. After 1885, especially, prostitutes in the Río de la Plata ports were often victims of what was then called "the white slave trade" from Russia and Eastern Europe. Of more than a thousand women in an 1887 enumeration of legal prostitutes in Buenos Aires (fewer than the illegal ones), 245 were Argentine, 145 German, 141 Russian, 108 Spanish, 99 French, 59 Uruguayan, 39 Swiss, 30 Paraguayan, 27 English, and 48 of other nationalities.[20]

If these women were inevitably classed among "the lower orders," certainly not all their customers were. The houses of well-known madams like "Laura" and "María la Vasca" attracted middle-class or even upper-class men ("bad boys from good families," said people in Buenos Aires and Montevideo).[21]

Prostitution was not absent from Havana, either, of course. The mentioned author of *Prostitution in Havana* devoted a whole chapter to the problem's choreographical dimensions.[22] Like Rio and Buenos Aires, Havana was a city of immigrants and a busy Atlantic port. All the factors already discussed for Rio and Buenos Aires were at work, too, in Havana. Yet their configuration was distinctive. Havana's immigrants were mostly young Spanish men come to seek their fortunes in Spain's last rich American colony. Eventually, they became enthusiastic dancers of danzón—but then, so did practically everybody else in the city. Havana was also the home of many black Cubans (none of them slaves, any longer, after abolition in 1886). The social space in which danzón emerged was not, as with maxixe in Rio, as specific section of the city, nor, as with the milonga, exclusively among the "lower orders." By the mid 1880s, danzón was being danced all over Havana, in gatherings of the humble and the well-to-do.[23]

The most significant commonality of maxixe, milonga, and danzón (at least for this book) is their intertwined African and

European roots. In his careful historical study of maxixe, Jota Efegê concurs with other authorities such as Nei Lopes, Artur Ramos, José Ramos Tinhorão, and Mario de Andrade in affirming that maxixe expressed an African influence in Brazilian music and dance.[24] Indeed, those influences seem never to have been doubted by anybody. The first recorded usage of any form of the word *maxixe,* located by Efegê in a 1880 Rio newspaper, refers to "*maxixeiras*" (women who dance maxixe). And newspaper references to maxixeiras generally suggest that they were women of African descent, e.g., "The mulata is the key/To the *requebrada* maxixe." As late as 1919, when maxixe had been the most popular dance of urban Brazil for decades, a national legislator and member of the prestigious Academy of Letters still scorned it as an unpleasant reminder of the dancing of Brazilian slaves.[25]

A six-volume memoir of turn-of the-century Rio offers a vivid description of cheap music halls. The black pianists of these music halls played in a syncopated style that evoked, for the memorialist Luiz Edmundo, "the cadence of African *batuque*"—batuque being the percussive music to which Brazilian slaves had danced. In other words, these pianists played maxixe.[26]

Edmundo describes the show of a performer named Mulata Farusca, who mounts the stage in revealing costume—see-through blouse and blue silk head scarf, with earrings, necklaces, and bracelets glittering in the stage lights—that loosely imitates the West African apparel worn by women of Bahia. The all-male audience calls for her to dance maxixe, thumping their canes on the floor in time with the rhythm. The performance culminates when Mulata Farusca executes "the screw," a whirling and spiraling movement of her body, that brings down the house. Quoth Edmundo: "Mulata Farusca finishes her sensational number amid a deafening roar. The pianist, delirious with enthusiasm, pounds out the last chords of the maxixe . . . bathed in sweat but covered with glory." Edmundo reports that the enterprising owners of Rio's music halls combed the city's poor black neighborhoods in search of performers.[27]

Milonga's African associations were necessarily different, because neither Buenos Aires nor Montevideo had a large black population at the end of the nineteenth century. Most milonga dancers were therefore white. Still, black (especially mulato) men seemed to hold pride of place on the floors of public dance halls such as Montevideo's San Felipe Academy. Stage representations of superior milonga dancing often connected it to a black identity, and any particularly showy display of milonga technique was called *bailar a lo negro* ("dancing black") in the slang of the Río de la Plata ports. An important early account (1883) says that milonga rhythms "had the movement of *candombe* drums."[28] Candombe, like Brazilian batuque, was the dancing of slaves and free blacks, who had formed a substantial part of the Río de la Plata population until the mid nineteenth century.

Just how did dances of black people become dances of white people? In a sense, this entire book is an answer to that question. But the question is particularly central to the history of milonga and tango. The 1883 quotation about candombe drums is interesting because it explicitly suggests an answer: "Milonga is danced by urban tough guys [called *compadritos*] who mockingly imitate the dance of blacks."[29] But how convincing is this answer? Something makes one skeptical about it at first blush.

It is hard to imagine just how this mocking imitation might have taken place, in what specific situations whites observed and caricatured black dancing, and why they would ever have done so persistently enough to propagate a full-blown dance genre. Yet, if milonga had some influence from candombe, and the scholarly consensus says it did, then the Italian and Spanish immigrants who flooded Buenos Aires and Montevideo in the 1880s had to have learned it through some process of imitation. Along with compadrito tough-guys, the 1883 description associates milonga with soldiers, cart drivers, the clients of "low-life dives," and the inhabitants of the city's outskirts in general. Argentine blacks must have mixed socially in these poor neighborhoods and "dives" with Galician cooks, Italian construction workers, and Polish or Russian prostitutes.[30] In a plausible scenario, immigrants learned milonga dancing through normal social interaction with Argentine blacks. Still, there is little direct evidence of white dancers imitating black dancers. We must return to this issue later.

The African influences on danzón are as plain as those on maxixe, and danzón is the best documented of the three cases because of a dispute that arose in the Cuban press in 1878. The dispute, which focused at first on dancing in the city of Matanzas, not far from

Havana, began with criticisms from Havana's important newspaper, *El Triunfo. El Triunfo* sneered sarcastically at "that stuff that the *morenos* and *pardos** of Matanzas call danzón." It sneered even more at a Matanzas paper's attempts to defend the dance as a practice "both of colored people and of the most distinguished circles of white society" in Matanzas. In that case, chortled *El Triunfo,* the Matanzas paper admitted that white society in the city danced this creation of colored people! *El Triunfo* explained: "We had preferred not to say that outright, but since Señor L., who is no doubt from Matanzas, has taken it upon himself to clarify matters, so much the better. We wash our hands of the matter." Such "dirty linen," concluded *El Triunfo,* should be washed in private by the white society of Matanzas.[31]

This airing in the press exposed racial undertones that normally surfaced only as veiled innuendo. *El aprendiz* (a paper from Regla, across Havana harbor) lamented that danzón was, after all, merely "a degeneration of African tangos."[32] (The word *tango* occurs here in its nineteenth-century Cuban meaning, to refer to any sort of African dancing. In nineteenth-century Brazil, the word *tango* had identical African associations and might, in fact, be used to refer to maxixe, too.[33]) The same theme was taken up, and elaborated in familiar terms, by a Matanzas paper, *La aurora de Yurumí*:

> Danza and danzón might have been born in Cuba, but their origin is African. The music of those dances has something of the concupiscence and voluptuousness that characterize the natives of sultry Africa. . . . The beat of the kettledrums shows this beyond doubt. Furthermore, the rhythm of danza and danzón is very much like the rhythm of the tangos that Africans dance in our streets.[34]

Not just African influence, but race mixing, was at issue in the controversy surrounding danzón.

Maxixe, milonga, and danzón often show up historically in encounters between dark-skinned women and lighter-skinned men of superior social position. Such men were the intended readership of Rio's 1905 journalistic chronicler João Phoca, who called maxixe "a fever that nobody of the masculine sex can escape." Phoca

* Both names referring to people of African descent.

exhorted Rio's shy, middle-class "Everyman" in the following terms: "Go, timid and curious. See the bizarrely limber limbs, that twisting and untwisting of couples to the sound of a languorous [maxixe]."* The dance is dangerously seductive:

> Go. Get to like it . . . and you're lost. In a while, imperceptibly, unconsciously, you'll be ready to ask a woman you don't even know to dance. And soon, without ever having learned those steps, those movements, you'll be swiveling clumsily, running into things, stepping on feet and getting stepped on, but *dancing maxixe.*[35]

Many of the women that our novice maxixe dancer was urged to seek as partners were poor maxixeiras of African descent, including paid dancehall girls. Unlike danzón, which rapidly gained a foothold in Havana dancehalls of all social descriptions, maxixe was a dance that "decent"† women of Rio rarely did before 1900. True, many stories circulated about "decent" women who attended carnival balls incognito as *dominós,* wearing a hooded cloak and mask. In one common variant, the disguised woman encounters and dances with her own husband who is, of course, eventually shocked and outraged when he discovers her identity. Still, middle-class women constituted a small minority of the available partners in any dance venue featuring maxixe. In a similar carnival story, the man "drools" all night for a dominó who, when the dawn light reveals her dark skin between glove and sleeve, turns out to be the family cook.[36]

Women presented as maxixeiras, maxixe dancers, became a standard attraction of dances given in carnival season, and there was rarely doubt about their social identity. For example, showy 1895 newspaper ads for Rio's Phoenix Dramática theater promised the presence of "three hundred splendid mulatas maxixeiras" at its dance. Not to be outdone, another theater advertised "a great abundance of mulatas" who would dance maxixe at its two costume balls. A few years earlier, a third theater, the Recreio Dramático, had announced for 10 p.m. "the triumphal entrance of the Group of Maxixeiras,

---

* The original uses the word *tango* here, though referring to maxixe.

† *Decente* was a word widely used to indicate wealth and priviledge, especially in the phrase *la gente decente,* "the decent people," who were more or less an upper crust.

made up of 450 damsels who will display sixty-nine choreographical evolutions." In all these cases, the implication was that the women would mingle at the dance after their act. An 1896 ad for the Santana Theater advertised a dance with three hundred maxixeiras "*do mundo equívoco*,"* women whose explicitly "iffy" background all but guaranteed their sexual availability.[37]

Common practice found expression in popular imagery. Brazilian women of color have been a national sex symbol for two centuries. Aluísio Azevedo's *O Cortiço,* one of the most widely read novels of Brazil in this period, provides a sample from the 1880s. In the novel, Rita Baiana, a woman "half black and half white," dances not maxixe but one of its Afro-Brazilian antecedents, which could be danced by one person alone. Significantly, Rita's surname Baiana signals her connection to Bahia, the center of neo-African culture in Brazil. Her Portuguese lover watches her dance, transfixed:

> The moon burst through the clouds at that moment, bathing the scene in a soft, silver glow and lending to the rich, warm skin of the mulata a pallor which made her really beautiful. With infinite grace she danced, simple, primitive, seemingly formed only to delight the senses, a creature from Eden's gardens, much of the woman and much of the serpent.
>
> She danced within the circle, her hands at her waist and her entire body in movement. Now her arms were outstretched and raised, and then lowered till her fingertips touched her neck. At times she sank till she appeared to be almost sitting on the ground, while the movement of her arms and hips never ceased. The she leaped into the air and danced faster and faster, her arms twisting and writhing, and her blood boiling with a passion that communicated itself to the onlookers.[38]

Obviously, the passage is riddled with the racism of its day, not to mention its leering male viewpoint: It takes an extra moonlit "pallor" to make "primitive" Rita "really beautiful." She seems "formed only to delight the [male] senses." Rita's serpent-like seduction of the Portuguese immigrant is intended, in the novel, to signal danger for Brazil. As a result of the affair, her formerly hard-working Portuguese

---

* Roughly, "the world of false steps."

lover becomes improvident, pleasure-loving, and lazy, just like Rita's other (Brazilian) lovers. He gives up wine for rum, cod for black beans and manioc, becoming, in Acevedo's word, "Brazilianized."[39] We need share none of Acevedo's outmoded assumptions, however, to sense the power of his imagery. As the passage illustrates, dance was already central to pre-1900 images of black women as Brazilian national sex symbols.

Similarly, the women who danced milonga in Montevideo or Buenos Aires were often of African descent. Overall, the Rio de la Plata cities were overwhelmingly white by 1900. Well before then, the black population of Buenos Aires had dropped below two percent of the total as the city's black population was diluted by massive European immigration and, in a famous metaphor, "disappeared like a drop of ink in a glass of water." This disappearance was largely a matter of proportion, as the population increase of Buenos Aires, driven by immigration from Europe, reached toward a million, with Montevideo showing a similar demographic pattern on a smaller scale. But the disappearance of the city's black population was also a matter of "passing," as light-complexioned people abandoned a black identity.[40] Whenever whites socialized with people of African descent, though, milonga dancing was unlikely to be far away.

Many of the women paid by the dance at the San Felipe Academy and other such "dance academies," were apparently of mixed race. The rooms of women called by the slang term chinas,* who lived around army garrisons, were another famous venue of milonga parties. The chinas, who took care of the soldiers in a variety of ways (even going with them on campaign in many cases), were often of indigenous descent.[41] Suggestively, some places of prostitution were called *quilombos,* the Brazilian word for settlement of escaped slaves. When "bad boys from good families" commemorated their escapades publicly, however, they were likely to brag of visits to fancy brothels staffed by European prostitutes. As a result, there is no parallel figure to the glamorous mulata Rita Baiana in the fiction or memoirs of Montevideo or Buenos Aires.

* The word *china* for woman was taken from the Quechua language of the Andes and has no connection with China. Its usage in Spanish dates from colonial days.

Havana, in contrast, had precise and extensive parallels. "Sugar-hipped" mulatas figured poetically, musically, and graphically in Cuban popular culture from the 1840s on. A beautiful mulata is the protagonist of *Cecilia Valdez* (1882), the most famous nineteenth-century Cuban novel.[42] Cecilia, like Rita Baiana, is a mulata with a white lover, in this case, a rich merchant's spoiled son. The young slacker seeks out Cecilia at dances arranged to facilitate such liaisons. There they mingle with black dancers of both sexes and also with white males (to quote the novel) "of decent, well-to-do families, who did not hesitate to socialize with people of color and take part in their favorite diversion, some for love of dancing, and others for motives less pure."[43] The author, who also reported on society dances for the Havana newspapers, clearly knew his topic. The quoted scene of the novel goes on to describe how the white men waited until late in the evening before dancing with women of African descent and how they stayed away from the windows when they did. The novel's main plot twist is relevant to the matter at hand, too: Cecilia and her white lover turn out to have the same father, a Spaniard who ruined Cecilia's mother just as his son will ultimately ruin Cecilia.

Cecilia Valdez is set in 1830s Havana, but choreographic encounters of this kind did not disappear in the late 1800s. A brief note in the 1879 Havana press makes that clear: "A few nights ago there was a little dance in the block between Aguila and Blanco on Animas Street. And there, *the two colors* [italics in the original] mixed together gaily, indeed. The male attendees were various apparently decent young men; the females—pure *caracolillo*."[44] Caracolillo here refers to tight, curly but not kinky, hair. In other words, the women were mulatas.

Erotic images of dark women were pervasive in Cuban popular culture in the nineteenth century. The memoirs of Lola Cruz, collected in the 1920s, contain many examples. Some are song lyrics that she learned from her mother, praising "the cinnamon flower " a poetic reference to mulata beauty.[45] Lola also remembered Havana's locally written light musical theater, Bufos Cubanos, in the 1880s and 1890s, particularly a piece called *La mulata callejera* (*The Street Vendor*). Although the lead in this sketch may have been played in blackface, it reeks of rosy romanticization rather than taunting caricature. The actress who played the mulata seemed, to Lola, quite glamorous when she flounced her white dress across the stage to a rumba beat and sang: "I am the mulata/Lovely and bewitching."[46]

It is hardly surprising, given their penchant for crossing lines, that maxixe, milonga, and danzón thrived at carnival, when the collective mood celebrates, even encourages, transgressive behavior. In fact, the first documented appearance of the word *maxixe* occurs in a 1883 comedy set at Rio's carnival. Several characters are gathered on the sidewalk of the Rua do Ouvidor, the main carnival parade route, when a woman says to a young *malandro* (a Brazilian tough-guy counterpart to the compadrito): "Hey, Manduca, don't go soft on me. Let's see that maxixe stuff!"[47] By the 1890s, maxixe had become Rio's carnival dance *par excellence.* Buenos Aires and Montevideo also had major carnival celebrations in the years when milonga was the rage of "the lower orders." In a 1934 interview, when Buenos Aires carnival had entered its permanent decline, a veteran musician waxed nostalgic about the carnival dances at "la Negra María's" establishment in the years before 1900—the years when milonga's cortes and quebradas were beginning to attract middle-class curiosity: "Ah, carnival in the old days. Can you imagine how long those dances lasted? Seven days and seven nights without stopping more than a moment to move the band to the patio when the house's wooden floor caved in!"[48] Also in the 1890s, with perfect simultaneity, danzón reigned supreme at Havana's carnival celebration. Direct press coverage of carnival in Rio, Havana, and Buenos Aires offers a special opportunity to study transgressive dancing that went on, less noticed, year round. We will begin, in the next chapter, with Rio de Janeiro's carnival.

Let us take stock before proceeding. Here are the main points so far: Maxixe, milonga, and danzón were like so many fingers of the same hand, variants of a single phenomenon that we might call the transgressive close embrace. Dances of this kind appeared throughout Latin America around 1900. These dances emerged as a new way of performing conventional dance music, adding rhythmic complexity and accenting hip movement. Maxixe, milonga, and danzón arose not so much *inside* communities as *between* them. They had particular associations with race mixing, both because people of mixed race created them and because they were typically present at racially mixed gatherings.

Having clarified what these dances had in common, let us see how diverse national contexts shaped them into distinct national rhythms. We will focus on the experiences of particular people involved in the popular culture of our Atlantic port cities: First, an Afro-Brazilian matriarch, "Aunt Ciata," at whose house in Rio's Cidade Nova district the canonical "first samba" was composed in 1917. Next, the Podestá family, Montevideans of Italian descent who put the milonga on stage and gave dance an important place in Argentina's national theater. Finally, Cuban band leader Miguel Faílde, who crystallized the musical form of the danzón and made it the music that Havana could not resist.

Chapter Three

Tia Ciata's House
(Rio de Janeiro)

The carnival parades of Rio's samba schools always have a theme, and each school has a new theme each year. The theme is established by a specially-composed samba that the school will sing and dance during its whole hour and a half under the flood lights of the sambadrome. Enormous floats illustrate the theme, as do the lavish costumes of the dancers who press around and between the floats. Themes are an important aspect of competition among the schools, but their annual change makes carnival exceedingly expensive for the dancers, mostly black residents of Rio's poorest neighborhoods. The dancers generally pay for their own costumes and need new ones each year.

Rather than a couple dance, carnival samba is a spectacle, a competition, a civic event. Understanding samba requires understanding that event. Brazil's is the world's most "nationalized" carnival, and its main focus is on Rio. Rio's carnival parades officially celebrate the African heritage in Brazil's mixed-race national identity. Whatever its annual theme, each samba school always presents some of its dancers as Baianas: women of African descent wearing a stylized version of folk costume from Bahia. Dancing Baianas represent a formative influence on Rio's carnival celebration, the important participation of free black migrants from Bahia who settled in Rio during declining years of Brazilian slavery and continued to arrive after abolition (1888). The most important of the historical Baianas, was Hilária Batista de Almeida, remembered in the history of Rio carnival as Aunt, or "Tia," Ciata.

Hilária was only about twenty two years old, still far from deserving the respectful title of Tia, when she arrived in Rio from Bahia in 1876. We know only the details of her life that could be recollected by her family almost a hundred years later. She first lived in a neighborhood of downtown Rio near many other recent arrivals from Bahia. We know that she became a *quituteira,* who prepared and sold on the street a variety of Brazilian sweets (among the more agreeable legacies of the country's four centuries of sugarcane production). We know that many of her delicacies, because of their color or ingredients, had a special significance in Candomblé, the Afro-Brazilian religion always strongest and best organized in Bahia. Hilária attended a *terreiro,* or ritual center, that had been transplanted to Rio by another Bahian named João Alabá.[1]

Hilária became the respected Tia Ciata, apparently, because of her role as Iyá Kekerâ (an important ritual office) in Abalá's terreiro. The Candomblé practiced by João Abalá closely resembled Yoruba religion in West Africa. In her role as Iyá Kekerâ, Tia Ciata took primary responsibility for organizing propitiatory offerings, an important dimension of Candomblé. And she was second in charge of directing the spirit possession ceremonies. The deities of Candomblé (Ogun, Oxum, Iemanjá, and many others, referred to as *santos*) enter the bodies of their devotees in rites that constitute the defining event of any terreiro. As Iyá Kekerâ, Tia Ciata helped worshipers experiencing possession to put on the color-coded ritual garb of their santo. She guided the unfolding of the ceremony, with its special drumbeats and distinctive dance moves for each santo. As Iyá Kekerâ, Tia Ciata's life revolved around the terreiro.[2]

Tia Ciata was no dancehall maxixeira. But she did like to dance at her own parties, which she threw on birthdays and occasions of the Candomblé calendar. The only specific recollection about her dancing links her to old folk dances in which the spectators formed a circle (*roda,* in Portuguese), singing and clapping hands, around a single dancer or couple. In such dances, the couple faced but did not put their arms around each other. These were Brazilian versions of the archetypal dance-of-two, discussed in chapter one. The Portuguese word for the circle around the dancers gave Tia Ciata's dance its classic designation, *samba de roda*.[3]

Tia Ciata seems more like a pillar of community than like the culturally intermediary cortiço-dwellers who created maxixe. Yet, for all her immersion in African religion, the mark of cultural hybridity was strong on her. She might dance samba de roda, for example, at a party for Nossa Senhora da Conceição or other Catholic saints, and she often attended mass before officiating at the terreiro. Another of Tia Ciata's projects—one she came to a bit unexpectedly—was arranging Catholic folk pageants that dramatized the three wise men's adoration of the Christ child at Epiphany.

Back in Bahia, such street pageants were lavish spectacles and occasions for affirmation of community, but in Rio the custom had largely disappeared by the 1870s. Rio—Brazil's urban showcase, its paragon of progress—frowned on black people dancing in the street. Even many religious processions had been curtailed because of the tendency of Rio's poor to turn them into street parties. The Ash Wednesday procession, once the biggest and most elaborate of all, was canceled for that reason in 1861.[4] The people of Rio did not dance in the street at carnival, either. During the 1850s, 1860s, and 1870s, Rio's festival was dominated by elite carnival societies, the so-called Great Societies, that paraded on horseback or on large floats decorated to represent literary allegories. This "Venetian" model of carnival was something for the rich to play at, something for the poor to watch, just as poor Brazilians today avidly watch the rich at play on television.[5]

The image of Rio's Venetian carnival is disorienting: carnival without the Afro-Brazilian participation that now defines the festival. But it should not be so surprising. Overall, the spirit of Rio's larger popular culture was far different, in the 1870s, from what it is today. In fact, mid-nineteenth century Rio was proverbially "dead" and lacking in nightlife. The transformation of carnival, precisely, did much to make sad old Rio into a party town. And African percussion and transgressive dance are what transformed carnival. The credit goes to Tia Ciata's Epiphany troupe (along with similar groups) that introduced dancing Baianas into carnival more than a hundred years ago. In so doing, they opened a new public space for Afro-Brazilian culture in the streets of Rio de Janeiro, and ultimately, made samba into Brazil's national rhythm.[6]

The first change at carnival was the appearance of noisy groups called Zé Pereiras that specialized in pounding various kinds of drums. The Zé Pereiras took their name, supposedly, from one José Pereira (Zé being the Brazilian nickname for José) who began this custom in 1846.[7] Zé Pereiras seem to have become common, however, only in the 1870s.[8] They are usually pictured as mere noisemakers who played the bass and snare drums of a military marching band. But newspaper descriptions of the 1880s show that a Zé-Pereira also became the percussion for groups of street dancers. In 1883, the carnival reportage of Rio's *Gazeta de Notícias* described Zé Pereiras led by a *velho* or "geezer," a dancer costumed as an old man with a cane and monocle.[9] These "geezers" staged comic dance showdowns when, in winding through the narrow streets, two of them happened to come face to face. Red-suited devils seem to have been among their most frequent followers.[10] Zé Pereiras spawned many other thematic variations. In 1887, the first Zé Pereira to pass down the Rua do Ouvidor parade route made "nastiness" its motif. This Group of "Nasties" (or *sujos*) seems to have been the prototype of many later groups by that name, who wore their clothes inside out or cross-dressed. The second Zé Pereira of 1887 was a group of Cucumbys, black men and women doing a folk pageant with strong African roots.[11]

In 1888, just before the final abolition of Brazilian slavery, the *Gazeta de Notícias* published an article by pioneer folklorist Mello Moraes Filho, explaining that Cucumbys was the Bahian name for a dramatic dance done throughout Brazil—though not in Rio since the 1830s.[12] Mello Moraes Filho provides a detailed description of the pageant as he had seen it performed by different groups of Cucumbys at 1888 carnival. The pageant included a cast of characters—especially a king and queen—and dramatic action involving the death of an infant prince. Women, dancing with babes in arms, had an important role. The dancers, about fifty in each group, wore feathers at their knees, waists, wrists, upper arms, and heads. They wore necklaces of coral, glass beads, and animal teeth. And they wore flesh-colored tights to simulate nudity. As they danced through the streets, occasionally raising their arms in time to the music, the Cucumbys played a variety of percussion instruments, including marimbas,* tambourines, and shakers (like the chocalho that gave maxixe its characteristic flavor).[13]

The Cucumbys were not simply "being themselves" when they put on feathers and beads to represent, somewhat ambiguously, Africans or Indians. Mello Moraes Filho's article stressed the idea of African origins in discussing the Cucumbys, declining to comment on the Indian feathers. Authenticity and purity were the qualities prized by early folklorists. But the reporters of other papers made the "Indian" theme explicit, confirming the cultural hybridity of the Cucumbys. Appearing the day after the folklorist's 1888 *Gazeta de Notícias* article was a description in *O Paiz* of one such group, Trump of Cucumbys "masquerading as Indians."[14] The paper mentioned a specifically-titled African Recreational Society, also "performing as Indians, to the sound of a collection of percussion instruments worthy of an anthropological museum." These "Africans performing as Indians" sang and executed dance steps that were much applauded for their originality."[15] Originality, mind you, not African authenticity, which the applauding crowd on Rio's Rua do Ouvidor would not have recognized anyway. These African Indians (the name chosen by a group in 1890) were not so much reviving an ancestral culture as they were simply playing "savage," assuming the demeanor of beings beyond normal social controls—a very carnivalesque, and very transgressive, attitude.[16] Black Indians are an old phenomenon in diasporic dance, and they can still be found among carnival paraders all over the Atlantic world. We will return to them in a future chapter.[17]

But for now, let us not stray too far from Hilária Batista de Almeida, nicknamed Ciata, who was still in her early thirties when the Cucumbys began to dance on the Rua do Ouvidor. Folklorist Mello Moraes Filho believed that what he saw was the work of Bahians recently arrived in Rio. Herself a Baiana, Ciata would not have missed the Cucumbys performance, surely. Might she herself not have been

* In Brazil *marimba* refers, not to the xylophone-like instrument, but to the "African thumb piano."

a Cucumby? In fact, there is no record that Tia Ciata paraded with any of the carnival groups she helped create during her long life. We do know that in 1893, when Ciata was almost forty, she finally got the chance to have her own Epiphany parade troupe, or rancho de reis, with Three Wise Men and lots of dancing shepherdesses. The opportunity came unexpectedly. Ciata had lived for some time near the house of Miguel Pequeno, who, despite his name Pequeno (meaning *small*), was a big man in Rio's Bahian community. Pequeno's house was constantly full of new arrivals from Bahia. Donga, one of the famous early samba players whose family lived in the neighborhood, told the story decades later: "Miguel Pequeno was a sort of consul for Bahians in Rio," explained Donga. His colorful description is worth repeating in detail:

> Houses back then always had four or five rooms, and there was always a papaya tree and some tobacco out back, plenty for everybody. People arriving from Bahia would stay at Miguel's until they could get on their feet. Now, Miguel was married to Tia Amélia Kitundi. Miguel was dark, but Amélia was a very pretty mulata. No kidding, people couldn't stop looking at her. A spectacle. Her presence brought more people to the house.[18]

Having plenty of personnel on hand, Miguel planned to start an Epiphany troupe to enliven the holiday season. He applied for and received a police permit for the group. He also attracted Hilário Jovino Ferreira, another influential Bahian, who wanted to leave his existing troupe, Rei do Ouro (a playing card, roughly, King of Diamonds), and join another. Donga tells how Hilário broke his ties with King of Diamonds, only to become angry when Miguel's project went nowhere. At that point, Hilário Jovino started his own, more successful project with the lovely Amélia. Miguel might have wished he had attracted fewer visitors. Amélia left Miguel, and the despondent Bahian abandoned his plans to form a new Epiphany troupe. Since he already had a police permit, he gave it to his friend Tia Ciata, who used it to create Rosa Branca, or White Rose—a famous name in the early history of Rio's carnival.

White Rose may never have paraded at Epiphany at all. By 1894, the year of these events, the Epiphany troupes were parading at carnival, instead. Hilário Jovino Ferreira himself had initiated the shift to carnival parading with his first troupe, King of Diamonds. Parading at carnival worked better, explained Hilário Jovino in a later interview, because the people of Rio were not used to the Bahian custom of Epiphany street pageants.[19] In carnival, after all, "anything goes," and the pleasure of these pageants was only tenuously linked to their Catholic significance, anyway.

Tia Ciata's troupe White Rose featured not black Indians but folkloric Bahians, or, more to the point, Baianas. Baianas in characteristic dress had long danced as shepherdesses. Shepherds (and plausibly, shepherdesses, too) play a traditional part in the Epiphany story, after all, since they were among the first to see the star of Bethlehem. But parading at carnival gradually undermined the traditional Epiphany script. Troupes like King of Diamonds and White Rose began to adopt a variety of different, secular motifs for their annual street performances at carnival. Unlike the "savage" Cucumbys, these ex-Epiphany carnival troupes went for elegance. Their music included strings, wind instruments, and considerable libretto. Their colorful costumes had a quasi-operatic style contrasting with the Cucumbys' feathers and animal-tooth necklaces. In the street, the new carnival troupes held aloft Japanese lanterns and waved showy banners. Sometimes they ended their trip through the streets at the house of Tia Bebiana, a friend and associate of Tia Ciata's. Tia Bebiana's special mission, one she took upon herself, was putting up a nativity scene to serve as the traditional festive destination of the parading troupes.[20] Troupes like White Rose represented a considerable investment of money and effort. They had a year-round organization and sometimes an official clubhouse. Readers who notice the resemblance to today's carnival parade organizations, the samba schools, are not mistaken. Troupes like White Rose were clearly the forerunners of the samba schools, which is why all Rio's carnival parades have dancing Baianas today.[21]

Zé Pereiras, Cucumbys, troupes of Baianas, and groups led by dancing "geezers" with monocles—all coexisted and cross-pollinated each other in the street carnival of turn-of-the-century Rio. Zé Pereiras became the percussion (*pancaderia*) that all groups had, rather than a separate sort of group.[22] The Cucumbys, who had really been the entering wedge of transgressive street dance in the 1880s, were rare by 1900—but many groups still had a few black Indians dancing vigorously in front to open a path through the crowd.

Elegant ex-Epiphany troupes like King of Diamonds and White Rose flourished particularly in the first decade of the new century. Soon there were troupes of guitar strumming students, red-suited devils, transvestites, and all sorts of other themes, including an occasional group in blackface, along with lots of nasty sujos. To some extent, different sorts of people paraded in each modality. Troupes that performed themes from Verdi, for instance, required fancy costumes and enlisted dancers who could pay for them. On the other hand, it cost nothing to get ragged and go out "nasty," so the poorest inhabitants of Rio were likely to parade as "nasties." But even members of high-tone troupes like White Rose sometimes paraded as nasties just for fun.[23]

Whatever their nature, all the new carnival parade groups were neighborhood-based. On one of carnival's three principal days, they would set out from their neighborhoods and move through the thickening crowds toward the city center. Not all, by any means, would make their way down the prestigious Rua do Ouvidor, where the Great Societies still paraded their allegorical floats on the model of Venetian carnival. But many black street-dancing groups did parade on the Rua do Ouvidor beginning in the 1880s.

So even the main parade route of Rio's carnival was no longer monopolized by the allegorical floats of the Great Societies at the beginning of the twentieth century.[24] Things had changed quickly after a handful of Cucumbys made their appearance in the late 1880s. In 1895, when the carnival crowd had become densely multi-class and multicolored, *O Jornal do Brasil* felt compelled to warn "families" (by which it meant white middle-class women and children) of the dangers inherent in the multitude that rubbed elbows on the Rua do Ouvidor.[25] Fifty groups paraded that year. By 1902, seven years later, *O Paiz* described "one, two, three hundred carnival parade groups moving back and forth, here and there, some in thunderous Zé Pereiras, some singing, some dancing."[26] In 1903, the *Gazeta de Notícias* sported a front-page illustration showing black and white carnival revelers pressed together in what was intended to appear, for middle-class Brazilian readers, repulsive proximity.[27] In 1904, another paper protested that two hours before the big carnival parades of the Great Societies, the narrow Rua do Ouvidor was literally packed with bodies: "not even covered with vaseline, from head to foot, could one squeeze through that human maelstrom."[28]

The crowd along Ouvidor would soon be decompressed, just a bit, when the parade route shifted to the broad, new Avenida Central. But now, and for the rest of the twentieth century, the prodigious energies of Rio's blossoming popular festival could fill any street in town. In 1908 even the wide Avenida Central was packed to capacity when an estimated half million people became street revelers or spectators. And there was plenty more activity in neighborhoods all over the city.[29] A 1913 observer decried the physical closeness "among young people of both sexes, right in the street, immodest, shameless, in the most scandalous contacts, without distinction of race, color, or education."[30] Carnival had been transformed. The Venetian elements had not disappeared, but they had been inundated by street dancers who moved to Afro-Brazilian rhythms.

Carnival street dancers had won new access to public space and a new audience for their performances. Rio's burgeoning press became their ally. Troupes of street dancers traditionally visited several houses along their route to dance and receive refreshments. The early Cucumbys did this in the 1880s, also stopping to dance in front of newspaper offices.[32] Annual visits to newspaper audiences became a carnival ritual for groups doing Afro-Brazilian dances. Visits to newspaper offices raised the public profile of the papers and created admiring publicity for the dancers. "Oh," effused *O Paiz* in 1898, "five typical Baianas danced a *fado** in front of our offices, and each outdid the last with the movements of her thighs!" The next year, the same paper saluted another group, Flower of Gamboa, who danced a big-circle *batuque,*† as "valiant perpetuators of Brazilian popular dance."[33] During carnival, maxixe groups were praised in terms far different from the usual moralizing criticism. In 1900, *O Jornal do Brasil* adored the "beautiful maxixes" performed at its door by Flower of Andarahy Grande, the "graceful maxixes" of the Mermaid's Sons, and so on.[34] No group that visited the paper got a bad review. In 1902, one group carried a banner with the names of all the city's newspapers emblazoned on it.[35] In 1906, the *Gazeta de Notícias* had a contest for the best street dance group, ran a long series of articles about their activities, and featured front-page photographs of the groups' glittering banners—banners which

---

* *Fado* was an old-fashioned dance-of-two.

† *Batuque* was the dance of Brazilian slaves.

the newspaper also displayed in its offices to help build excitement in the weeks before carnival. Not to be outdone, *O Jornal do Brasil* recruited its own associated groups of street dancers and displayed their banners in its offices.[36]

Women were prominent in Rio's new popular carnival. When street dancers paraded, it was always women who carried the banners. These standard bearers were often praised for their beauty and poise. "The rich banner" of such-and-such a group, for example, "was held aloft by a comely and graceful *morena*."[37] Standard bearers were often richly dressed in long velvet capes, but other women showed a lot of flesh and "could be called semi-naked" according to *O Paiz* in 1899."[38] Many street dance groups were composed purely of women. Commonly, they dressed as Baianas, like the ones who so impressed *O Paiz* with the movements of their thighs. Other groups were mixed—the Lieutenants of Hell, for example, included both he-devils and she-devils, the Flower of China Society had both *chineses* and *chinesas*, and so on.[39] Women street dancers, like early street dancers generally, and, indeed, like the people who parade in the sambadrome today, were most often of African descent. The word *mulata* rarely appears in the turn-of-the-century sources, however.[40] *Morena* is the word most used in newspapers, and not just by the reporters. The groups called Flower of the Morenas and the Moreninhas of the Cidade Nova presumably chose their own names.* Both these groups of morenas had light skin. The White Pear Society, on the other hand, was "a handful of lovely and vivacious *crioulinhas*," a word suggesting women of quite dark complexion.[41] One group of black men called themselves—with carnivalesque immodesty—Pleasure of the Morenas. Interestingly, few groups chose to call themselves Morenos, the masculine form of the word, which just did not have the same ring.

As at carnival today, some of the dancing women were men. Cross-dressing, especially male cross-dressing, goes back to the 1840s at least in Rio's costume balls at carnival time. In the new popular carnival of the turn of the century, it was fairly common on the street. For example, a group of ersatz (bearded) Baianas provoked a lot of laughter dancing inside a circle with an equally ersatz padre.[42]

---

*In Portuguese and Spanish, a diminutive suffix like the *–inha* in *moreninha* was (and is) often used to impart an affectionate tone to racial descriptions.

A close-up look at Rio's street dance groups in the first decade of the twentieth century comes from the *Gazeta de Notícias*'s 1906 contest, already mentioned. In the weeks before carnival, reporters visited dozens of the groups' modest clubhouses to observe their preparations, and they treated their hosts' artistic efforts with respectful seriousness. The reporters noted the names of each group's officers, its colors, banner, and other emblematic paraphernalia, and the address of its clubhouse or headquarters. They described each group's percussion battery—its pancaderia or Zé Pereira. Then as now, percussion was the beating heart of popular street carnival. Assorted drums, tambourines, chocalhos, and empty kerosene cans were molded, through long practice, into each group's signature sound, the rhythmic energy of everything it did in the street.[43] The roar of practicing pancaderias floated over many Rio neighborhoods, but most especially the Cidade Nova, all January. Apparently the groups did not dance for the visiting reporters of the *Gazeta de Notícias,* for their reports say much about the music and little about the dancing. Most street groups had their own music and lyrics. The reporters make clear that beautiful morenas supplied the dominant lyrical theme, the subject of "hundreds and hundreds" of marches, maxixes, and sambas. "The Morena" was Rio's "tenth muse," they rhapsodized. "During pancaderia practice, she is there at the clubhouse . . . and then, during the three days of carnival, with the group, amid thunderous batuques and endless dancing, like an unassailable queen, continually exalted." Rhetorically, most of these lyrics seem to have been pure exaltation: "Let's go now, friends,/To the Rua Ouvidor,/To see the Moreninha/With temptations galore."[44]

Brazilian carnival discourse had featured lyrical tributes to an idealized Morena as early as the Constant Polka Society of the 1850s. Since that time, the lyrics themselves had changed less than the world around them. In the 1850s, the idealized Morena of Rio carnival was a rare, and *rarefied,* literary image cultivated in white clubs. In 1906, the idealized Morena had become queen of a popular street carnival that engulfed the entire city. Literary image she still was, but neither rare nor rarified. Thousands of flesh-and-blood black women literally danced down the middle of the street while these songs were sung by the group Pleasure of the Morenas ("When I see the Moreninhas/I go crazy with happiness") and groups like it, their Zé Pereiras filling Rio's public space with percussion.[45] They came into the center of town from their poor neighborhoods, like inner-city kids with boom boxes in late twentieth-century New York or Detroit. Freed slaves and the children of slaves had joined prosperous Bahians like Hilário Jovino and Tia Ciata in transforming Rio's carnival. And gradually, samba and popular carnival made sad, boring old Rio into a different place altogether, both in its own eyes and in the eyes of the world.

The eclipse of Rio's elite Venetian carnival by popular Afro-Brazilian carnival occurred, as we have seen, between 1886 and 1906. Yet most histories of Rio carnival date the transformation much later, to the mid 1920s. Why the confusion? The main reason is simple. The first modern samba schools were formed in the 1920s, the period when music called samba began to dominate carnival. Today, earlier troupes like Tia Ciata's White Rose are often considered to have been too elegant to represent a truly popular Afro-Brazilian tradition, but that is plainly a mistake. Ex-Epiphany troupes did not play music called samba, because no musical genre of that name yet existed, but their dancing was quite Afro-Brazilian. In fact, the dance moves now called samba had become central to the Rio's carnival street dance repertoire by 1900, as a careful examination of the newspaper reportage shows beyond question. In order to interpret that reportage, however, one must consider that the writers were not observing a series of discrete, well-defined dance genres. They were struggling to describe a fluid field of dance practice where names partially overlapped in meaning. *Samba* was only one of the words they used to characterize Afro-Brazilian dancing.

Let us visualize what the reporters saw during the parades. When street dancers visited newspaper offices, they usually pushed back the crowd to form a circle in the street out front. People entered the circle and strutted their stuff, one at a time or as couples, amid the roar of Zé Pereira percussion and clapped hands. Eventually, the troupe danced off double-file down the street, singing and playing percussion as it went. What the dancers did in the circle was often described, around 1900, as *fadinho* or *sapateado*—two words associated, during most of the nineteenth century, with Afro-Brazilian dance styles.* And, occasionally, almost any

* *Fadinho* is simply *fado* plus the Portuguese diminutive suffix inho. *Sapateado*, from the Portuguese word for shoe (*sapato*) was a style not dissimilar to U.S. tap or buck dance.

kind of dancing in the circle was also called the samba de roda.[46] The name *samba* was used by reporters to highlight the street dancers' connections with Afro-Brazilian tradition. It was applied particularly to "the beloved and celebrated customs" exemplified by troupes like Tia Ciata's White Rose; "a multitude of charming and beautiful Baianas dancing samba," in the words of *O Jornal do Brasil* in 1900.[47]

However, the reporters of the period described the movement style of samba with exactly the same vocabulary they used to describe fado, sapateado, batuque, or especially, maxixe. *O Jornal do Brasil* saluted the samba-dancing Baianas of Rosebud (yet another troupe formed by the irrepressible Hilário Jovino) for their "swaying hips" (*cadeiras requebradas*). *O Paiz,* as well, mentioned Rosebud's graceful "sways" (*requebros*), but more warmly praised the *bamboleios* ("bouncing thighs") of their competition.[48] *Gazeta de Notícias* mentioned a group of baianas whose swiveling hips made maxixe "hurt so good."[49] It is interesting to see maxixe, as well as samba, associated with Baianas. Likewise, the "loose-jointed" devils who called themselves Sons of the Flames were hailed as "meticulous maxixe dancers" also "well-versed in samba."[50] The main difference in the reporters' usage of the words *maxixe* and *samba* lay not in movement style but choreography. A man and woman who faced each other inside a circle were dancing samba. But if the couple moved into close embrace, they were dancing maxixe. A second difference was that *maxixe* had modern, urban connotations in contrast to *samba*'s traditional, rural ones. Finally, the word *maxixe* suggested a more transgressive mood. To speak of an "infernal, unrestrained" maxixe—or a "furious" or "incorrigible" or "madly shaking" maxixe—was to signal an outrageous mood particularly appropriate for carnival. It is no surprise, then, that the Sons of the Flames made *maxixe* their specialty; no surprise, either, that *samba,* with its connotations of wholesome, back-to-the-land traditionalism, ultimately won out as a label for Brazil's national rhythm.[51]

Tia Ciata lived into the mid twentieth century, plenty of time to see black street dancers become, not just the soul of Rio's carnival celebration, but a quasi-official symbol of Brazilian national identity. Tia Ciata's house was, in fact, at the center of the process by which that symbol arose. In 1917, more than twenty years after she formed White Rose, Tia Ciata lived in a big house on Praça Onze, a neat tree-lined square in a district of Rio's Cidade Nova sometimes called Little Africa. Little Africa had become the stronghold of Rio's popular carnival after the turn of the century, when the Pereira Passos urban reforms demolished much low-rent housing downtown and pushed many poor residents out.[52] Tia Ciata was not among the poor, however. She had prospered during her long marriage with João Batista da Silva, a talented man who studied a few years at Bahia's medical school, and then, in Rio, worked at *O Jornal do Comércio,* at the customs house, and finally in the office of the Chief of Police. Tia Ciata and João Batista had fifteen children before he died, some time before 1917. It was especially after his death that the house on Praça Onze became known throughout Rio as "Tia Ciata's house," scene of some the city's most famous parties.

Now, around 1917, samba was becoming a musical genre. Today's histories of samba music usually date its emergence to "On the Telephone," a song invented during collective improvisations at Tia Ciata's parties. "On the Telephone" became the great carnival sensation of 1917.[53] Tia Ciata's parties filled her big house: conventional couple dancing in the front room, samba de roda in the back yard, lots of food. "It was a black party," recalled one who was there, "but whites went, too, just to have fun." This anonymous reminiscence then continues:

> Only the best dancers participated in the sapateado, though. Somebody willing to get in the roda was somebody you knew was good. Back then I was a carpenter. I'd get home from work and say "Ma, I'm going to Tia Ciata's house," and she wouldn't worry because they had everything there. The parties went on for days and days. We sort of lived there."[54]

Tia Ciata had been cooking sweets for sale on the street all her life. Now she had employees. As Tia Ciata of Oxum (for Oxum was her special deity, a bit like a patron saint, in Candomblé), she produced superb chicken *ximxim* with dendê palm oil and coconut milk, a dish sacred to Oxum. Most of her guests were working-class blacks: artisans, city employees, stevedores, many Bahians like herself. Attracted by the growing national glamour of samba and popular carnival, curious whites from aristocratic Botafogo across town—people to whom Tia Ciata sometimes now rented Baiana dresses to use as carnival costumes—were beginning to drop in, too.

In later years, the old samba players remembered police repression of their parties as repression of samba. For example, João da Baiana, a famous early samba player and son of another Bahian matriarch, Tia Perciliana, was in and out of Tia Ciata's house from the age of ten. "Now, samba was prohibited so they had to get a police license," he recalled. "You had to go down to police headquarters and explain there was going to be a samba, I mean, a dance, you know, a party."[55] But getting police permission to hold a dance was fairly routine, and Tia Ciata was not likely to be refused, given her husband's connection to the police department. At Tia Ciata's parties, the only policemen present were sent to stand guard there as a courtesy of the Chief of Police.

During carnival, many groups of street dancers visited the house of Tia Ciata. "She was one of the first Baianas, always in demand, and she helped make Praça Onze famous," remembered Tia Carmem do Xibuca, Ciata's friend and contemporary:

> At carnival, all the clubs stopped at her door to pay their respects and get her blessing. She'd open the doors and serve whatever she had on hand. They'd party inside a while, then head off. What a pity to have lost the only photo I had of her. I lent it to a reporter, and he never gave it back.[56]

New groups called samba schools—rowdier, more free form, endowed with heavier percussion than the old-fashioned Ex-Epiphany troupes—appeared in the 1920s. They became the enduring main event of Rio carnival, incorporating floats like those of the old Great Societies as well as street dancers like those of White Rose. By World War Two, all the principal parades of Rio's festival celebrated samba.[57] Not everyone was happy with this situation. "Our carnival has turned into a big African party," lamented one columnist in Rio's illustrated magazine *Fon Fon* in 1922. "The monotonous drone of barbarous drums" assaulted his ears everywhere he went, it seems, during the three days of carnival madness. He asked himself: Was this Brazil or Senegal?[58] Rejecting popular carnival, *Fon Fon*'s reportage focused on Rio's upper crust. Photo after photo showed well-heeled whites at high-tone society gatherings.

But other *Fon Fon* writers reacted positively, noting the apparent unanimity of carnival revelers, rich and poor, all humming the same tunes and repeating the same lyrics. If samba's detractors called it African, its defenders called it quintessentially Brazilian. Samba dancing retained strong rural/provincial associations in the 1920s. In other words, it was the stuff of which folklore is made, and folklore had important political applications throughout Latin America in these years.[59]

Defenses and appreciations of samba became key expressions of an emerging cultural nationalism in mid-twentieth century Brazil. Bit by bit, the influence of coffee-planters—and the landowning class generally—had weakened with the deterioration of the international market for their crops. At the same time, the growth of working-class and middle-class populations in Brazilian cities created the potential for new political alliances capable of challenging the domination of rural oligarchies. Urban political alliances required a new style of politics, however. Rio's twentieth-century populace, like other urban people throughout Brazil, could not be herded to the polls at election time the way landowners did with poor rural people who lived on or around their great estates. Urban constituencies were more anonymous, less easily compelled to support the candidate of some powerful patron. Urban constituencies had to be wooed through new methods.[60]

The collapse of the international import/export trade, beginning in 1929, further weakened a system of oligarchic rule already in crisis. As a result, Brazil's Revolution of 1930, spearheaded by urban reformers of various stripes, reconfigured political power. The fifteen-year rule of Getúlio Vargas brought unprecedented efforts to engage and rearrange the political loyalties of urban Brazilians. In Rio, a populist mayor began to offer official sponsorship to black street dancers early in the decade. An annual competition was held in the Praça Onze. In 1938, the relationship was institutionalized in a government-linked Union of Samba Schools. From then on, samba acquired a quasi-official status as Brazil's national rhythm. The markedly patriotic carnival festivals of the World War Two years further solidified that status. In the 1950s and 1960s, Rio's carnival would become Brazil's number one image for export, a major attraction for international tourism. Brazil had become the Kingdom of Samba.[61]

Government support came with strings attached, however. Samba schools were to choose "Brazilian," meaning *nationalist,* themes for their parades. Even their music and dancing were to follow certain (supposedly traditional) guidelines. Interestingly, these guidelines were not intended to make their samba seem less African. In fact, the contrary was true. Wind instruments like clarinets and flutes were banned in favor of massed drumming, which had not been used by the first samba schools.[62] Vargas-era populism fostered a new ideology of race in Brazil, an ideology that celebrated the country's African heritage as a root element of its racial mixture. No matter what its annual theme, each samba school was required to have Baianas to commemorate the early contributions of women like Tia Ciata. The African/Bahian roots of Rio's carnival were now appropriated to serve the festival's consensual political meaning. Here is the paradigmatic case of "dirty dancing" turned "national rhythm."

Chapter Four

The Podestá Brothers' Circus (Buenos Aires)

Argentina's national rhythm turned out very differently from Brazil's, though around 1890, Argentine milonga and Brazilian maxixe were quite similar, as we have seen. To understand the forces shaping Argentina's national rhythm we will have to look at nineteenth-century Buenos Aires carnival. Perhaps the reader will, by this time, not find that an odd approach. After all, if tango history is full of brothels, why should it not include carnival? We will begin our tango history, however, with something even more incongruous: the circus.

Let us begin with a particular circus performance of 1889, when the first stage milonga was danced in the Río de la Plata as part of a melodrama called *Juan Moreira,* about a good gaucho* gone wrong. Rather oddly, given its significance in the history of the Argentine national theater, the performance took place in Montevideo, and

* Gauchos were the Argentine and Uruguayan equivalent of American cowboys—plainsmen whose dress, speech, and equestrian culture became symbols of national identity.

the performers were Uruguayans. For the purposes of a gaucho melodrama, however, the difference was immaterial. The hinterland of Montevideo had been gaucho country, no less than had Argentina's province of Buenos Aires. An Uruguayan could play the outlaw protagonist of this Argentine story perfectly well.

The startling success of the *Juan Moreira* circus melodrama defined an epoch in the popular culture of the Río de la Plata. The show played forty-two straight performances during its first Montevideo season.[1] Then it became an even bigger hit in Buenos Aires, where it packed applauding audiences into its downtown circus tent through the mid 1890s. People saw *Juan Moreira* over and over again. A reporter for *Sud América* described an 1895 Buenos Aires crowd where doctors and politicians rub elbows with the hoi poloi. The number of well-to-do circus-goers was obvious from the expensive carriages outside. The street in front of the tent was habitually clogged for several blocks with double-parked carriages. But the show attracted people of various social classes. Huge, crudely lithographed bills showing the gaucho on his horse were plastered all over Buenos Aires: *Juan Moreira, drama criollo.*[2]

Criollo. The word has appeared in chapter two, the reader may recall, to describe dancing with cortes and quebradas—the basic choreography of first milonga and then tango. Criollo signified something essential in emerging notions of Argentine national identity. Anything that had resulted from centuries-old Spanish colonization was criollo—as opposed to later importations.[3] Criollo horses and livestock were the old Iberian breeds that Spanish missionaries had introduced to the grassy plains of the Río de la Plata in the 1500s—as opposed to the fancy pedigreed livestock recently imported from England. Criollo speech was full of metaphors taken from rural life, without the Frenchified expressions favored by the elegant "swells" of the Buenos Aires upper class. And popular Criollista* fiction, like the novel *Juan Moreira* from which the melodrama was taken, dealt with rural people, especially gauchos. Townspeople could be criollo—but not quite so criollo as country people.[4]

* The Spanish and Portuguese suffixes *–ista* (-ist) and *–ismo* (-ism) mean just what one would suppose.

The *Juan Moreira* melodrama was part of a *circo criollo,* a one-ring circus with clowns, trapeze artists, and lots of equestrian acrobats. The "low-brow" tone of the show contrasted with that of the opera or other refined entertainments requiring considerable carriage parking space. Yet, like the street samba that Tia Ciata was promoting in Rio, *Juan Moreira* attracted spectators in the 1890s who might not have attended a criollo circus before. Like Brazilian street samba, the criollo circus represents a new middle-class interest in popular culture. Criollista pulp fiction and the criollo circus were simply Argentine variants of a transnational social phenomenon, exemplified in the United States by "dime novels" and "Wild West" shows.[5]

By inviting audiences to identify themselves with what was "of the country," *Juan Moreira* made a *nativist* appeal. Nativism—and its accompanying xenophobia, the other side of the same coin—might be expected in cities so full of immigrants as Montevideo or Buenos Aires. In addition to celebrating gauchos, the *Juan Moreira* melodrama poked fun at immigrants. The show's pathetically comic Italian immigrant character, Cocoliche (wearing outlandish clothing, leading a skinny nag, and speaking fractured Spanish) put the expression "to speak *cocoliche*" into the lexicon of the Río de la Plata. But Río de la Plata criollismo was more agglutinative than exclusive, more didactic than mean-spirited. Immigrants like the Cocoliche character could be redeemed culturally, *acriollandose* (becoming "creolized"). Cocoliche needed a better horse, and he needed to ride it well—two prime elements of criollo self-respect. A change of clothes would make a big difference. And, as always, speech was a crucial marker of identity. Immigrant children who arrived young enough to speak like Criollos were considered native in all but birth. As for the native-born children of Italian immigrants, they were Criollos by definition.[6]

Native-born blacks were Criollos, too. In fact, black music and dance became a key element of what was criollo—and therefore, of what was *national*—in the 1890s, just as carnival samba was emerging in Rio de Janeiro. The two national rhythms drew on analogous energies, and they satisfied similar needs for inclusive national identities. But the Brazilian and Argentine national rhythms constructed inclusiveness differently. Samba foregrounded blackness, while tango dissolved it into whiteness. Certainly, it is no mere coincidence that these opposite processes occurred as Brazilian cities swelled with black migrants from the countryside, while, in contrast, the black population of the Río de la Plata seemed physically to disappear under massive waves of European immigration.

These waves of European immigration to Buenos Aires recall a problem raised earlier. How did the black tango of the nineteenth century become the white tango of the twentieth? Rio forged a national rhythm at carnival, and, as promised, we will look at Buenos Aires carnival for clues, too. First, however, let us return to the Podestá Brothers, their circus, and their criollo melodrama *Juan Moreira.* As will become evident throughout this book, theater is a crucial "site" of dance history—especially for the stagey tango.

The Podestá brothers surely spoke Italian with their parents, who were both Genoese. The family had left Italy in the 1840s and moved back and forth between Montevideo and Buenos Aires several times before ultimately settling in Montevideo. The father worked at the city's slaughterhouse—not a prestigious occupation, but one lucrative enough for him to buy a modest house. Pepe, the future actor and protagonist of *Juan Moreira,* was born in 1858, making him four years younger than Tia Ciata. Pepe Podestá's published memoir tells us much more than we know about Tia Ciata, however.[7]

At the age of about fourteen, Pepe Podestá began practicing acrobatic stunts with his friends and brothers. Within a couple of years, in 1874, they had started a makeshift circus in a vacant lot, the same boys doubling as acrobats, musicians, and ticket takers. Music was a big part of their act. Pepe played several brass instruments. He had also formed a dance troupe of sixteen members, doing mostly quadrilles.* The troupe (eight boys and girls in their late teens) practiced partly for fun and partly for public performances. From then on, dance always figured in Podestá circus acts. In the late 1870s, Pepe and his older brother Jerónimo bought a real circus tent and made a few tentative forays into the well-populated rural hinterland around Montevideo. During 1880, they crossed the Río de la Plata

* Quadrilles were a kind of square dance.

and did their first tour through Buenos Aires province, where the whole family later resettled.[8]

The Podestá staging of the *Juan Moreira* melodrama began in 1884. Like the carnivalesque version of Brazilian folklore appearing on Rio streets that year, the Podestás' gaucho theatricals presented a stylized version of rural/provincial culture. So dominated by foreigners were the performing arts of 1880s Buenos Aires that a convincing criollo melodrama was hard to cast. The first who tried were the Carlo Brothers, another Italian circus family.[9] The Carlo Brothers approached Eduardo Gutiérrez, author of the *Juan Moreira* pulp novel, who reportedly told them the idea would never work: "To put on Moreira you'd need a criollo actor," he said, "someone who rides like a Criollo, who knows how to act, sing, dance, and play the guitar like one." So the Carlos (who were quite an international family, U.S. citizens, in fact) contracted the Podestás to stage a melodrama of the Gutiérrez novel. The melodrama's first version was a pantomime accompanied by music. In it, Pepe Podestá sang a rustic folk song that the audience was charmed to hear performed on stage, a novelty at the time. Two black musicians were hired to play traditional rural music for the big dance scene.[10]

Why would black musicians be brought in to perform a music associated with gauchos? Gauchos were not all white, and black gauchos had a reputation as musicians. Rustic *payadores* (singers and guitar players skilled at improvisation) were often black. The literary gaucho Martín Fierro, protagonist of the 1872 poem by José Hernández, has a famous musical showdown with a black payador, for example. Black gauchos have tended to be forgotten in Argentina, just as black cowboys have in the United States. In the 1890s, however, black payadores were understood to be an authentic part of the criollo scene. The payadores presence in the circo criollo was part of a more general nativist vogue. Rustic payadores were performing in various urban settings at the time. Conditions were right. No wonder *Juan Moreira* inspired a host of imitators, becoming emblematic of popular culture in the 1890s Río de la Plata.[11]

The Podestás' interest in social realism went hand in hand with their interest in Criollismo. When they re-crafted the *Juan Moreira* pantomime in 1886, now for their own circus,[12] they added dialogue and many realistic details, like horses (this was an equestrian circus—half stage and half earthen-floored ring), even lighting fires and roasting meat on stage. Once, the realistic behavior of secondary characters—suddenly quarreling over a card game—prompted a watchman to jump on stage to stop the fight. It was their desire for realism, apparently, that prompted the Podestás to choose a milonga for the grim final scene of *Juan Moreira,* set in a gritty dance hall on the urban outskirts.[13]

Not coincidentally, gritty dance halls—and similarly fabled locales of early tango lore—must have been chief venues for the mystery we need to explain: how white dancers learned a style created by black dancers. But one can glean only so much from the existing evidence. Here, for example, is a particularly detailed newspaper account from *La Patria Argentina* in 1880:

> Generally public dances are hidden in establishments where one sees on the dirty white–painted glass, black letters made bold by the interior lights: "Café So and So." In the front room there really is a café . . .
>
> The door to the next room is closed, and all one hears are the voices of customers and the sounds of waitresses about their work. But then someone wanders through that door and stays a while, or someone else appears, looking a bit fatigued, and goes to drink something at the bar—generally French wine and fizzy water in equal parts, a drink invented by the Italians. . . . And each time the door opens one hears an odd brushing sound on the floor, like a lot of people dragging their feet.[14]

So the writer, too, goes through the door into a stuffy room full of cigarette smoke and oddly quiet. He then describes how thick padding has been strapped around an organ-grinder's organ so that it produces mostly a percussive thumping, as if on wet wood:

> And to that strange music, men dance with only two, three, or four women hired by the owner. These poor women dance all night every night without a rest, passing from the arms of a Criollo dancer, who twists her in a milonga, to the arms of an Englishman man who shakes her stiffly in a waltz, to the arms

> of an Italian who disjoints her in a *peringundín*. The room fills up with men, and since the women are few, some men dance with each other just to take advantage of the music, which costs a peso per song. When the piece is over, someone quickly calls out "lata," referring to the tokens used to pay for the songs and signaling his request.[15]

Otherwise, the people barely speak, intent on dancing, and the rhythmic shuffling of feet is the dominant sound.

No mention of *tango,* only of *milonga,* which appears as the dance characteristic of a Criollo. On the other hand, the quotation does mention men practicing with men, a still mostly unexplored aspect of tango/milonga history.[16] The account also illuminates the meaning of "Dame la lata" ("Give me the token"), the title of a well-known milonga of the day. There is definitely nothing on "mocking imitation" in this description, however. The next year, a different paper, *La Pampa,* reported on similar peso-per-dance-halls. According to this article, around the barracks at the Plaza del Parque "dance halls alternate with houses of prostitution for whole blocks." In addition to muffling the sound, this article points out, some cagey owners stationed lookouts at both corners of the block and another at the door, who would reach inside to ring a bell at the approach of a police patrol. On the other hand, the patrol might be deaf to the music, since those charged with enforcing the prohibition against illicit dancing were not uncommonly bribed. When one operator failed to get a license, then tried to bribe the police in 1881, he was able to offer the appreciable sum of fifty to one hundred pesos and, when the trusty officer turned him in anyway, the owner quickly (and with revealing ease) paid one thousand pesos to stay out of jail.[17]

The police who licensed dance halls left very little evidence in the official records of the dancing at such places. Their main concern was with prostitution. They inspected the premises of applicants who wanted to hold public dances, even just occasionally, and very often refused permission to dance. "It is well-known that dances in such places, replete with women of ill-repute, are hotbeds of scandal and immorality," affirmed one inspector. The inspectors refused permission, as well, to applicants who wanted to start little businesses in conventillos.[18] The big parties of immigrant mutual aid societies also required special permission for dancing. For example, when the Círculo Italiano applied to put on "some honest diversions" in 1886 the inspector found "perfectly hygienic conditions" at the locale. Soon, though, he returned to inquire just what diversions were planned. "Dancing exclusively among the family of our members," explained the Círculo Italiano. Unpersuaded, the city government then asked for a report on the *type* of dances planned—and the unfortunate Italians gave up, apparently because the planned date had already passed. The Círculo Italiano may have run afoul of ethnic profiling, because, to judge by the names in the city records, most of Buenos Aires café and dance hall owners (suspected, *ispso facto,* of abetting prostitution) were Italian.[19]

The infrequent mention of milonga dancing, despite the indubitable popularity of the practice, is partly explained by the associations of the name *milonga* itself: vulgar, pejorative, signifying a dance "exclusively of the lower orders." Even people who liked the style might be squeamish about saying—much less writing—that they danced milonga. That squeamishness is plain in the dignified black newspaper *La Broma,* which shows that dancing was central to the social life of the black community in the 1870s and 1880s but, much concerned about respectability, never uses the word *milonga.*[20] On the other hand, the paper indicates that the preferred music at black parties was habanera—the Cuban music which, more than any other, inspired Río Platense dancers to invent "cut-and-break" choreography. "That milonga descends from habanera is something few have ever questioned," wrote Héctor and Luis J. Bates, the best early chroniclers of tango history, in 1936. So, *La Broma*'s frequent references to habanera music no doubt indicate frequent milonga dancing at gatherings of Buenos Aires blacks. Some whites could obviously have been in attendance, of course. But dances of the black community were surely not occasions for "mocking imitation" of black dancers by white ones.[21]

If we have no eye-witness descriptions of white dancers learning milonga from black ones in brothels or dance halls or black parties, what about carnival? In 1890s Rio, press reporting on street carnival frankly celebrated maxixe and samba, producing a lot of evidence. It is time to look at carnival in nineteenth-century Buenos Aires.

From the 1860s through the 1880s, carnival was just as lively in Buenos Aires as in Rio—and fully as elite-dominated.[22] Venetian-style parade groups like Rio's Great Societies were the main event on Calle Florida, the fashionable downtown street of Buenos Aires analogous to Rio's Rua do Ouvidor. In Buenos Aires, these groups were called *comparsas,* which is a common term in Spanish for carnival street musicians and dancers. Somewhat horrifyingly, many elite comparsas in Buenos Aires were performed in blackface, as if for a U.S.-style minstrel show. One would not choose to dwell on their performances, perhaps, were they not precisely the "smoking gun" that we seek. Could there exist a more obvious instance of "mocking imitation of blacks by whites"?[23]

The Buenos Aires vogue of blackface comparsas had begun in the mid 1860s with the Dramático-Musical Society Los Negros, a carnival group formed by young men of the city's richest and most powerful families. The group played both stringed and wind instruments and paraded wearing the Hungarian-style "zoave" uniforms so widely copied in the mid nineteenth century—with kepis, blue jackets, and baggy white pants tucked into knee-length boots. Los Negros danced at carnival balls but not in the street. Their principal activity in the street was marching around in double file, stopping to play and sing popular melodies of the day beneath the windows of "decent" young women. The confident young men of Los Negros thought nothing of blocking the street and stopping the parade to serenade a strategic balcony. In 1869, their membership stood at about fifty, twenty of them musicians, with a permanent clubhouse where they held dances year round. Soon, Los Negros had many imitators. In fact, blackface characterized Buenos Aires carnival for the rest of the century.[24]

Not only did the domineering young men of Los Negros blacken their faces. They also actively impersonated blacks. Each member took a persona identified by a nickname: "the old black man, the black street vendor, the black kid just-off-the-boat" (*negro viejo, negro de los pasteles, negrillo bozal*). The group's members also practiced caricatures of black speech (*no señola, yo soy güeno, no digo mentilas*) and, in song after song, they returned to the same theme, dramatizing the love of humble, docile slaves for their masters' untouchable daughters.

The musical group Los Negros,	La comparsa de Los Negros,
Most trusty and most true,	La más constante y leal,
Greets every sweet missy,	A las amitas saluda,
To give her this year's due.	En el nuevo carnaval.
And each Negro offers, Missy,	Y a las niñas, como esclavos,
Slave in body and in soul,	Se ofrece para servir,
To remain your faithful servant,	Esclavos de cuerpo y alma,
Until his life is o'er.	Y fieles hasta morir.

And then the chorus: "Oh, white missies! For pity's sake, hear our sad black voices . . ."[25]

Let us take a moment to absorb this ditty. The male-lover-as-black-slave metaphor was not original with the lyrics of Los Negros. Like blackface—with which it obviously had a symbiotic relationship—that metaphor was widespread in nineteenth-century lyrics. In addition, theatrical stylization of black music, dance, and speech had been happening in Spain since the sixteenth century. The 1860s Río de la Plata was also clearly influenced by U.S. blackface performances. It must be kept in mind that blackface minstrelsy was then among the most popular stage entertainments in the United States. The elite of Buenos Aires had an opportunity to see the blackface minstrel version of *Uncle Tom's Cabin* performed in Spanish adaptation as early as 1856, and a series of blackface theatrical tours visited Buenos Aires in the late 1860s. In 1867, the city celebrated a Panamanian actor's impersonation of a black broom seller, "Negro Schicoba." In 1868, theater goers in Buenos Aires heard a U.S. minstrel performer render Stephen Foster songs in blackface to banjo accompaniment. The next year the famous Christy Minstrels visited from the United States. The stylish youth of Los Negros organized their comparsa at just this time—a coincidence, perhaps.[26]

In sum, blackface performances were commonplace in the Atlantic world at mid nineteenth century. But Buenos Aires embraced blackface with particular enthusiasm. For example, although Los Negros did not parade in 1881, their absence may not have been noticed among comparsas that included Los Negros Cocineros, La Estrella de Africa, Los Primitivos Negros Azúcares, Los Negros Porteños, Los Pobres Negros Orientales, Las Negras Mucamas, Los Negros Alegres, Perla Africana, Los Negros Triunfantes, Grupo Negras Porteñas, Los Negros del Sud, Los Negros Esclavos, Los Negros Chichones, Las

Negritas Unidas, Los Negros Americanos, Las Hijas de Africa, and Los Negros Candomberos.* These were more than a quarter of the sixty-one comparsas parading that year at Buenos Aires carnival—amounting, all told, to two thousand participants with an audience estimated at 150,000 (counting the people in their balconies).[27] Of course, there were comparsas with many other themes, too. Italian and Spanish immigrants paraded specifically as such, for example. Furthermore, some of the groups named above were not blackface comparsas, but comparsas of real black people. Yet others were comparsas of real black people wearing blackface—a practice we are about to address. Still, the question remains unanswered: blackface was far more important in Buenos Aires (and Montevideo) than Rio or, as we will see, Havana. Why?

Romance, it must be said, was the main concern of Los Negros' Venetian-style carnival revelry. So Los Negros, when singing beneath the balconies of privileged young women, were impersonating specifically black *males.* At some level, no matter how indirectly, this entertainment involved white peoples' imagining the black male as a lover of white women. That scenario, one cannot help noticing, reversed the commonplace of Latin American life, with the idealized Morena and her often-white partner. To understand what was going on, we should observe that in historical societies where social roles narrowly defined people's lives, role reversals had an inherent dramatic interest. The imaginative life of such societies is less about choices (*what if I became an astronaut?*) than about how well people play their assigned roles (*what if I were in his shoes?*). This particular role reversal was a volatile one—the sexuality of black males carrying, as it did, an imaginative charge, the same charge that fueled lynchings of thousands of black men in the United States around the turn of the century. The fascination of Los Negros has its own logic. And, well-to-do whites in Buenos Aires, with its rapidly dwindling black population, could permit themselves this provocative fantasy. Perhaps that is why blackface performances were less popular in Rio and Havana, where large black populations made black men's desire for white women a riskier imaginative game.[28]

* Translation of these names would be too tedious. By glancing at the list, however, even non-readers of Spanish can form a sense of their variety and their insistent representation of a black identity.

In 1902, a black grandmother's reminiscences about Buenos Aires carnival were quoted in the city's illustrated magazine *Caras y Caretas:* "In 1870, before the [yellow] fever, young men of good families started dressing up as blacks, even imitating the way we talk," she said. "And after a while, there wasn't an Italian in this whole city that didn't dress up as an African, make faces, and do truly ridiculous dances." This woman had danced in real street candombes, an elaborate pageant with king and queen, similar to the Brazilian Cucumbys. "We had no choice but to shut ourselves up in our houses," she said about the post-1870 period, "because we were poor and felt ashamed."[29] Real street candombes did disappear at that time. Partly, though, they just changed form.

Almost immediately after the appearance of Los Negros, blacks formed musical comparsas of their own. They followed the blackface model closely—adopting their uniforms and serenades, even the mock-black dialect of their lyrics—but rejected the obsessive theme of black men loving white women. *La Broma,* the black newspaper, gave a lot of space to the organizational efforts of carnival comparsas in the 1870s—lyrics, rehearsals, fund-raisers. In 1878, for example, *La Broma* celebrated the following male comparsas: Musical Primitiva Los Tenorios, Estrella del Sud, Los Tenorios del Plata, El Progreso de la Creación, Los Negros Esclavos, Los Negros Libres, Símbolo Republicano, 6 de Enero, Los Tunantes, and La Aurora. And it saluted female comparsas, too: Las Negras Bonitas, Las Unionistas, Las Negras Libres, Las Humildes, Las Soberbias, Las Negra Esclavas, Las Verduleras, Las Tenorias del Plata, and last but certainly not least, the paper's own official comparsa, Las Amigas de *La Broma.*[30] Plainly, the new-style carnival comparsas became important vehicles of community life, much like the candombe associations remembered by the grandmother of 1902.

As in Rio, black carnival paraders staked their claim to public space partly in the street and partly in the press. In Buenos Aires, though, it was the black press. When a writer from the black newspaper *La Broma* visited Montevideo in 1881, he called on that city's black comparsas (Los Negros Ferreros, Las Negras Lavaderas, Raza Africana, Los Changadores, Estrella del Este, Los Negros Congos, Las Negras Minas) even though he was not there during carnival.[31]

By 1882, though, *La Broma* had become ambivalent about black participation in Buenos Aires carnival. In the early 1880s, new blackface street groups were performing a satire of candombe at carnival. Instead of wearing smart military-style uniforms like the older comparsas, these *candombero* groups dressed as slaves, or even as African tribesmen in imitation leopard skins and black tights. Candombero groups featured drums rather than strings and wind instruments, and, unlike the uniformed musical comparsas, the candomberos more or less danced during their street performances. That is, they did a mocking imitation that was meant to represent—but was very far from really replicating—the elaborate choreography of real candombes.[32] *La Broma* remained silent on the subject of white candomberos in blackface, but it blasted the *black* candomberos that were soon mirroring the blackface groups, even darkening their own faces to do so. "There are countless among those young fellows," said *La Broma,* "who would act ashamed if one of our *tías** were to beg them to play the drum at one of the few remaining candombe houses . . . and yet they shamelessly put on blackface and expose themselves to the hilarity of the general public in the middle of Calle Florida."[33] In darkening their faces, black candomberos were quite explicitly imitating those who imitated them. Obviously, they had mocking intentions of their own.

Let us leave this troubling hall of mirrors with a clear lesson. By the end of the nineteenth century, Buenos Aires whites had considerable practice at "mocking imitations" of black people. Blackface carnival comparsas, most popular in the 1870s and the 1880s, had institutionalized blackface as a participatory activity, practiced by thousands of men. So, the idea of white people learning black people's dances, even amid the prevailing racism of nineteenth-century Latin America, clearly has validity. This look at Buenos Aires carnival has confirmed the mocking, but also erotically charged, spirit of their imitation.

But were the blackface paraders of Buenos Aires dancing tangos between 1870 and 1900? The answer is "no" if by *tango* one means couples doing "cut-and-break" moves. Buenos Aires street paraders rarely, if ever, danced as couples. But the blackface comparsas and

* "Aunts," meaning neo-African matriarchs like Tia Ciata.

candomberos certainly did use the word *tango* a lot. Entirely too much has been written already about the etymology of words like *tango* and *milonga.* Let's merely sketch their range of meanings to show how milonga was more or less absorbed into tango around 1900.

So far, we have established that the name *milonga* was strongly associated, in the 1890s, with cut-and-break choreography. As for the word *tango,* over two centuries it has meant, variously, a place where slaves were kept on the African coast, a free association of blacks in Buenos Aires, any African-style dance to drums, a candombe house such as the one mentioned in *La Broma* and a dozen other things. A new meaning of the word became salient among the blackface performers of the mid nineteenth century—like Los Negros. This new tango was a musical, but not a dance, genre. When a Spanish touring company presented its adaptation of *Uncle Tom's Cabin* in Buenos Aires, its blackface chorus sang "tangos." When Germán MacKay—the Panamanian blackface actor who presented El Negro Schicoba—sang his mock-dialect songs about liking to dance and making the girls blush, it was called a "tango."[34] In one sense, the new meaning was not different, however. Before acquiring its current meaning as the name of Argentina's national rhythm, the word *tango* was always somehow associated with the African diaspora.*

During the mid 1800s, musical tangos were identified partly by use of mock dialect. A Madrid dictionary of the period defined tango as "a song with black slang."[35] For example, the blackface comparsas of Buenos Aires carnival played waltzes, polkas, and other music from a "straight" repertory, as well as "tangos." They did "straight" numbers out of character, apparently—then reverted to their blackface caricature when the drums announced a "tango," normally sung in mock dialect. Even the *black* comparsas sang numbers called "tangos" in mock dialect. A lyric presented by the black Sociedad de Negros Humildes at carnival in 1881 shows the switching of "r" and "l" conventionally used in Spanish to imitate the speech of African slaves. The same lyric also illustrates how milonga was created. In the lyric, "Mundele and Cagombo" (two caricatured Africans) dance the European rhythms of mazurka and

* The word *tango* also has uniformly African associations elsewhere in Latin America, as in Cuba, for example.

schottische, "only requebrando their waists/and shuffling their feet."[36] That "shuffling" sound, the same sound the reporter heard in the back room of the clandestine dance hall, signals the groundedness and lateral hip motion typical of African-influenced dance.[37] This theme tango by a black—not a blackface—carnival comparsa offers an affectionate and choreographically well-informed caricature. But it is still a caricature. Otherwise, it would not have been a "tango."

In sum, from the 1860s until the 1890s, tango meant above all a caricature of black identity. Most "tangos" were blackface tangos. This was, at least, the most common documentable meaning of the word and certainly the word's main meaning among whites. Future applications of the word would necessarily have to absorb this baggage.

The modern meaning of *tango*—referring to a closed-couple dance using cut-and-break choreography—does not appear in the historical sources until the 1890s. Very clearly, the words *tango* and *milonga* were converging in meaning during that decade, becoming synonymous. Popular musical theater again provides clues to changing meanings. The dialogue of the short musical skits called *sainetes* often paired *tango* and *milonga* in the 1890s: "We'll give it some tango and milonga!" Sheet music for pieces labeled *milonga* might be advertised for sale as *tangos.*[38] Then, around 1900, the word *milonga,* referring to a distinct dance genre, disappears from the historical record altogether. The word *milonga* retained several meanings within the vocabulary of tango dancers: a gathering where people dance tango; a fast, early sort of music within the tango repertory; and, in the form *milonguita,* a woman who dances tango. Overall, however, cut-and-break dancing had changed names. From around 1900 on, people would use the word *tango* to define the style of music and dance that had developed under the name *milonga.*

The name change happened just as middle-class people began their collective flirtation with the transgressive close embrace. White Buenos Aires was learning, en masse, a dance style associated with black dancers. But these dancers were rarely present to do the teaching. At this point, black Buenos Aires had been submerged under a flood of European immigrants, dwindling to less than 2 percent of the population. The main teachers of the all-white new generation of tango dancers were whites who had learned cut-and-break technique in gritty dancehalls and conventillos back when cutting-and-breaking in close embrace was still usually called milonga. Their pupils, the rising generation of 1900–1920, learned basically the same moves as tango. The situation was analogous to what happened in the 1950s United States, when the basic elements of black *rhythm and blues* became white *rock and roll*. The new name reflected more a sociological than a musicological or choreographical difference.

Still, the legions of new dancers just off the boat from Europe had their own impact on the genre. Very few probably learned to dance exactly like Argentines of African descent. And yet, "dancing black" was unquestionably what they had in mind. The adoption of the name *tango* confirms that. As we have seen, the word *tango* carried a salient allusion to blackness: not the real-life black experience of poor neighborhoods, but the caricatured—and therefore safer, more distanced—attitudes of blackface carnival. The new label *tango* invited white Buenos Aires to approach close-embrace cutting-and-breaking in a spirit of temporary appropriation. White Buenos Aires wanted to flirt with danger but not to marry it. It wanted to dance a "low-life" fantasy without really joining the "low life." It wanted to "dance black" without the color's rubbing off. The name *tango* suggested a carnivalesque mood for middle-class experimentation with transgressive popular culture.

So, just as in Rio, carnival in Buenos Aires helped loosen up the middle class for the close embrace.[39] Middle-class men, of course, had dabbled with the dance even before 1900. At the turn of the century, middle-class women rarely danced tango at all, except when their husbands or brothers showed them a few steps picked up here and there in situations they declined to explain. Tango was not for "polite company." Carnival dances were the great exception. In the words of a Spanish traveler quoted by the Buenos Aires press just after 1900: "With carnival here, the tango has virtually taken over dance programs because, being so libertine, it can only be tolerated during those days of temporary madness."[40]

Precisely for this reason, carnival often figures in twentieth-century reminiscences about the advent of tango. According to a mid-century memoir, for example: "Tango spread through the city via the Politeama theater, the dance's Mecca during carnival." Back in 1903, when the process had just begun, *La Tribuna* reported an invasion of "cheap dances" at the city's carnival balls.[41] The illustrated magazine *Caras y Caretas* announced the phenomenon again in 1904: "One could say that the tango criollo has been glorified in this year's carnival." Tango seems to have been that year's novelty even in up-scale venues, and more so at popular ones. "Of the popular theaters," continued *Caras y Caretas,* "the favorite among Criollos has been the Argentino. There, tango with cortes and quebradas predominated, and some truly notable couples won ovations from spectators in the boxes."[42] At the Victoria Theater, "people gathered round to see a *china orillera,** an acclaimed mistress of the difficult art, whose prodigious quebradas garnered applause."[43]

Gradually, during the first half of the twentieth century, Buenos Aires as a whole embraced tango dancing, and the dance continued to evolve. In 1905, the Argentine navy frigate Sarmiento made its famous second voyage to Europe carrying one thousand copies of sheet music to a tango called "La Morocha,"† of which 280,000 more copies soon had to be made. The dance of Buenos Aires brothels had been launched on the path to international celebrity.[44] After 1910, most tango dancers abandoned the bouncy, hunch-shouldered funkiness of milonga, and their hips became less mobile. The original association with black dancing faded quickly in the popular imagination. Tango music became much slower, and its spirit changed completely. Sad or bitter lyrics accented its new, often melancholy mood. Tango music and dancing were becoming, in a word, more Europeanized.[45] No wonder the tango today is so unlike other dances influenced by the African diaspora. No wonder, too, that it is so easily caricatured. The spirit of caricature has been inherent in its history, infusing tango with "attitude" and exaggeration.

Thus did Argentina's modern national rhythm—a dance with an African name but apparently little else African about it—turn out so differently from Brazilian samba. Before turning to our third national rhythm, Cuban danzón, we should notice an important ambiguity of the Argentine case (and of the Uruguayan case, which is identical in most respects). Tango is unquestionably Argentina's signature music and dance when viewed from outside the country.

---

* *China orillera* means here a poor and not-quite-white woman from the outskirts of Buenos Aires.

† Yet another slang term for a woman of dark complexion.

Inside the country, however, far from metropolitan Buenos Aires, another genre of music and dance competes with tango for the prestige of national rhythm.[46]

The principal competitors to the tango as Argentina's national dance come from rural criollo folklore. Like tango itself, criollo folk dances belong to the great family tree of Latin America's national rhythms. One of them is, in fact, called *zamba,* and the resemblance between samba and zamba* is clearly a family resemblance. The point is that the tree of national rhythms has branches that diverge *within* countries as well as between them. In Argentina, the most prominent internal branching parallels the great divide in Argentine history: the port capital versus "the interior," city versus countryside, immigrant Argentina versus Criollo Argentina. Tango and criollo folklore today represent opposite poles of the national identity.[47]

Therefore, it is surprising to find that, at its inception around 1900, the modern tango—so strongly associated today with the immigrants and their cosmopolitan port city—was heralded as *tango criollo.* On the other hand, if we recall that the Podestá circus put the first milonga on stage in their gaucho melodrama, *Juan Moreira,* we will be less surprised. The Podestás were an urban family, and their audience was mostly urban, too—but their gauchesque theatricals dealt in the imagery of rural life. Argentine rural traditions (like rural traditions throughout the Atlantic world) were viewed nostalgically as the repositories of each nation's authentic spirit and distinctive values. Urban culture, on the other hand, was viewed as *inter*national, rather than national—corrupted by outside influences and a permissive environment. An imagined connection with rural traditions made cut-and-break dancing more palatable, even patriotic, for new middle-class dancers.

Turn-of-the-century carnival illustrates the point. Just when Rio's Rua do Ouvidor filled with carnival Baianas in traditional costume, Buenos Aires's Calle Florida filled with carnival gauchos in traditional costume.[48] In both cases, urban popular culture was masquerading as rural tradition. The carnival gauchos' years of greatest vogue in the street celebration coincided precisely with the tango

* The pronunciation of these words is almost identical because z sounds like s in American Spanish.

criollo's debut at carnival balls all over Buenos Aires. Many carnival gauchos paraded in a long-haired wig and false beard to look like Pepe Podestá's stage characterization of Juan Moreira. Even the greatest tango singer of them all, Carlos Gardel, appeared as a carnival gaucho in 1907. Later, he occasionally performed tangos wearing gaucho costume on stage, as well.[49]

The great success of the Podestá Brothers' circus depended, in part, on their ability to bridge the rural/urban divide. The Podestás had become a kind of Argentine national institution in the 1890s. They performed more and more in theaters and eventually left their circus tent behind. A quarrel split them into two rival theatrical troupes, both portraying "national," often "gauchesque," themes, to which they added light musical theater with nativist resonances.[50] Soon they were putting tangos on stage. A description of their remarkable 1898 theatrical review *Ensalada Criolla* (roughly *Criollo Potpourri*) is a good place to end our discussion of tango history.

The Podestás' *Criollo Potpourri* was the first Buenos Aires musical review ever done with all local material and actors. The show contained a fascinating early representation of tango dancing in an *arrabal* (a poor neighborhood far from the center of town) where three *compadritos* (small-time punks) are seen to establish their pecking order, partly according to how well they dance. One normally imagines a Buenos Aires compadrito to be a first generation Criollo of, say, southern Italian background. But these compadritos appear in the libretto—and presumably on stage—as black (Negro Pantaleón), blond (Rubio Pichinango), and mulato (Pardo Zipitría). Typically, for compadritos, they are all knife fighters of renown. Typically, too, they pride themselves as *tangueros* (tango dancers). Without question, though, Negro Pantaleón is the master tanguero, and the white Rubio Pichinango seems distinctly unimpressive by comparison. *Justicia Criolla* (*Criollo Justice*), a sainete presented in 1897 by a different company, also featured a black virtuoso tanguero, Negro Benito. The sainete culminates with a party in a conventillo, where Negro Benito calls for tangos—just the thing, he proclaims, for "good Criollos" like him.[51]

Over the course of the twentieth century, as Brazilians increasingly highlighted the African roots of samba, Argentines gradually forgot the African roots of tango altogether. Memory of tango's

African roots is dim, indeed, on the streets of Buenos Aires today. Cuba constitutes an interesting third case. Cuba's large population of African descent naturally makes its national rhythm more like samba than tango. But there are also contrasts, as we will see.

Chapter Five

Failde's Orchestra
(Havana)

One night in October 1871, Miguel Faílde, a black cornet player hardly twenty years old, was hired by several young men of "the very best society" to assault a posh private residence in the Cuban city of Mantanzas, just to the east of Havana. This "assault" was a musical one, an impromptu party organized by the young men, "with no other purpose," in the words of a subsequent newspaper social note, "than to pass a few happy hours surrendered to the pleasure of music and dance."[1] The respectable señora whose house was assaulted would bear no responsibility for the absence of Spanish guests at the party, since the partiers had arrived uninvited, bringing Faílde's dance band and refreshments along. To exonerate the host family of responsibility for the guest list was one purpose of these festive *asaltos.* Cuba's first war for independence had recently begun and tensions ran high. Only weeks later, in Havana, a young man who danced to Faílde's music figured among eight medical students executed for defacing a Spanish tomb. The martyred medical students became Havana's prime symbol of Spanish ignominy, a symbol that gained poignancy, for the elite, from the students' connections to "the very best society."[2]

For our purposes, the most interesting symbol of contemporaneous events on the island might be the massacre two years earlier at Havana's Villanueva Theater, which occurred during a performance of the musical comedy genre called Bufos Cubanos. Like Buenos Aires sainetes, Bufos Cubanos often featured popular music and dance. The Bufos also included many black characters, played mostly by whites in blackface. In Havana, though, despite the inevitable blackface caricature, political tensions between Spaniards and Criollos made these black characters, above all, *Cuban*. Most of the men who swelled Cuba's patriot ranks were black. And it was black characters, especially, who sang the *guarachas,* a musical form that (Havana newspapers smugly affirmed) Spanish actors never got quite right.[3] Bufos performances at the Villanueva clearly gave vent to Cuban nativist feeling in the weeks before 22 January 1869, when members of the Spanish resident militia entered the theater and fired on the crowd during a Bufos performance. It was a hated colonel of that same Spanish resident militia, precisely, whose tomb the medical students defaced two years later with such grave consequences.[4]

The late timing of Cuban independence struggles made Miguel Faílde's world different from Tia Ciata's or Pepe Podestá's. In most of Latin America the wars of independence occurred between 1810 and 1824, whereas in Cuba the years were 1868–78, 1879–80, and 1895–98. Faílde's remarkable success as a band leader occurred precisely in the tense interlude between armed fights for Cuba Libre. The island remained under Spanish control, but nationalists organized vigorously in New York, and the passions raised by a decade of fighting naturally lingered.

Music and dance expressed Cuban popular nationalism pervasively, but also subtly, in Spanish-controlled Havana. A stronghold of Spanish political and military power, boasting Cuba's densest Spanish immigrant population as well as a social elite of risk-averse Criollo planters, Havana was no cauldron of insurgent activity. Young men, especially the students of the University of Havana, might speak loudly of their patriotic sentiments in cafés. Young women of "decent" family might braid their black tresses with ribbons in Cuban patriotic colors for their afternoon carriage drive. But no major uprising disturbed Havana's hinterland in western Cuba, with its large sugar plantations, center of the island's booming economy. The armed struggle for Cuba Libre occurred, for the most part, far from Havana, on the eastern side of the island. Patriot guerrillas occasionally fired down on patrols of Spanish-resident militia from a Havana rooftop, then clambered away amid a clatter of broken roof tile, never seriously threatening Spanish dominance in the city. Havana remained firmly under Spanish control throughout the independence wars.[5]

Still, the independence movement did have a nationalizing impact on popular culture in western Cuba, as the practice of musical asaltos shows. Many Criollos made a point of not fraternizing with Spaniards. The Cuban case, then, illustrates the power of armed conflict to polarize group identities. A vague sense that it was patriotic to enjoy (Afro) Cuban popular music seems to have accelerated middle-class acceptance of danzón, Cuba's transgressive national rhythm. The story of Miguel Faílde and of his longtime associate Raimundo Valenzuela, another black band leader, will make that clear. In a nutshell, while samba gestured proudly toward African roots and tango actively forgot them, danzón remembered and incorporated African roots but did not flaunt them. The broad gestures of samba and tango give way to something more subtle and insinuating in danzón. Danzón was the close embrace under military occupation.

Miguel Faílde's composition "Las Alturas de Simpson," or "Simpson Heights" (1878) is usually called "the first danzón."[6] The music—and the way people danced it—quickly attracted criticism from Havana's important daily *El Triunfo,* resulting in a scandal already recounted in chapter two. The reader may recall *El Triunfo*'s bitter denunciations of "that stuff that the morenos and pardos of Matanzas call danzón," or the newspaper's expressions of shock that danzón had infected "the most distinguished circles of white society" in Matanzas, or perhaps the publication's pleas for a discrete laundering of provincial "dirty linen." (Readers who recall none of this have just been reminded of everything they need to know.) The stink raised by *El Triunfo* lingered for a few years, then quickly abated. Faílde's musical star was unstoppably on the rise during the 1880s.

Although his band often played in Havana, only a few hours away by rail, Faílde lived always in Matanzas, where he was highly respected. Matanzas matron Lola Ximeno y Cruz, who was a teenager at the time Faílde came out with "Simpson Heights," recalled the advent of danzón as a great event in her life. Her memoir of nineteenth-century Matanzas salutes "the artist Miguel Faílde, widely-applauded musician and composer, darling of the city's youth."[7] Faílde was remembered as an elegant dresser, seldom without an amber cigarette holder, a gold watch and chain, and an umbrella hooked over his left arm. He was notably well-spoken and maintained excellent relations with the high-society types who were his principal clients for several decades. Faílde belonged to the same generation as Tia Ciata and Pepe Podestá, having been born in 1852. His father was a Galician immigrant, and his mother, a free Cuban woman that Miguel's birth certificate calls parda (of mixed African and European descent).[8]

The Faíldes were a musical family. Miguel's father played trombone and both his brothers played in the family band for years. Miguel's brothers did not quit their day jobs as tailors to play, but Miguel did. As the Faíldes gained impetus, they moved toward the full line-up of the period's standard dance band: kettledrums and double bass, a deep-toned brass *figle,* two clarinets, two violins, trombone, cornet, and güiro. In these early years, the Faíldes played for "dances of color," and for the baptisms, weddings, and birthdays of better-off people. For example, *La Aurora de Yumurí,* a Matanzas paper, carried the following announcement in November 1874:

> **Baile de color.** One took place on the day of San Carlos in a house on the Calle del Teatro, crowded with colored folk and also visited by many families of our society. The well-known orchestra of Los Faíldes provided music, including their own version of "El Baile de los Pájaros," from the magical comedy "La Paloma Azul." All in all, they say our *cinnamon* had a great time, which is just as it should be.[9]

In time-honored style, the Faíldes put melodies from current theatrical hits to their own dance rhythms, and white Matanzas society was showing a clear interest. *La Aurora de Yumurí* presented this interest in paternalistic terms: "families of our society," meaning of course white society, had visited the "cinnamon" party. In fact, white Matanzas society was dying to hear the Faíldes' music, which is why barely two weeks later, in the words of another ad, "the Faíldes delivered a magnificent serenade to Señor don Eugenio Domínguez on the eve of his saint's day." The serenaded family did not listen sitting down, either.[10]

Miguel Faílde's band inaugurated danzón for Matanzas society at a dance to honor the holiday of Santa Aurora in 1878. The name "Simpson Heights," referring to the heights of a mostly black Matanzas neighborhood, was added at a 1879 New Year's dance in the city's elite Club de Matanzas. But too much weight should not be given to the inaugural date of "the first danzón." Miguel Faílde was not a lone creative genius, not the only musician infusing the dance repertory of Matanzas with the new rhythmic excitement that defined danzón in the 1870s. The scandal created by *El Triunfo* in the early 1880s occurred specifically because of Faílde's performances at places like the exclusive Club de Matanzas on the city's downtown Plaza de Armas. The scandal, in other words, was triggered less by the existence of danzón than by the music's intrusion into elite settings.[11]

The Club de Matanzas had only recently reopened after being closed during the 1868–1878 decade of civil war. The war years, according to *El Triunfo*'s exposé, had been the secret genesis of the danzón scandal. Because Matanzas society's normal recreations were discontinued during the war (still according to *El Triunfo*), the city's "decent" young men found themselves at loose ends. So they arranged *bailes de candil* (called "candle dances" because of their semi-clandestine character) where they could dance with pretty mulatas and learn danzón. We should be careful about locating the origin of large social phenomena in any single setting, but given the situations in which transgressive dances generally arise, the story seems far from incredible. *El Triunfo*'s cautionary tale accents the dangerous consequences of elite male "slumming." It also describes the prior existence, as far back as the 1850s, of another kind of danzón.

This earlier danzón, according to *El Triunfo,* was a coordinated figure dance put on by groups of Matanzas blacks, in which dancers held the ends of colored ribbons and carried flower-covered arches. The evolutions of the dancing group twisted and entwined the ribbons in a decorative manner.[12] There is plenty of independent corroboration of the existence of this earlier sort of danzón. For example, an 1854 travel account describes black Cubans doing "a kind of wreath dance, in which the whole company took part, amid innumerable artistic entanglements and disentanglements."[13] This early danzón was obviously not a spontaneous social dance. Rather, it was the performance of a group, a carnival comparsa such as those we have already encountered in Rio and Buenos Aires. Most references to danzón before the late 1870s call it, precisely, a dance of black carnival comparsas.[14] Lola Ximeno y Cruz recalled that black carnival comparsas had danced in the streets of Matanzas "carrying flowered arches." Faílde, in his own words, first composed danzón music for "twenty couples who carried arches and flowers."[15]

In a response to *El Triunfo*'s sneering commentaries, the *Diario de Matanzas* admitted that a dance of carnival comparsas was not proper for decent society, above all for women. The danzón of mid-century black carnival comparsas was, in the words of the *Diario de Matanzas,* an "ardent and provocative" music produced by "African brains in this tropical land." But the paper maintained that white Matanzas society did *not* have a tradition of improper flirtation with that music. "The dignified mothers of today's beauties," specified the *Diario de Matanzas* "did *not* dance danzón." Before the recent decay of proper standards, in other words, white women were only spectators to danzón, and then only at carnival.[16]

So we have a plausible narrative: Until the 1870s, danzón was a dance of carnival comparsas, especially black ones. Comparsas must practice for weeks before carnival, and—because their practice sessions are parties in themselves—such practice sessions were probably the encounters that *El Triunfo* called "candle dances." Young white men turned up at the rehearsal parties of black comparsas, not to rehearse the show, but merely to participate in the sociability and the music of the evening. Sociability and music in this setting meant couple dancing, and the partners of the white young men can only have been the black young women of the comparsa. They danced the cinquillo rhythms of the comparsa in a close-embrace adaptation with ample lower-body movement . . . and afterward were never quite the same. After the peace treaty of 1878, when the Club de Matanzas reopened, these "bad boys from good families" convinced Faílde to play danzón there, which he did, producing a scandal.

Because of its clear association with black dancers, something (anything) called danzón was likely to be somewhat scandalous at an all-white dance in 1879. But Faílde's danzón (like the older variety) also seemed *musically* transgressive. All forms of danzón had the Afro-Cuban cinquillo rhythm[17] that had come to Havana from Cuba's Oriente Province as early as 1853, when the song "Maria de la O" made such a hit at Havana carnival. While not new in the 1870s, music with cinquillo was considered provocative stuff among the "decent" families of Matanzas and Havana, music suitable only for carnival and not for proper young women to dance even then.

When *El Triunfo* began its polemic against danzón, the "contagion" remained limited to Matanzas. Fortunately, snickered *El Triunfo,* danzón was not in style in Havana, "and probably it would never be."[18] Within the year 1879, however, young people of Havana society were exposed to danzón at an outing in nearby Marianao—the sort of outing for which special trains were hired to return to Havana after the dance at two in the morning. "All the newspapers of Havana have censured the danzón of Marianao," announced *La Voz de Cuba,* also of Havana, "and we have received letters from respectable matrons complaining that it was not announced in the program."[19]

All this indignation accomplished nothing, however. The most remarkable thing about the battle waged against danzón by Havana journalists and matrons was how quickly they lost. "Because I love my country it hurts me to see danzón at gatherings of decent people," lamented *La Voz de Cuba*'s social reporter in November 1879. "But if there is no way around it, if this blindness continues, then I beg of you, at least don't play danzón, and don't dance it, when foreigners are around."[20] Six months later Havana's *El Diario de la Marina* ribbed *El Triunfo* on the failure of its anti-danzón campaign, because the new dance was "growing, extending, and propagating itself amazingly." Skirmishing in the press would go on for two more years. The anti-danzón forces might even be said to have won in the newspapers, but on Havana dance floors resistance was futile.[21]

The orchestra that played the offending "danzón de Marianao" was probably Raimundo Valenzuela's. Valenzuela, too, almost certainly played at the Society of Colored Coachmen, Cooks, and Bakery Chefs' danzón contest in 1878.[22] Without doubt, Valenzuela's band could take most credit for the "amazing propagation" of danzón in Havana, where Valenzuela lived (while Faílde always lived in Matanzas). Faílde and Valenzuela were associates and compadres.* The two band leaders often performed together in Havana—at a five-band bash in 1881, for example. In 1883, when Faílde and Valenzuela did a double bill for carnival at the Tacón Theater, the biggest public dance in Havana, the two bands alternated all night for non-stop music, mostly danzón. It was in 1883, too, that Valenzuela added a third segment to the two-part structure created by Faílde, perfecting danzón's musical form.[23]

By the mid 1880s, danzón was the centerpiece of most successful dance programs in Havana, and almost everyone had stopped complaining about it. Danzón reigned from Havana's Firemen's Ball to exclusive elite venues like La Caridad de Cerro, El Casino Español, El Círculo Vedado, El Círculo Habanero.[24] Both Faílde and Valenzuela created backup bands so that each could play, in effect, two places at once. Havana's taste for danzón did not fade in the 1890s, either. According to *El Fígaro,* the "true followers of the danzón cult," seized by a kind of delirium during carnival 1892, and not content to dance danzón in some of Havana's toniest clubs and all its public dance halls, took the train to Matanzas looking for more, then returned to Havana the next day to dance danzón with the very dregs, at a joint called La Valla, The Cockpit. *El Fígaro*'s social chronicler makes a classic, tongue-in-cheek avowal of innocence to his "decent" middle-class readership: "None of you, obviously, can know what goes on in such a place as The Cockpit, nor can I, never having been there. But the name is enough to give us an idea!" No fewer than 150 dances were announced for Havana's 1893 carnival. Danzón had become the focal point of what some regarded as dance mania.[25]

Talk of dance mania was not new in Havana. To the contrary, by the late nineteenth century it had become proverbial. "In Havana it is a scandal," wrote the noted poet José Fornaris who found that mania "taking on more alarming proportions every day." He railed at "the cheap dance halls vulgarly called *escuelitas,*" and complained of "an organ grinder on every corner all day long, annoying the neighbors and unsettling innocent girls with his shrill

*There is no English name for this important relationship, which exists between the parents of a child and that child's godparents.

notes." He also pointed out that the city's dozens of middle-class recreational societies gave dances almost every Sunday and on holidays. "Today the man who doesn't dance is considered a ridiculous being to be pitied."[26]

When *El Triunfo*'s social chronicler himself sheepishly confessed dancing a danzón in 1882, the occasion of his pecadillo was, of course, a carnival dance. Another chronicle, this one appearing in Havana's *El País,* provides a vivid look at how the carnival spirit facilitated middle-class flirtations with transgressive dance: It is 1888, exactly midnight at the Círculo Habanero's big carnival piñata dance. The chronicler speaks to a woman whom he found watching by herself from an elevated box. (Such dances were held most often in theaters with the seats removed from the floor.)

> —Don't you dance?
> —Only the figure dances [the old-fashioned stuff like quadrille].
> —On a night like this, you might try a danzón . . . render unto carnival what belongs to carnival, you know.
> —Nevertheless, I think I'll just watch from this box.
> —These days, the most up-standing people, those with soundest judgement, all dance.
> —So I see.

The pair watches various respectable people "swaying softly to the rhythm of clarinets and kettledrums." Judges, doctors, and army officers—everyone seems enthralled. "Carnival is a tempting demon that unsettles even the most prudent and quiet spirits," the chronicler explains. Then he adds, "they say that Valenzuela's musicians put a witches' essence on their violins, clarinet, and drumsticks."[27]

Mention of the drumsticks is significant. Faílde and Valenzuela brought a new emphasis on percussion to Havana ballrooms. Their kettledrums, güiro, and double bass produced a rhythmic groove showcased, occasionally, when the melodic instruments fell silent. Faílde's drummer was a star performer to judge by poetic appreciations that appeared in the newspaper. He "did everything but stand on his head," and sometimes "came apart bone by bone," phrases that indicate the virtuoso style of African-influenced percussion.[28] The enemies of danzón focused on the rhythm as well, calling it *verde* ("dirty").* According to a criticism that appeared in *La Voz de Cuba* in November 1879, this "dirty" rhythm forced the dancers into obscene movements. Even the innocent, who would have refused knowingly to participate in "the deplorable novelty," according to *La Voz de Cuba,* might be ambushed "by a changed rhythm in the middle of a dance."[29]

For dancers, a change in rhythm translated into a change in movement. What were the movements that Havana's purest virgins might slip into so easily, given the right rhythmic stimulation? In a word, it was the transgressive style of lower body movement and close embrace (with or without "slippage") that also characterized Rio maxixe and Buenos Aires milonga. An 1884 poem in *El Triunfo* contrasted carnival dances, present and past, precisely because the "chaste virgins" of the old days had avoided "marked and lascivious movements of the hips."[30] But middle-class women of Rio and Buenos Aires never danced maxixe or milonga before the 1900s, not even at carnival. Middle-class women in Havana, on the other hand, were hip-deep in danzón by the mid 1880s. Here is the remarkable asynchronicity of the Cuban case when compared with the Brazilian and Argentine cases. A transgressive national rhythm in close embrace penetrated the ballrooms of "decent" Havana a generation before that occurred in Rio or Buenos Aires. The early social rise of danzón has led some writers to overlook just how transgressive the dance was originally. The current practice of danzón—a dance of grey-haired people today—contributes to the oversight. But the risqué qualities of the dance in the 1880s should now be clear.

Comments about women's dancing constitute the best evidence. In Rio and Buenos Aires, moralists warned that "decent" men were dabbling in transgressive dance. Havana moralists, in contrast, warned that "decent" *women* were, too. In 1888, *La Habana Elegante* fired off a typically ineffective salvo:

> We recommend the proscription of danza and danzón because they are vestiges of Africa and should be replaced by essentially European dances such as quadrille and rigadoon.

* This meaning of *verde*, literally *green* also occurs in the common expressions *chistes verdes* ("dirty jokes") and *viejo verde* ("dirty old man").

> We give our gentleman's word of honor to our feminine readership regarding this: There is nothing more prejudicial to a woman's reputation in the eyes of Cuban men, including young men, than her enthusiasm for danza and danzón. Those who defend these dances in drawing room conversation, laughing at the critics, whom they call "stoic moralists" and "puritan goody-goodies," are the same ones who, in a gathering of men, express fear and disgust, in the harshest terms, at the idea of marrying a woman who "has danced a lot of danzas and danzones."[31]

"Just between us," smirked another journalist, "I'll say that, if I had dancing daughters or sisters, I'd try to see them dance *as few danzones as possible.*" Keeping them away from danzón altogether was apparently not an option.

Warnings of the menace that danzón posed to "decent" women often highlighted the African associations of the dance. Take three examples from 1881. First, the poem "To Rosalía," about lost innocence: "Fortunate, you who/Pure of heart/Have yet to taste/The spicy danzón," which the poet calls a "tango" of "Congo and Mozambique." The poet then invokes the *ñáñigos,* members of a secret black society that haunted the imagination of white Cubans. The ñáñigos, he says, feel a thrill of pleasure at hearing a white woman addressed as "*mi negra*"—a term of endearment extremely common in the lyrics of danzón and other Afro-Cuban music.[33] *El Almendares,* a Havana women's magazine, delivered a similar blast: "First we had danza, then came danzón . . . next it will be rumba, and finally we'll all end up dancing ñáñigo." The horrified writer imagined a future in which "Valenzuela's orchestra does away with all instruments except drums," and "decent" white families appear as carnival comparsas, dressed as Africans, playing maracas and *clave.*[34]* Finally, a columnist in *La Aurora de Yumurí* reveals the full profile of the disquiet that danzón had provoked in the upper strata of Cuban society: "The black race has introduced into our decent white families a malign influence, one to which we have become so accustomed as hardly to notice it. And the power that the black race has over us begins with dance." A few days later, in a column entitled

*The clave, played by striking two short wooden rods together, provides a basic rhythmic marker in Cuban dance music.

"Poor Cuba," the same writer mentioned dances that occurred every Sunday in Matanzas, where "certain pardos" (although not darker morenos) were admitted along with whites, threatening to produce an "amalgam of races."[35]

Despite the racist protests of writers such as these, the vogue of African-influenced dance music grew at all levels of Havana society after the patriot victory of 1898 was hijacked by U.S. occupation of Cuba. Although Miguel Faílde seldom performed in Havana after 1900, Raimundo Valenzuela's bands played all over the capital, from the black society of La Divina Caridad to the elite Sociedad del Vedado. When Raimundo died in 1905, his brother Pablo Valenzuela carried on. Until around 1920, when the music called *son,* danzon's successor, began to eclipse it, danzón remained indisputably the most important social dance in Havana, unofficially but undoubtedly Cuba's national rhythm, a prime element of *cubanidad,* or Cubanness.[36]

So danzón, samba, and tango finally became middle-class dances in very different ways. In white Buenos Aires, the children of European immigrants learned to tango mostly in the 1920s and 1930s, when the city's once-numerous black population was a fading memory. The distant Afro-Argentine roots of the dance became quaint and exotic, totally absorbed into an *argentinidad* (Argentineness) defined by whiteness. On the other hand, Faílde's orchestra embodied cubanidad, much the way Tia Ciata's White Rose embodied *brasilidade* (Braziliannness)—through Euro-African cultural hybridity. To be Cuban or Brazilian meant, by definition, to share that cultural hybridity. But the Cuban and Brazilian styles wore their hybridity differently. Carnival Baianas emphasized Afro-Brazilian folk traditions remote from the experience of middle-class Rio. The eventual "nationalization" of Rio carnival (in the 1930s) was a state-orchestrated gesture of inclusiveness that highlighted Brazil's African roots. Danzón, in contrast, had a less rustic, more cosmopolitan style than early samba.[37] Its rise was purely unofficial and subversive in the Spanish-controlled Havana of the 1880s. Cinquillo rhythms revealed African influences, but danzón did not flaunt its African roots. The conditions of its rise made danzón necessarily more seductive than spectacular, more about participation than peformance. The Cuban embrace of danzón seemed sudden and total. Rio absorbed samba more gradually and less completely.

For most middle class Brazilians, street samba was (and is) a show to be watched, rather than joined. Not until the 1970s would a few residents of Rio's prosperous south zone actually begin to join samba schools.

Cuba's music and dance heritage *is* extraordinarily rich. But that does not explain why, in the same years when maxixe and milonga remained confined to low-life dives, danced occasionally by middle-class men but never by middle-class women, danzón became the sensation of all Havana. Danzón, as danced in the 1880s, was no less transgressive than maxixe or milonga. Therefore, the readier acceptance of danzón surely owes something to the political context of its emergence. This is where Cuba's on-going independence struggles seem to have made a difference.

Here and there, we can glimpse a direct connection between dancing and the fight for Cuba Libre. One connection was the practice of "asaltos" (allowing Cuban Criollos to avoid socializing with Spaniards) like the one Miguel Faílde played in 1871, when the wars for independence had just begun. Asaltos continued throughout the independence period. Vedado, Havana's most exclusive neighborhood in the late nineteenth century, had its own asalto-organizing society in 1878. By 1885, *danzones criollos* were being danced at a ritzy asalto chronicled by *La Habana Elegante.* In 1893, we find Valenzuela playing a Vedado asalto at which caterers were hired to provide the buffet.[38] Another direct connection between danzón and the independence movement was Faílde's involvement with the Simpson Baseball Club, whose name refers to the same mostly black Matanzas neighborhood as does Faílde's famous composition, "Simpson Heights." Faílde's band sometimes traveled with the team to away games. The trips were useful because the Simpson Baseball Club, like many teams in the Matanzas league, served as a cover for patriot organizing. When the last installment of Cuba's independence struggle began in 1895, the organizer of the Matanzas baseball league fielded eight hundred fighters from Matanzas clubs, all of them black. After the victory, in 1899, Faílde and Valenzuela played a benefit dance to raise money for reconstruction in Matanzas.[39]

The main argument for the influence of Cuba's independence struggles on its dance culture is circumstantial but nonetheless persuasive. As we have seen, the rise of danzón occurred during a sort of intermission in Cuba's independence struggles. Historically, wars of independence have generally conferred a patriotic aura on local culture, and Latin America is no exception. Everywhere in Latin America, the goal of independence was unachievable without wide support. In Brazil, Argentina, Cuba, and most other countries of the region, white elites flirted with popular dance in the patriotic spirit of shared national identity essential to a common cause. Once independence was won, however, white elites became more concerned with reproducing European cultural models. So the patriotic aura of popular dance waned after independence in country after country. In Cuba, the post-independence change of mood could not stop danzón, but it did close down that perennial venue for transgressive dancing, street carnival.[40]

Havana's "decent" people had always enjoyed carnival, but street carnival had never been their particular cup of tea. Their attention was on the society dances whose number at carnival surpassed any other time of year, a time when, in the words of one 1863 observer, "everyone who does not dance with a mask . . . dances without one."[41] Havana's elite males were not enthusiastic carnival paraders like those of Rio and Buenos Aires. Havana had no long-term, high-profile carnival organizations—such as the Great Societies of Rio or the blackface comparsas of Buenos Aires—to link street carnival to the circle of elite soirées and focus general attention on the parades. Havana had plenty of street carnival, but the Havana press had little interest in, and no praise for, the popular comparsas that composed it. The most important street activity of Havana's "best society" during carnival was the *paseo* in carriages, pulled by fine teams of horses, driven by a liveried coachman, to see and be seen—an activity that existed, by the way, in Rio and Buenos Aires carnival, too. Because Havana's rich were in the habit of taking a similar carriage drive almost daily, however, they did not particularly prize the carnival paseo, either.[42]

Whereas carnival reporting in Rio and Buenos Aires demonstrated an increasing appreciation of popular carnival in the 1880s and 1890s, that did not happen in Havana, where journalistic discussions of the street festival speak perpetually of decline after the 1860s. The supposed golden age of Havana's street carnival, in other words, was the mid nineteenth century, and in all three cities these were carnival's most elite-dominated years. Havana's "satirical, economic, and literary" magazine, *El Moro Muza,* provides a word picture of Havana carnival in 1860: "It would be hard for me to give an idea of the noise, the hubbub, the clamor, and the shin-digging (*rumbantela*) that took place in the streets, both within the old walled city and without." The reporter goes on to mention ubiquitous stands selling meat and drink, public dances in theaters, coaches loaded with ladies and servants, acrobats preceded by a band of amateur musicians, rascals picking fights, gangs of misbehaving kids "of all classes and colors," and "a thousand comparsas that fill the streets." That single phrase is all he has to say about those comparsas, however.[43] A slightly later illustration in the same magazine shows a coach of "decent" people mired in a disrespectful crowd of maskers tussling in the streets. Very few women can be discerned in the crowd, and the most obvious one is a prostitute. Without important elite parading to focus attention on a central parade route, street carnival in Havana was more diffuse than in Rio or Buenos Aires. The most animated area was normally around the Tacón and Escauriza theaters, venues of the city's biggest carnival balls.[44]

Stray phrases in press reports on carnival document the existence of popular comparsas, mostly black, through the second half of the nineteenth century. "The essential Japanese lantern" carried by these comparsas is mentioned as early as 1863. Carnival during the war years 1868–1878 seems to have been quiet in the streets (by government order, no doubt), but there are new signs of "comparsas criollas made up of persons of all colors" in the 1880s and 1890s.[45] Even when they rate no press coverage (which is usually) the comparsas' members show up occasionally in police reports because of scuffles or disorderly drunkenness. An angry comment in *El Triunfo* suggested in 1883 that the Spanish colonial government seemed intent on prohibiting everything except "the comparsas of ñáñigos that go around in the streets singing insolent things in chorus." Obviously, this kind of negative press coverage tells us little about how these comparsas danced.[46]

Consequently, most descriptions of carnival comparsas in nineteenth-century Havana are based on twentieth-century observations projected into the past. For example, Fernando Ortiz, the chief interpreter of Afro-Cuban popular culture in the early twentieth century, describes comparsas of Kokoríkamos in monstrous costumes that marched double file down the street to a rhythm that their leader beat on a frying pan. Periodically, the leader would accelerate the rhythm and each Kokoríkamo would cut capers, "leaping, dancing, climbing up the window grills," and (according to Ortiz) trying to startle the women who watched the street from inside. Some groups carried a large effigy of a scorpion or a snake that they ritually "killed" at intervals. Other groups represented the black social organizations called, in Havana, *cabildos,* to which we will return in a moment.[47]

Havana's elite recoiled from such "awful spectacles" in the streets, and they worried particularly about the negative impression that the comparsas might make on foreigners (these words and sentiments from *La Habana Elegante,* in its new slick-paper format of 1893).[48] In 1894, *El Fígaro* published a large double illustration that contrasted "carnival past" with "carnival present" in paired drawings. "Carnival past" is the "Venetian" variety, in which the passengers of an impressive coach cavort with other upper-class revelers while orderly spectators line the streets to admire the rich at play. "Carnival present," in contrast, is presented as a shabby crowd full of dark faces and makeshift costumes, with knives and guns around the edges of the picture as a decorative border. The menace of popular energies unleashed is palpable in this 1894 illustration. The menace was confirmed—for the government, at least—when the final rebellion against Spanish rule began, precisely, on the first day of carnival 1895.[49]

Once again, carnival celebrations were suppressed during the fighting, but they returned to the streets in a brief efflorescence of popular participation on the heels of the 1898 victory over Spain. After the emergency of war had passed, however, Havana's powers-that-be had little patience with street carnival. U.S. occupation and subsequent U.S. tutelage constantly reminded the Havana elite of their need to banish "savagery" and "backwardness," and demonstrate "progress" and "civilization." It simply would not do, any longer, to have Kokoríkamos climbing window grills and comparsas of "Africans" symbolically immolating giant snakes in the streets. In April 1900, the mayor's office (having "had enough," apparently, with that year's festival) prohibited black comparsas "at odds with the seriousness and elevated culture that ought to characterize the inhabitants of this country." The same decree also banned "drums of African origin at all kinds of gatherings, whether in public thoroughfares or inside buildings."[50]

As most often happens with prohibitions like these, neither one "stuck," so, in 1908, certain influential "friends" of the festival tried a different sort of reform initiative, announcing, with great fanfare, a Temporada Invernal, or Winter Festival, to replace carnival altogether. The 1908 Winter Festival was strictly elite-organized and elite-dominated. It included the election of a Queen of carnival, a paseo of flower-covered automobiles, contests for the best costumes and the most beautifully adorned balcony, and a few allegorical floats of the kind constructed by Rio's Great Societies.[51] But the Winter Festival flopped, hardly outliving its first year, and at that point Havana's fashionable society retreated totally from involvement in street reveling. In 1910, the fashionable magazine *El Fígaro* that had lavishly promoted the failed Winter Festival, omitted any coverage of street carnival. "Boring carnival," the magazine lamented in 1911, "your presence in the streets is bothersome and mortifying."[52]

In 1913, Havana's chief of police ordered "the strictest compliance" with an order that banned transgressive street dancing by comparsas. He prohibited "any instrument that sounds like an African drum." He forbade the use güiros or marimbas and as well as "dancing or moving the body to the sound of the music." He also proscribed comparsas from the main route of the elite automobile paseo. So comparsas of black street dancers disappeared from the city's main streets, taking with them the heart of the popular celebration. Finally, in 1937, a period when Cuba's African heritage had begun to gain the intellectual validation of cultural nationalists such as Fernando Ortiz, street comparsas were reauthorized and six shiploads of tourists were imported to observe them. But Havana's carnival did not then, or ever after, regain the popular energies that once characterized it.[53]

In sum, both the early embrace of transgressive danzón by Havana society and the post-independence repression of street carnival illustrate the political context's impact on popular culture. Wars of independence, as we can observe in the Cuban case, have played an under-appreciated role in the development of Latin America's national rhythms. We will address that role directly in a later chapter. For now, though, we have a more pressing agenda.

Again and again, our story has mentioned black social organizations that had little to do with race mixing, little to do with nation-states, and much to do with a sense of Africanness. João Abalá's Candomblé terreiro was one, the "black Indian" Cucumbys, another. The candombe houses of mid-century Buenos Aires and Montevideo constitute a third example, and Havana's black cabildos (who also danced in the street), a fourth. Africans, and occasionally their children, too, created social organizations like this all over Latin America. They were mutual aid societies, in some ways, but their most important functions were ceremonial. Often, they were "nations" whose members spoke the same African language and shared a sense of common African origins. Such organizations chose a ceremonial leader, almost always called a king. They buried their dead with appropriate pomp. And always, they danced. These organizations were the strong stem of African dance traditions transplanted in the New World, and it is time that we give them our attention.

The Deep History of Latin American Popular Dance

Chapter Six

The Drums of Epiphany

(African Roots)

So far, we have traced national rhythms back to nineteenth-century carnival in Rio, Buenos Aires, and Havana. Beyond carnival in our search for the deep history of Latin American popular dance lies . . . an epiphany—in this case, the Epiphany of the Christian calendar, or, as people say colloquially in Spanish or Portuguese, the Day of Kings.

Havana's *El País,* in 1886, expressed pleasure at seeing blacks rent public carriages to join the carnival paseo. The coming of abolition to Cuba in 1886 had ended the major street celebration of Epiphany, 6 January, when slaves and free Africans danced in the streets all day. Said *El País:* "It is well known that most of the costumed people who go to the paseo in rental carriages are colored people who do well to take advantage of carnival to substitute . . . for the old Day of Kings."[1] Havana's carnival comparsas of the 1880s also seem to have inherited energies displaced from earlier Epiphany celebrations. The attentive reader will recall that just about this time in Rio de Janeiro, such a displacement led Tia Ciata and others to parade their Epiphany troupes at carnival rather than on 6 January. In

Buenos Aires and Montevideo, candombe organizations had their oldest and strongest links to the very same spot on the calendar, 6 January, and several black carnival comparsas in those cities were called *6 de enero.*[2] Why this connection should exist is not known exactly, but we can make a good guess. It is part of the story of how Africans reinvented themselves in the diaspora, creating "neo-African" culture in the process.[3]

Neo-African expressive culture took shape in the context of four centuries of Latin American slavery. Catholic holidays, while not always respected by masters, nevertheless provided slaves with their main chance to socialize with each other in New World captivity.[4] Furthermore, Catholic ideology and state ideology intertwined in the mentality of masters and slaves. Therefore, slaves took advantage of some Catholic celebrations, making them their own and infusing them with neo-African meanings. The Day of Kings provides a notable example. Pageants reenacting the Magi's adoration of the Christ child at Epiphany, an old Iberian custom, provided the perfect focus for slave sociability, *especially if the get-together involved black kings.*

Not for any Catholic reason, and more probably as a reflection of African lineage-based social organization, Africans in Rio, Havana, and Buenos Aires identified collectively through ceremonial leaders. Their neo-African *nations* (or *cabildos* or *candombes*) most frequently represented language groups. Cabindas, Congos, Benguelas, Mozambiques, Angolas, Kasanjes, and Quilimanes were common in Rio, for example, but there were many dozens more. Gathering to choose a king and to recognize themselves as a nation was a great event in the lives of enslaved people. The black nations of Rio "danced with an air of heartfelt gaiety, so strongly, so naturally expressed, that I could not for one moment suppose it to have been affected," wrote an English visitor of 1810.[5] Like any great social event, gatherings of neo-African nations called for pomp and circumstance, in this case, drums and dance. These gatherings of hundreds of people, celebrating to the rhythm of vigorous African drumming, were hardly unobtrusive—especially when they paraded through the street. And when might the assiduously Catholic colonial authorities allow Africans to parade through the streets behind their kings and drums?

At Epiphany, precisely, when the presence of a black king symbolized not insubordination, but *submission.* One of the three Magi who came to adore the baby Jesus was black according to Christian tradition—usually Baltazar (in Cuba, Melchor). Visions of a black Baltazar became the special motif of Epiphany for Spanish- and Portuguese-speaking people of African descent. The lyrics of some seventeenth-century Portuguese *vilancicos,* carols that were sung and danced at Epiphany pageants, even used mock black dialect like that of nineteenth-century blackface tangos in the Río de la Plata.[6] The Iberian monarchies had long used the street dancing of subject peoples—Moors, Jews, and Gypsies, as well as blacks—in public spectacles, too. So, when black nations danced before their kings in Rio, Havana, or Buenos Aires on 6 January, they were maintaining neo-African social forms in a state-sanctioned, Catholic framework. Commonly, they gained permission (always subject to withdrawal, of course) to dance every Sunday at some spot on the edge of town.[7]

Black nations existed throughout the African diaspora. As with other, associated neo-African cultural manifestations, such as drumming, however, nations were rare in the English colonies. Blacks yearly elected their own ceremonial governors or kings in certain localities of colonial New York and New England, and neo-African nations danced on Sundays in New Orleans' Congo Square. An 1819 visitor to New Orleans, out for an afternoon stroll, reported hearing a sound like "horses trampling on a wooden floor," and, on going to investigate, found the dusty square on the back side of the city filled with hundreds of slaves forming several large dance rings, each one of them doubtless a nation.[8] The dancing in Congo Square took place within earshot of the house where Louis Moreau Gottschalk lived as a child, and it was probably the Creole pianist's first exposure to a dance called *bamboula.* It was Gottschalk's piano piece "Bamboula, Dance of Blacks," that first established his reputation as a composer and virtuoso in 1840s Paris.[9]

Widespread and enduring, black nations are a key to understanding dance in the African diaspora. As early as the 1540s, writings on the settlement of Hispaniola mention the Congo, Wolof, Sape, and Berbersi nations, each with "its own king or governor." Black nations began getting permission to dance in the streets of Cartagena de Indias in 1573. There is evidence of black nations electing kings in both Brazil and Mexico by the early 1600s. The nations of Rio, Havana, and Buenos Aires appeared later, however, during the 1700s, apparently the heyday of this neo-African cultural form in Latin

America as a whole.[10] The following look at the dancing of black nations in our Atlantic port cities will range widely over sparse and uneven evidence from the mid 1700s to the mid 1800s. The documentation from Rio, where we will begin, is oddly thin, that from Montevideo and Buenos Aires, surprisingly abundant. And what does it show, overall? Let's see.

The Campo de Santana, on the back side of Rio de Janeiro, was a peripheral urban space exactly analogous to Congo Square in the early nineteenth century. On Sundays the two places must have looked much alike. A British merchant described the presence in the Campo de Santana of Moçambiques, Angolas, Cabindas, Benguelas, and other nations in 1808:

> The dense population of the Campo de Santana was subdivided into capacious circles, formed each from three to four hundred blacks, male and female. Within these circles, the performers danced to the music, which was also stationed there: and I know not whether the energy of the musicians or that of the dancers was most to be admired.[11]

But black street dancing was limited in Rio soon after that time. Even dancing sponsored by the lay brotherhood of Nossa Senhora do Rosário was prohibited in 1817. Another British traveler, Maria Graham, reported in the 1820s:

> A king of each tribe is annually elected, to whom his people are obedient, something in the way of the gypsy monarchy. Before 1806, the election took place with great ceremony and feasting, and sometimes fighting, in the Campo de Santana, and the king of the whole was seated during the day in the center of the square under a huge state umbrella. This festival is now abolished.[12]

Ejected from the Campo de Santana, some nations apparently danced for a time on moonlit beaches, where the sound of the surf helped muffle the music.[13] Overall, though, public manifestations of neo-African dance faded in the 1830s and 1840s, only to be revived by the carnival parading of migrants from Bahia in the 1880s.[14] In the meantime, Rio's black nations continued to function for a time, although we know almost nothing about them, except their insistence on maintaining their funeral activities at all cost.[15]

Probably, Rio's black nations continued to function informally within the Catholic Church. The neo-African nations of Brazil had linked themselves closely to colonial institutions through devotional brotherhoods dedicated to particular saints.* Of these, the most important were the brotherhoods of the Nossa Senhora do Rosário, mentioned above, and that of the black Santo Rei Baltazar. The virgin of Rosário had her own church in Rio—the home, it should be added, of devotions to the black São Benedito. Devotions to the Holy King Baltazar took place at his image in Lampadosa church. Melo Moraes Filho (the pioneer Brazilian folklorist who explained the Cucumbys to Rio newspaper readers in 1888) reports that the Moçambique nation did a funeral dance in front of Lampadosa church in 1830—a time when, according to him, the church was also served by black clergy.[16]

This nineteenth-century folklorist is also the source of the fullest single description of Rio's neo-African nations in action. It depicts the coronation of a black king at Lampadosa church in 1748, when Moraes says that the associated brotherhoods were composed of both African and Brazilian-born blacks, most of them slaves. Moraes begins by transcribing a document from the church archive. The petition is addressed to one of the city's chief magistrates on behalf of "the emperor, king, queen, and other members of the nation of the Holy King Baltazar." The petitioners remind the magistrate of their custom of dancing in the streets on Sundays and other church holidays to collect contributions for their patron saint's celebration on 6 January. They ask permission to collect those contributions and to crown a king during their celebration. They clearly hope that their case will be strengthened by the identity of their prospective king, a man named António (probably a slave, since they give no surname) who is a servant of the viceroy himself. The document is signed with X's and dated 3 December—none too soon to prepare for a major celebration on 6 January.[17]

* These are often called "lay brotherhoods" (*irmandades* or *cofrarías* in Portuguese—*cofradías* in Spanish) because they are gathering of laity, not clergy.

The document teaches us several things. Nations did not just gather spontaneously on 6 January. First they planned, raised money, and secured written permission from the authorities. They also made material preparations for ceremonial costumes and constructions, as we are about to see. These activities kept the group in motion for weeks during the holiday season. (Troupes like Tia Ciata's White Rose or Hilário Jovino Batista's King of Diamonds could switch their focus easily from Epiphany to carnival in the 1890s in part because the new day was part of the same holiday season, extending from Christmas to Lent.) We also see in the document that neo-African nations did not define themselves only in reference to an African ethnicity. Particularly in Brazil, where the nations were most closely linked to Catholic lay brotherhoods, they might describe themselves as something like "the nation of the Holy King Baltazar." In this case, António would be crowned "king of the Rebôlo nation," so the brotherhood of Baltazar may have been merely a front for the Rebôlos. We see, finally, that nations needed patronage connections, such as the one implicit in the identity of António's illustrious master, the viceroy. Moraes further cites an 1811 document, also from Lampadosa, concerning the coronation of a Cabinda king and queen, "having been elected by their nation and possessing the requisite license from the Chief of Police."[18]

Next, without revealing his sources, Moraes offers a detailed description of a coronation. Let us view it with caution: First, dancing groups go through the streets (and also visit the nearby Jesuit sugar plantations) collecting contributions for their devotion, while others prepare the church, adorning the altar of Baltazar, raising thrones for the coronation, and carefully weeding and sweeping the space in front of the church. They erect structures of bamboo and foliage to provide shade for spectators. At 10 a.m. on 6 January, the brothers of the Holy King Baltazar gather inside the church wearing silken gowns and chatting loudly as the church bells resonate overhead. Outside, the roar of the arriving procession gets louder. At the head of the procession, just behind several pirouetting boys whose function is to open a path in the crowded street (exactly as the leading "Indians" of a carnival dance troupe still did 150 years later) come the king and queen wearing capes of scarlet velvet, their crowns carried by vassals, their hair plaited with strings of shells, coral, and beads. Of all these, only the royalty and a few of their ranking followers enter the church. As the crowd waits outside, the king and queen sit on their thrones and the chaplain crowns them. The chaplain then escorts the king and queen to the sacristy, where they hear the official coronation act and sign it, each with an X. The most popular part of the ceremony is the dance that will last in front of the church all afternoon. Moraes indicates that blacks of many other nations are among the spectators.[19]

The nineteenth-century folklorist's vivid description of the ceremony must be a composite recreation. Melo Moraes Filho was born after the latest coronation we know about in Rio, so he cannot have been an eyewitness. Rather, he seems to have collected oral tradition more than half a century old. Even if we take the details "with a grain of salt," however, the description is illuminating. Obviously, the coronations of Rio's neo-African nations were lavish, noisy, public events. Exactly the same point emerges from a similar description in the pages of Luiz Edmundo, Rio's most important turn-of the-twentieth-century memorialist. Edmundo's sources are just as obscure as those of Moraes, yet he, too, clearly knows a lot. He concurs that church altars were especially lit and their bells rung for neo-African coronations in eighteenth-century Rio. Enthusiastic crowds carried their king and queen on canopied litters through the central streets, spilling finally into the square beside the palace to dance under the viceregal balcony. The memorialist describes the king and queen in particular detail, the king wearing a gold paper crown, a brown tailcoat, yellow vest, and red velvet cape spangled with brass stars and crescent moons, the queen wearing a hoop skirt and velvet cape. To evoke the dance of the nations, Edmundo describes a performance of Cucumbys, which he probably took from Moraes but easily could have seen himself at Rio's turn-of-the-century carnival.[20]

Despite their flaws, Melo Moraes Filho and Luiz Edmundo reliably signal the importance of neo-African nations in Rio de Janeiro during the eighteenth and early nineteenth centuries by confirming the collective memory of frequent, boisterous public coronation ceremonies. Such confirmation is useful because the activities of the Rio's black nations left many fewer traces of documentary evidence than did those of Havana or Buenos Aires. In fact, the primary indicator of how common the public dancing of the nations once was in Brazil lies, not in any documentary proof, but in the folk tradition of street pageants itself. Dozens of these pageants (termed "dramatic dances" in Brazilian folklore) were still performed throughout Brazil in the early twentieth century. Many of these dramatic dances involved kings or shepherds that clearly link them to earlier Epiphany pageants, and they were traditionally performed at celebrations associated with the black saints Nossa Senhora do Rosário, São Benedito, or, most especially, the Holy King Baltazar. Among the most common pageants were Congos and Congadas, of which Cucumbys were a Bahian variant. Many included a uniformly dressed chorus of dancing shepherdesses, the spiritual progenitors of carnival Baianas.[21]

In sum, a shortage of documentary evidence has reduced Rio's black nations to mere street spectacles in the historical record. Given that our particular interest in the nations lies in their spectacular dancing, this reduction is not a total loss for us. Without the descriptions of Moraes and Edmundo, one could only refer generically to the nations of Rio dancing batuque. However, better evidence allows the nations of Buenos Aires to emerge before us in a more fully rounded form.

The reader will perhaps remember the black Buenos Aires paper *La Broma* and its distress, in 1882, about young people who "acted ashamed" if a tía of their community asked them to drum at "one of the few remaining candombe houses." These houses were called, in the common parlance repeated by *La Broma*, "*sitios, naciones, o tambores.*"* Here was something missing from our recent look at Rio: meeting places owned by black nations. *La Broma* urged the black community to honor "what could truly be called monuments" built with great sacrifice by their grandfathers.[22] Buenos Aires archives also contain an 1802 inventory of such a meeting place, here called a "tango place" or "tango house," a two-storied structure with fenced yard and fruit trees.[23] A few were still active in the 1880s, as *La Broma* itself had evidenced on 27 January 1881, when it reported that excessive noise at a candombe house led neighbors to petition for a prohibition.[24]

*The words for "place" (*sitio*), "nation" (*nación*), and "drum" (*tambor*) all refered to these meeting places. The nations used their places especially for drumming—which means, for dancing.

Did the black nations of Rio not have analogous places? Or has evidence of them simply not come to light? One can make only tentative comparisons of nations across the African diaspora. Clearly, though, much about the black nations of Buenos Aires was quite reminiscent of Rio's black nations.[25]

For example, in 1786 the black brotherhood of none-other-than San Baltazar in Buenos Aires asked permission to collect funds for their celebrations, precisely as in the Rio document of 1748. They hoped to gather pious contributions in the street: "especially when the government permits us to dance on Sundays and holidays, those being the main days of attendance among our people." They did not request permission for a coronation, though.[26] The authorities of the Río de la Plata had apparently limited overt expression of ceremonial kingship among neo-African nations. In other documents, the brotherhood of San Baltazar mentions "the *moreno* named Pablo Aguero, to whose command these nations are subject." Aguero was a free black man, a landlord of rental properties, and a crown official who went around on horseback. He was charged with supervising the black population of Buenos Aires, a charge that included pursuit of escaped slaves and, apparently, suppression of coronations among the black nations. In 1787, he had trouble with his orderly, Manuel Farías, a Guinean, who denounced Aguero to the city authorities for allowing the coronation of black kings in various nations. The government's investigation of the episode is dated, significantly, just after Epiphany.[27]

Several witnesses gave testimony of what had transpired. The brotherhood of San Baltazar apparently had no meeting place, during these years, because it gathered to dance in a vacant lot. The man accused of being a black king, Pedro Duarte (who had a surname and was therefore not a slave) testified in his own defense that "he had merely gone with those of his nation, wearing a hat, cape, and skirt, and carrying a parasol, so that they could recognize him as great, but not as king." (Whether "king" or merely "great," Duarte was clearly assuming the regalia of neo-African ceremonial kingship, complete with the parasol. He naturally avoided the word *king* because he knew that the authorities frowned on its use by the black nations.) Another Guinean who testified, Josef González, a man who distributed water in Buenos Aires neighborhoods from a sort of barrel on wheels, said that "on feast days, when the blacks meet at a certain vacant lot" he had on occasion seen Pedro Duarte under a big parasol, wearing some kind of crown, and that all the people of the Congo nation obeyed him. Asked if the Congos still obeyed Duarte, the water carrier said they did during the celebrations of San Baltazar.[28]

Better records in Buenos Aires allow us to see tensions between and within nations. There was apparently no love lost between Guineans and Congos. Nor were individual nations always harmonious. In the 1780s, for example, two free black men petitioned the government about "a difference that has arisen between blacks of the south side and the north side of the city." Currently, they explained, people from the north had to cross town to attend dances of the nations. Therefore (continued their very diplomatic argument) "after the dances they cannot return to their houses as quickly as good service to their masters would warrant." But the southern-based leaders of the nations in question pronounced themselves satisfied with the current southern location of their dances and "expected for those of the north to show up" all the same.[29] Nations might in fact split and regroup under such circumstances, as later records from the 1800s enable historians to document in considerable detail.[30]

As in Rio, Catholic lay brotherhoods devoted to Baltazar had become frameworks for neo-African nations. Buenos Aires had several such. For example, the Black Brotherhood of Guinea, dedicated to San Baltazar, solicited in January 1791 "to parade a dance of our nation through the streets of this city, visiting private houses along the way [just like Brazilian Epiphany troupes], as honestly and decently as can be." The Guineans stressed "honesty and decency" because the city's black overseer, Pablo Aguero, was now campaigning against the dances of the nations. Aguero was angry because the nations had disobeyed him, "every black in the city parading through the streets and plazas" after their license to do so had expired. Aguero also raised the alarm about secret gatherings "to dance the *tambo** and other indecent dances."[31]

Aguero found an ally in the city's public prosecutor. The official's concern had been raised, no doubt, by revelations about the secret crowning of black kings in 1787. In 1788, the public prosecutor

* A word related to *tango* or *tambor* (drum).

informed the city council about the menace presented by gatherings of the nations. He argued that the celebrations threatened the moral order of the city. (His litany of pernicious effects strongly recalls later denunciation of maxixe, milonga, and danzón.) Slaves sometimes resorted to prostitution to raise funds for their celebrations, alleged the prosecutor, and their work suffered when "all they can think about is going to the dance." He expressed concern that the exaltation of the dance made the slaves forget their place and undermined their devotion to Catholicism by reenacting pagan rites. The rhythm itself goaded the dancers to "obscene movements," the prosecutor asserted, and he worried that the obscenity infected white spectators, principally "maidens and other innocents" who observed and inevitably learned "things they should not, by any means, know." The prosecutor closed his report with a threat. "Everyone knows," he declared, that these dances attracted at least two thousand blacks, and "if they all acted together for any reason, who could control them?"[32]

The city council concurred. Dances of the nations seemed to encourage insolence among the city's blacks, making it harder to "reduce them to rationality" and instill "a proper understanding of their own lowness." Furthermore, both the dancers' example and the drumming itself could incite lechery among impressionable youths. Therefore, the council recommended to the viceroy that all such dances be banned.[33] There is no record of what action the viceroy took, if any. Still, the fears expressed by the public prosecutor of Buenos Aires help us imagine what forgotten arguments must have been brandished to repress the black nations of Rio.

Evidence from Buenos Aires suggests that the dancing of the nations was quite transgressive in some ways. From the perspective of colonial authorities, large gatherings of slaves or free blacks—or worse, the two mingling together—strained certain social controls. White spectatorship, obviously eager, also worried the authorities.[34] Still, when a new viceroy was about to make his ceremonial entry into Buenos Aires in 1795, the Congo nation petitioned "to dance through the streets of the city (according to the custom of the nations) amusing and entertaining the residents of the neighborhood, with harmony and good behavior among the dancers." Their request had centuries of precedents in Iberian monarchical spectacles, in which dancers represented different ethnic groups among the king's subject peoples. These precedents gave bona fide "national" dances a kind of protected status. For that reason, clearly, the Congos specified in 1795 that "each nation would dance according to its own style with all purity." They seemed to be responding to a complaint from the public prosecutor to the effect that the nations' dances were "no longer those of the people among whom they had lived" in Africa. A note addended to the Congos' petition by an administrative hand states that they could join the public festivities for the new viceroy, though "without a king."[35]

Dire denunciations of dirty dancing did not prevail completely in Buenos Aires. The city's black nations did not disappear for several more generations. With the end of Spanish colonial control in 1810, they became African Associations chartered by the republican government. But political connections to old monarchies and new republics are the stuff of later chapters. Let us now focus our attention on the dancing itself.

Dance was the beating heart of the neo-African nations. The members of each nation shared not only the moment of the dance—an ecstatic "time out of time," spiritual solace and respite from drudgery—they also shared a particular style of dance, indeed, a national rhythm defined by a distinctive drumbeat. And their dances were indeed "no longer those of the people among whom they had lived" in Africa—just as their nemesis, the public prosecutor of Buenos Aires, suspected. Even nations defined by linguistic similarity or the geographical proximity of their African homelands contained significant cultural diversity. Many nations had distinct minority groups within them. And some nations seemed entirely diasporic constructions. So, if some dancers were preserving an African identity, many others were acquiring a new one in an African mode. To understand their dance is to understand their recovered sense of identity and belonging in the lonely experience of slavery. The black nations of Buenos Aires left many traces in the historical record, far more than did the nations of Rio. But the most helpful descriptions of their dance come from across the Río de la Plata, in Montevideo. The richness of the Montevidean evidence justifies an extended excursion to that city.

Overall, the African nations of Montevideo seem to have resembled those of Buenos Aires rather closely, which is not surprising. The same slave traders supplied both ports, and movement back and forth between them was frequent. Montevideo's population was about one quarter enslaved in 1800, precisely the case of Buenos Aires. And the African population of Montevideo was roughly similar in ethnic distribution to that of Buenos Aires.

"Every nation had its trampled-smooth place to dance, and all were located not far apart, outside the south end of the city wall," wrote Montevidean chronicler Isidoro de María. On Epiphany in 1827, a French traveler to Montevideo observed that each nation elected a king and queen, "very originally dressed," who heard mass before leading their nations through the streets to the market square, where each nation danced. The traveler, like most observers, was impressed at how absorbed the dancers seemed and how much they enjoyed their dancing. "There, in an instant," he noted, "more than six hundred blacks appeared to have reclaimed their nationality in the bosom of an imaginary country" and to have forgotten, at least for one day, the privation and suffering of slavery.[36]

Overall, Montevideo seems to have been more hospitable to its black nations than was Buenos Aires.[37] In an account clearly rose-tinted by the intervening eighty years, Isidoro de María presents the dances of the nations as a popular destination for the Sunday strolls of bourgeois families. Black tías delighted the strollers with sweets sold from trays just like the one that a young Tia Ciata carried daily through the streets of Rio de Janeiro. The high point of de María's nostalgia was Epiphany. At the words "We're off to see the Kings," wrote de María, "the children leapt for joy."[38] Another retrospective account, a 1922 memoir looking back to the mid-nineteenth century, recalls that the dances of the nations commonly attracted "spectators out for a Sunday paseo, including distinguished figures of Montevidean society."[39] Although dances within the city were prohibited by law in 1816 (then again in 1842, showing the inefficacy of the first law) they still took place regularly on the southern outskirts.[40] On 6 January 1862, there were six thousand spectators on hand to see the dances and the parading of the nations, according to a contemporary newspaper, and the only problems were caused by three inebriated Spanish sailors throwing bottles.[41] A final recollection published in 1934, that of Marcelino Bottaro, an Uruguayan writer of African descent, lamented that the dances of the nations virtually became performances for tourists before finally vanishing altogether in the 1880s.[42]

Montevideo's last street candombes were described by a problematical but essential witness, Vicente Rossi. Rossi argued (contrary to the prevailing wisdom of the 1920s) that tango had its rhythmic roots in candombe. Like Rio's folklorist Mello Moraes Filho or its journalist Luiz Edmundo, Rossi clearly knew a great deal. His discussion of Montevideo's San Felipe Academy, for example, is the single most important description of the milonga. Much of Rossi's knowledge came from personal experience, but his observations are never documented, and he insists on describing everything in cinematic detail. Certain passages of Rossi's writing reek with the racial ideas of his time. Still, his overall argument for the creative power and importance of African roots in the popular culture of the Río de la Plata is undoubtedly correct.[43]

Montevideo's black nations had substantial meeting houses, and as a young man Rossi visited that of the Congos, a crumbling colonial mansion with cracks in the roof, a shrine to the black San Benito, and a throne room with two worm-eaten chairs on a platform.[44] At Epiphany, a band (which Rossi says was usually excellent, many of its members being professional musicians) warmed up outside while the Congos gathered. Then, led by their king, they processed through the narrow streets of the old city to the Cathedral, where they heard mass at a lateral alter dedicated to San Baltazar. Montevideo's black nations would dance by the presidential palace at Epiphany, too. And their kings dressed in republican styles, as generals or doctors of law, rather than wearing the crowns we have seen in colonial Rio and Buenos Aires. Rossi says that after this tribute ended in the 1870s, a few old Africans still went individually to pay their respects to the president each year on 6 January.[45]

As for the dancing itself, the distinctive drumbeats and dances that characterized each nation gradually faded into a shared black culture. During the 1830s, the common name for the dancing of the nations on both sides of the Río de la Plata became *candombe.* Like the words *tango* and *milonga, candombe* meant many other things besides a dance. It referred to the nations themselves, to their street celebrations on 6 January and at carnival, and to their meeting places or "tango houses."[46]

Uruguayan candombe has been the object of various folk revivals, but there are no reliable descriptions of its choreographical details in the nineteenth century. Not until the mid twentieth century did Uruguayan folklorists working with elderly informants reconstruct (and, no doubt, partially reinvent) a precisely choreographed candombe dance that unfolds in several stages: Men and women sometimes move in parallel columns, zigzagging[47] or circling the room. Sometimes they face each other and do figures clearly influenced by contradance. But the lines also move together until the men and women briefly touch bellies, a move apparently of Central African origin[48] called an *ombligada* in Spanish, an *embigada* in Portuguese.* An interesting mix of African and European influences, this twentieth-century candombe choreography reconstructs a very late form of the dance and presents it in an artificially static formula. Nineteenth-century candombe was not a single dance at all. In fact, candombe could also be "the dance-of-two," a single man and woman facing within a circle, just as in samba de roda.[49]

After Eva Canel, a Spanish traveler to Montevideo, visited the Congos' meeting house in 1874, she described this dance-of-two version of candombe, which was evidently used as a social dance among more prosperous elements of the city's black population. To paraphrase her description: the dancers were well-dressed and carefully observed conventional bourgeois ballroom etiquette. With a bow, a gentleman asked a young lady to dance. Rising primly, she followed him to the center of the room, her long dress extending behind her. Facing, the two inched toward one another with soft undulating movements, hands on hips. When a few feet apart, both made a sharp hand gesture (as if to say "stop right there!"). They were suppressing the ombligada, no doubt, as too unrefined for this setting. Instead, they turned away to circle back and repeat the process two or three times before being replaced by another couple.[50]

Montevideo's black population did not decline quite so precipitously at did that of Buenos Aires. Around 1900—long after street candombes had ended in both cities—some version of candombe remained a favorite first number at parties in Montevideo's black

---

* Another Portuguese version of the word, *umbigada,* like the Spanish version, *ombligada,* serves as a reminder of its meaning, *umbigo* and *ombligo* both translating "navel."

conventillos.[51] The Uruguayan painter Pedro Figari, who depicted Montevideo candombes in the early twentieth century, left a notebook with sketches of such parties—including one titled Celebrating San Baltazar. Figari's 1922 sketches clearly reveal candombe's "breaking" hips and dragging feet (just as did *La Broma*'s 1881 caricature of two Africans dancing by "requebrando their waists/and shuffling their feet"). The slightly hunched shoulders of dancers in many of Figari's candombe sketches were characteristic, as well, of milonga and the early tango.[52] Clearly, candombe interacted vigorously with other styles of social dance, lending them an African style of body movement. As we saw, samba was doing just that in the streets of Rio carnival during these years, too. Thus did neo-African nations influence Latin America's emerging national rhythms at the dawn of the twentieth century. The story in Cuba was much the same.

Havana had neo-African nations that lasted well into the twentieth century, and it had its own problematical witness to document them. The great Cuban anthropologist Fernando Ortiz was far more erudite than folklorist Mello Moraes Filho or journalists Edmundo and Rossi. Like all three, Ortiz made nationalist arguments in favor of African diasporic music and dance while still reflecting early twentieth-century racial determinism. Ortiz's 1906 study *Los Negros Brujos* (or *Black Witch Doctors*) presented neo-African religion as a social problem. His work of the 1950s, on the other hand, had evolved enormously. Ortiz's later work on African influence in Cuban music and dance introduced the concept of transculturation (interactive change that does not privilege one culture as superior) to replace acculturation, a more one-way conceptualization of cultural influences. His studies of Cuba's neo-African nations (1921) and their Epiphany celebrations (1920), in which he defended Havana's embattled black street comparsas but continued to disapprove of African-derived religious practice, stand somewhere between the early and the late Ortiz.[53]

Ortiz recognized that neo-African nations—called black cabildos* in Havana—were a diasporic phenomenon of hemispheric scope, and

* *Cabildo* refers more commonly in Spanish to the city council. Black nations were called cabildos in Lima, as well.

he traced their link with Catholic lay brotherhoods back to fifteenth-century Sevilla. Ortiz cites Havana ordinances of 1792 which show black cabildos owning their own meeting houses. As so often happens, the documentary evidence is a prohibition, or rather, a series of prohibitions. In their meeting houses the black cabildos were not to "raise altars to Catholic saints for dances in the style of their country" (article 8), nor were they to dance at funeral wakes (article 9). Their dances on Sundays and holidays were permitted only between mass and noon, then from three o'clock to the time of evening prayers (article 36). Two more articles (38 and 39), disposed that the nations' meeting houses be outside the city walls and that "in no case shall nations go out as a group to follow a flag or other insignia, nor go to seek their leaders at the leaders' houses, much less play their instruments in the street for simple diversion." The punishment for unauthorized street dancing was eight days at public labor. Fifty years later, in 1842, a new ordinance prohibited street dancing all over again, but this time a special exception was made for Epiphany.[54]

Havana's Epiphany celebration outshined all others as a time for black nations to dance in the street. During its mid-nineteenth-century heyday, 6 January was regarded as a free day for slaves, who poured in from the surrounding countryside. On that day, wailed an up-scale mid-century witness, "the carriage driver leaves us without transportation, the cook without food, the laundress without clothing" because all take to the streets for their traditional Day of Kings.[55] Parading nations and other street dancers stopped all traffic downtown, in the area around the Palace of Government, their special destination. A press account of 1843 describes "groups of black men and women crisscrossing the great city in all directions to the sound of drums." They wore "a profusion of ribbons, glass beads, small mirrors, old feathers, and parti-colored pieces of cloth."[56] According to an 1856 French travelogue, "myriads of them passed through the streets until four o'clock, shrilly singing local songs to the accompaniment of rattles, tambourines, and tin pans. . . . It was enough to drive one mad."[57] In 1866, a Spanish abolitionist paper reported that "innumerable comparsas of black Africans fill all the streets of the capital, an immense crowd."[58] In 1878, when the black Epiphany festival was rained out, Havana's *La Voz de Cuba* expressed disappointment. The paper then reported warmly on the postponed activities that took place a week later: "From early hours of the morning one could see interesting groups of black men and women of all ages and conditions who, to the rhythm of their odd music and with the funniest expressions, filed down the streets of Havana, lending them extraordinary animation."[59] In 1880, again *La Voz de Cuba:* "The cabildos and comparsas with their banners and drums in the lead came, as always, to receive their tribute from our highest authority, then paraded down various streets and, in the afternoon, the Calzada de la Reina [a wide main street] resembled a true Bohemian encampment."[60]

The leaders of Havana cabildos had many names (*jefes, capitanes, capataces, presidentes*)* but, by any of them, these leaders were the exact analog of neo-African kings elsewhere. Like many black kings in Montevideo and Buenos Aires, some wore a Napoleonic-era general's uniform, including a theatrical sword and scabbard. Others wore a sheep fleece and painted their faces. Interestingly, however, some of Havana's nations elected only queens, called *maestras* (normally, "teachers") who then chose royal consorts for themselves. Obviously, black nations were complex and variegated social institutions that changed over time. A particularly full 1887 account appearing in *La Habana Elegante* enumerated the many roles of the cabildos' leadership. The leaders kept the cabildo's money all year, served priestly functions, imposed fines on delinquent members, cared for sick ones, helped buy freedom for elderly ones, and arranged funerals for deceased ones. Symptomatically, the 1887 account in *La Habana Elegante* brought Havana's black nations to the attention of the city's elite readership at Epiphany, the one moment of the year when such readers customarily recognized the cabildos' existence.[61]

By 1887, however, abolition had ended Cuban slavery and, along with it, official tolerance for the black Day of Kings celebration, which had always been regarded as an act of paternalistic generosity on the part of masters. The paternalism of the festival was clearest in the visits that the cabildos made to the Palace of Government. "One by one the cabildos entered the central patio of the palace," recalls the suddenly nostalgic 1887 chronicle, "its high ceilings echoing for hours with the thunder of drums." And, "from the windows

---

* Chiefs, captains, overseers, presidents.

above the patio cigars and coins rained down." Each black king, hat tucked under his arm, ascended the stairs amid rising cheers to pay his respects and receive a substantial *aguinaldo* for the coffers of his cabildo. The aguinaldo was a gift customarily given by the wealthy to social dependents at this time of year, and it represented a special relationship between the Crown and its African subjects. Significantly, the banners carried by the nations were generally red and yellow, the colors of the Spanish royal arms.[62]

In the last years of the celebration, these monarchist sentiments were rewarded with further official paternalism. For example, the conservative newspaper *La Voz de Cuba* concluded its 1878 report on the black Epiphany celebration by congratulating the celebrants:

> All the cabildos came to receive their inevitable aguinaldo, and the greatest of good spirits reigned through the whole affair, among Congos and non-Congos alike, without the slightest regrettable disturbance or disorder. In such peace ended the festivities, that the cabildos' Mister Presidents and Madam Presidents should be proud, having applied their moral force to good effect.[63]

In 1880, the same conservative paper even defended the cabildos against implied criticisms: "It should be noted that an admirable order reigned both in the city center and the outlying neighborhoods. The only bother suffered by anyone was the inharmonious singing of the *diablos negritos,** and it is only fair that they, too, have their day of recreation."[64] Here was a vote of confidence, indeed, given that the *diablos,* their identities concealed by imposing masks, were often associated with the secret societies of ñáñigos.

Critics were not far away, however. "Although many try to hide it, Africanism is the secret sickness of our social organization, a great danger to our civilization," complained the leading liberal newspaper, *El Triunfo,* at Epiphany in 1882. *El Triunfo* feared that the celebration was no longer the "natural" expression of African culture by Africans, but rather the perpetuation of African culture among Cuban-born blacks. Street dancing facilitated a dangerous contagion

* *Diablitos* or *diablos* wore African costumes in Cuba. They were not the red-suited "Lucifers" of Rio Carnival.

of "Africanism" that ought to be wiped out. These complaints from *El Triunfo* were not new, and they appear here just two years before the traditional Epiphany activities were forbidden permanently in 1884.[65] These contrasting views of the Day of Kings are consonant with various political tendencies in the 1880–1895 intermission in Cuba's independence struggles. During those years, conservative proponents of Spanish rule sought to undermine black support for independence-minded Cuban liberals. Spanish sponsorship of abolition, as well as other conservative overtures toward blacks, had transparent political motivations.[66]

In Cuba, just as in Brazil or Argentina, black dancing often served as an occasion for blacks and whites to interact. The Day of Kings celebration was the face that the cabildos showed to white society. For that reason, precisely, the street activities of mid-nineteenth-century Epiphany in Havana are so abundantly documented. Virtually no account fails to stress the importance of white spectatorship on 6 January. "Spectators invaded the balconies, the sidewalks, the windows." The comparsas of street dancers performed for these spectators, directly underneath balconies and windows crowded with "niñas" and "niños" (as Cuban slaves called their young masters).[67] If pleased, the spectators might toss an aguinaldo to the dancers below, who carried a small chest to collect what they received. Lola Ximeno, our Matanzas memorialist, claims nostalgically of her nineteenth-century girlhood that the windows "rained silver and gold coins" on the Day of Kings. She asserted that giving "the aguinaldo was obligatory for anyone not a slave."[68] While some dancers dressed "outlandishly" (i.e. according to a non-European aesthetic) others dressed "up," in their masters' clothing. These were Cuban-born slaves who did not belong to a cabildo. Particularly attractive young women sometimes turned out "like a Parisian fashion plate," wearing silk stockings, fringed shawls, ribbons and bows, large earrings, and bracelets.[69] Illustrations in an 1868 Havana magazine show a gentleman in a top hat accosted by pretty dancing women in frilly, white, low-cut dresses, soliciting an aguinaldo.[70] A press description of 1859 specifies that feminine comparsas "were more warmly received and produced a more positive result [than male ones], being invited into the patio or dining room of many houses to dance for ten minutes in return for coins that they then divvy up and spend at some pastry shop."[71] "The aguinaldo! The aguinaldo! That is the word that rings incessantly in your ears," reported *El Abolicionista Español* in 1866.[72] One is reminded a bit of Marcelino Bottaro's 1934 complaint about the commercialization of the last candombes in Montevideo. Havana dancers even offered unsolicited performances to individual, well-heeled pedestrians in hopes of an aguinaldo. An account of 1856 tells that one dancer suddenly dropped to his knees in front of two French passersby and commenced to shine their shoes with the embroidered handkerchief that he had just been flourishing in the air—clearly a maximum effort inspired by the evident wealth of the foreigners.[73]

"Left and right," at Epiphany 1880, "people danced the proverbial tango* in the center of close-packed circles of onlookers, who shouted and applauded the dancers' grace and skill."[74] "Big circles were formed everywhere, a battery of enormous drums to one side, each drum straddled by a tireless drummer with calloused hands." And within each circle, someone danced solo, or a couple (sometimes several couples) danced face to face, the dance-of-two.[75] Local descriptions are generally more helpful than travelers' descriptions of dance. But local descriptions do not provide much detail on what happened inside the circles of excited spectators at Havana's Epiphany celebrations. Nor do we get much help from a French traveler's 1851 account of dancers "leaping like Salamanders in the flames," their feet, arms, hips, and chests moving in ways he could not describe.[76] Therefore we are quite fortunate to have the 1854 testimony of Swedish traveler Fredrika Bremer, who produced some of the most admiring and carefully observed descriptions extant anywhere of neo-African nations dancing.

Unfortunately, Bremer left no account of the Day of Kings per se. But she saw Cuban blacks dance at every opportunity, in Havana and elsewhere. She visited the meeting house of Havana's Lucumí cabildo and saw dancing there. And she likened what she saw to the dancing of nations she had observed a bit earlier, during a visit to a nearby sugar plantation:

> [The dancers were] between forty and fifty Negroes, men and women, all in clean attire, the men mostly in shirts or blouses,

* *Tango* in this Cuban usage refers generically to the dancing of slaves, like Brazilian batuque and Argentine/Uruguayan candombe.

> the women in long plain dresses. I here saw representatives of the various African nations—Congoes, Mandingoes, Luccomées, Caraballis, and others dancing in the African fashion. Each nation has some variations of its own, but the principal features of the dance are in all essentially the same. The dance always requires a man and a woman, and always represents a series of courtship and coquetry, during which the lover expresses his feelings, partly by a tremor in all his joints, so that he seems ready to fall to pieces as he turns round and round his fair one, like the planet around its sun, partly by wonderful leaps and evolutions, often enfolding his lady with both arms, but without touching her; yet still, as I said, this mode varied with the various nations.[77]

Bremer called this "dancing in the African fashion." The dances of Congos and Mandingos, Lucumíes and Caraballis certainly shared powerful African influences. Like most observers, Bremer thought she was observing a simple African transplant in the Americas. But she was observing something diasporic, rather than African per se: the dance-of-two, in which European influences are clearly visible, as well.

In Havana, just as in Rio, Buenos Aires, and Montevideo, neo-African nations created dances unlike any in Africa. Diasporic styles melded the European choreography of "courtship and coquetry" to African styles of body movement. While each nation found a way to express its distinctness in the dance (a Caraballi man, for example, placed a silver coin on his lady's tongue at the end), each also displayed similarities, a product not of their diverse African homelands but of their common experience in the diaspora.

Despite a few glowing accounts like Bremer's, whites often scorned black dancing as "contortions that offend the eyes."[78] Furthermore, white spectators were indubitably drawn to the dancing of the nations as spectators, but white *participation* in the dancing of the nations was rare. Whites generally learned the style of body movement preserved by the black nations only after it flowed into the choreographical framework of European social dances. This is the process that created maxixe, milonga, and danzón, as we have already observed. This process did not begin only in the late 1800s, however. To the contrary, African dance ideas interacted with European social dance ideas in many social settings over several centuries to produce Latin America's national rhythms. Now that we have given the drums of Epiphany due attention, let us turn to the conventional social dance venues that absorbed neo-African influence.

Time for some basics of European dance history.

Chapter Seven

The Latest Steps (Direct from Paris)

The dance history of the Atlantic world saw distinct waves of choreographical fashion beginning in the 1400s. These were waves of couple dances, something new in Europe and uncommon in the rest of the world. In medieval Europe most dancing had been choral dancing, meaning men and women participated as groups. Couple dances, on the other hand, dramatized the relationship between individual men and women. In the 1400s, basse dance was the principal form of Europe's royal courts. Basse dance featured complex sequences of small steps and slow glides followed by a more sprightly second section. Basse dancers paired off and enacted stylized European attitudes of courtship, the man eager and insistent, the woman reticent and coy. By the 1500s, courtship dances, like the slow-fast duo pavanne/galliard, had spread outward from noble courts to become pervasive in Europe. These were the open-couple dances that lent their basic form to the diasporic dance-of-two.

A second wave of dance fashions spread through European society in the mid 1600s. The French minuet, a modified open-couple dance, became the standard slow number, first at the French court, then gradually in most of Western Europe. The rollicking English country dance—which became "contradance" upon arriving in Paris—offered an enjoyable change of pace. Together, minuet and contradance dominated Western European dance fashion throughout the 1700s. Contradance was the ultimately the more important, not only because it was more frequently and more enthusiastically danced, but also because it introduced the choreography of interdependent couples. Interdependent couple dances involved formations of couples—arrayed in lines, squares, or circles—who interacted in highly structured ways. U.S. square dance, with its "caller" announcing what the couples should do ("now swing your partner . . ."), is a good example of an interdependent couple dance. Contradance spin-offs like square dance, quadrille, cotillion, and lancers—all interdependent couple dances—were among the most popular social dances in the Atlantic world for over a century.[1]

Beginning in the early 1800s, however, the popular interdependent couple dances competed with a third choreographical wave. These were the closed-couple dances (like waltz and polka), in which the dancers put their arms around each other (generally, the man's arm around the woman's waist, and her arm around his shoulder). Many closed-couple dances are obviously still with us. In addition, the 1900s witnessed a return of several open-couple formations.

Each of these waves radiated internationally from Paris, the European capital of choreographical fashion, into the rest of Europe and the larger Atlantic word. After crossing the Atlantic, each wave arrived first at major ports like Rio, Havana, and Buenos Aires, spreading from there to provincial capitals and eventually to the surrounding small towns. Fashion-conscious, urban people were usually the first to learn new dances, but gradually the new dances spread down the social hierarchy. Poor people of the countryside were the last to learn the newest European fashions. Therefore, rural practice often preserved dances of an older generation. In dance, as in so much else, nineteenth-century Latin America was dominated by the systematic, top-down diffusion of European fashions.[2]

It is worth asking how all this diffusion occurred. The nineteenth-century United States, for example, fairly overflowed with published dance manuals, but these were less common in Latin America. Instead, dance ideas arrived from Europe in the heads (and bodies) of human travelers. Today, when Latin American artists often perform for European audiences, we may forget that in the 1800s things were usually the other way around.[3]

Musical theater has already entered our story as an early venue for national rhythms. In fact, however, musical theater in nineteenth-century Latin America usually modeled European imports, constituting a primary mechanism for the diffusion of European dance styles. Dancing on stage was routine for actors and actresses in the Iberian theatrical tradition. Some plays, especially comedies, included dancing in their plots. A dance involving the whole cast symbolized festive reconciliation of all conflicts in the weddings that often concluded comedies. Dance also served as an index of characters' cultural affiliations. For example, Luís Carlos Martins Pena, Brazil's most popular nineteenth-century playwright, characterizes a "country bumpkin" in *A Backlander at Court* by making the bumpkin fail to recognize the dances performed at Rio's elite Foreigners' Ball. In a second comedy, a more progressive young backlander proudly reports of his visit to Rio: "You might not believe it, but I went many times to the Foreigners' Ball." (He only stood outside and listened, as it turns out, but he had the right idea.)[4] Even when not in the dramatic action, dancers usually came on stage at some point—between acts or, especially, at the end of the evening's program. While arranged for the stage, the dances belonged mostly to the normal ballroom repertoire: contradances, polkas, mazurkas, habaneras, and so on. "After the opera there was some fine dancing," reported a U.S. naval officer who visited Rio in the early 1830s, but he thought the actresses "should increase the thickness and longitude of their dresses."[5] Finally, theater and social dance also went together at public balls, especially carnival balls, which were often held in theaters. In Havana's Tacón Theater, the entire orchestra section could be elevated to stage-level, making a continuous dance floor.[6]

European dance masters, another sort of traveling choreographical model, appeared on the scene quite early, too. A Spaniard known as "Ortiz the Musician," for example, was among the residents of Cuba who joined the 1519–1521 Cortés expedition. Following the destruction of the Aztec Empire, Ortiz the Musician taught dance in Mexico City.[7] During the colonial period, dance masters were rarely absent from Latin America's major urban centers. They offered private lessons in the houses of the rich—and were often picked up in carriages, unlike the humble language teachers, who trudged on foot to teach the same wealthy clients.[8] In the nineteenth century, dance masters taught studio classes to people who could not afford private lessons. Husband-and-wife teams were common. Yet solid bourgeois families looked a bit askance at dance masters, just as they did at actors and actresses. (Professional dancers were somehow "Other" in the eyes of their elite patrons or middle-class students. The dance instructors of early modern Iberia, for example, were often Jews.) The important dance masters of Rio de Janeiro in the first half of the nineteenth century were all French: Lacombe, Milliet, Chevalier, Caton, Toussaint. The first of these served as choreographer for the Brazilian imperial court and published a dance manual, *Coleção de 67 contradanças francezas,* advertised in an 1836 newspaper (with score for fiddle and flute sold separately). At various times and places, dance masters of African descent predominated. That seems to be the case in 1600s Mexico City, for example, and in 1800s Havana.[9]

The U.S. naval officer who worried about the "longitude" of Rio actresses' dresses found the city's opera audience "promiscuously mixed," in racial terms, but thoroughly male, women being confined mostly to private boxes. Like theater audiences, the students of dancing masters were mostly men. Let us ponder the implications of that fact. Women learned to dance the way they led the larger part of their lives, in family surroundings. Men, too, relished dancing, but they had more diverse public contacts in their lives. So the dance as a public event loomed larger for women. For example, tailors and seamstresses were proverbially swamped, on the eve of society balls, with orders for dresses, not tailcoats.[10]

The seclusion of women is an insistent theme particularly in Brazilian travel accounts of the early nineteenth century. "I have yet to lay eyes on any women of society," remarked one traveler sourly, "They come out, I'm told, on moonlit nights."[11] In the first years of the nineteenth century, a young Portuguese resident wrote to his family about his Brazilian fiancée that "she doesn't know much about fashion, can't dance or play an instrument, and doesn't know how to receive visitors or discuss the wars." Far from complaining about this, he meant merely to reassure his family that he was not marrying a frivolous "modern" type.[12] Here, again, is the sad old Rio de Janeiro so distant from the fun-loving stereotype of the twentieth century. In general, the elite ladies of Buenos Aires and Montevideo were more conversant with theaters, balls, and salons, making them more to the taste of European travelers.[13] Havana women may have been somewhere in between. Travelers to Havana often remarked on the relentless supervision of women's contacts with men.

Women had ways of evading supervision. In Havana and Rio, there was an extensive "language of the fan" (which could be used to send messages from the windows where chaperoned young women spent so many hours). There was a language, too, of flowers. An Italian jasmine signaled jealously in Rio, for example, whereas the bud of a white carnation meant "I'm waiting for an answer," and three blossoms of a certain kind of rose meant "today or tomorrow." A glance down many a street revealed young men "sidewalk gargling" (according to Rio slang) as they whispered to a girl seated in a second story window.[14] Girls constantly exhorted to piety could, at least, go out to hear mass, making the church door a common venue for amorous encounters. Especially in Havana, afternoon carriage drives offered women a further opportunity to see and be seen.[15]

Imagine what a dance meant in the lives of these relentlessly shut-in and chaperoned young women. "The mazes of the contradance alone are free," rhapsodized a U.S. visitor to Cuba in 1854, who apparently spoke from experience when he added: "in that brief season of sunshine, flirtations spring up like flowers in the fleeting Scandinavian summer."[16] Dance offered these fleeting flowers a chance to bloom. And, by the 1850s, such limited flirtations were regarded as mere social pleasantries by the sophisticated Europeans whom Latin American elites so yearned to imitate. The nineteenth century was a time of uniformly wide enthusiasm for social dance in the Atlantic world. "The women of Havana really love to dance," concurred the Havana-born Countess of Merlin. "They stay up all night, agitated, madly whirling and dripping sweat until they collapse, exhausted."[17] "The feet of the Havana ladies are made for ornament and for dancing," concurred a French traveler in 1854. He then waxed lyrical: "They glide and whirl through the mazes of the dance for hour after hour, until daylight breaks upon the scene of fairy revel[ry]."[18] In a personal letter of 1855, one Cuban gentleman chided his sweetheart for the "intemperate cult" she made of dancing's "brief delirium."[19] Havana was perhaps an extreme case, but it pointed in a direction typical of the mid-nineteenth century. A British traveler to Buenos Aires found the women there "passionately fond of dancing" in these same years, and his comment is typical.[20] Finally, regarding women's special relationship to dance, it is worth remembering that bourgeois girls commonly had more musical training than their brothers. As early as 1807, a British general in the Río de la Plata found that Montevideo's well-bred daughters often played piano or guitar and "waltzed exquisitely." A French traveler remarked in the 1830s that they could play a contradance or an aria by ear after hearing it once or twice. Auguste de Saint-Hilaire, who visited Montevideo in the 1820s, confirmed the testimony of these travelers, adding that "almost all the women play contradances and waltzes on the piano and do not need to be asked twice before doing so."[21]

It had not always been thus. In fact, many eighteenth-century authorities took a dim view of any kind of dancing. In 1746, for example, the Bishop of Buenos Aires, drastically prohibited all dances in private houses. The edict threatened nothing less than excommunication for "any person of whatever dignity, rank, character, quality or condition" who frequented *fandangos** held in rented rooms or patios in houses on the edge of town. These impromptu fandangos attracted large numbers of people, and in his extreme condemnations of them the bishop left no doubt of the threat that they presented in his eyes. The dancing men and women, wrote the bishop, "look at each other, not just in passing, but quite on purpose, and there is no barrier between them at all." The bishop blamed their ardor on a new element of the choreography. "Quite without hesitation," he fumed, the dancers clasped hands, "lingering in that dangerous gesture just as long as they like."[22]

It is notable that the bishop threatened men of "whatever dignity or rank" who were caught far from the door when the authorities busted a fandango. Here, in the mid 1700s, are the great-great-great grandfathers of the "bad boys from good families" who learned to dance tango at brothels in 1900 Buenos Aires. So

* Fandango was a contemporary Spanish dance-of-two. Here, though, the word refers to the event: a dance party of the popular class.

the presence of "dignity and rank" at fandangos on the edge of town should not surprise us. The rigor of the bishop's edict is the more unusual aspect here. Unfortunately, the bishop died in the same year that his edict was issued, and it remained in force for several years, although the Buenos Aires city government continued to grant licenses for "honest" dances (where dignity and rank stood around uncomfortably in the presence of its own daughters and wives). When the new bishop arrived from La Paz, the town fathers appealed for revocation of a penalty that applied, in their own not-so-impartial estimation, "to most of the city." The new bishop nonetheless renewed the edict in 1753. The next year, the city council finally placated the bishop by promising to oversee "honest" private dances (those limited to "decent" people) and to eliminate the popular fandangos altogether.[23]

Prohibitions of dance rarely eliminated the practice, but they did limit it. Even dances to be attended exclusively by Spaniards, dances endorsed by the viceroy himself, might be suppressed by higher order. In 1783, when the progressive viceroy Juan José de Vértiz built the first theater in Buenos Aires, he soon proposed to offer carnival balls in the building as well. Profits from a few such dances (destined to support a public orphanage also founded by Vértiz) apparently warranted considerable effort. After a trial run, the city government carefully transcribed sworn testimony from more than a dozen men who attended the ball. The witnesses, including many city officials, solemnly agreed that the bright illumination in the hall prevented any possible misbehavior. Men were required to remain standing when asking the seated women to dance, and guards segregated the dancers who stepped out into the dark to cool off, men to one side, women to the other. All in vain—royal officials in Spain soon renewed the ban on all carnival dances, and the viceroy had no choice but to obey.[24]

Even Havana, so proverbially warm to dance, was noticeably cooler to it in the eighteenth century. Responding to that chilly climate in 1792, a writer in Havana's early *Papel Periódico** argued the utility of an "honest dance" where well-bred young people could meet "with the eyes of the Public incessantly on them." Parents, grandparents, and a magistrate should be present, according to this

* *Papel Periódico* would translate simply as Newspaper.

proposal. They would sit in a designated area towards which the dancing couples could bow deeply upon entering or leaving the floor. Such a venue would facilitate marriage choices (otherwise hampered by the limitations placed on the associations of "decent" young women) and promote "the conservation, concord, and prosperity of the republic."[25] But the very idea that parents should take their children—or husbands their wives—to a *dance* "smelled of libertinism" to a reader who offered an angry response to the proposal. In order to clinch his point, the respondent demanded, ad hominem, of the original article's author: "Would you, esteemed Sir, marry the maiden who gives her hand to everyone?"[26] Denunciations of promiscuous hand holding (the same behavior that incensed the Bishop of Buenos Aires) indicate that the offending dance was contradance, because every man meets and touches hands, in contradance, with every woman.

When the closed-couple dances arrived in the early nineteenth century, a new breach in the barriers of shame worried guardians of sexual morality. Waltzing couples moved around the floor in rough synchronization, but otherwise, each of the rotating planets was a world unto itself, a place of unsupervisable intimate transactions, an eternity lasting many minutes. Had he lived to see that, the Bishop of Buenos Aires would surely have been mortified beyond words. Indeed, the casual touching involved in closed-couple choreography (like polka) remained unaccustomed (and therefore provocative) for some even in the radically freer twentieth century. How much more significant it must have been, then, in the lives of historical Latin American women so closely hemmed in by the ethic of honor. Closed-couple choreography entered the most strait-laced balls only gradually. It was never danced, for example, by Queen Victoria, at whose court quadrilles predominated through the nineteenth century. As late as 1887, the great Brazilian novelist Joaquim Maria Machado de Assis scornfully dismissed polka as a lascivious business of "arms around waists and ties sniffing bosoms."[27]

The Atlantic waves of choreographical fashion broke differently over the particular social landscape of each surrounding coast. Indeed, the whole process was less orderly than the model implies. Almost always, choreographical waves overlapped. Between 1800 and 1850, for example, the social dance repertoire of Rio, Havana, and Buenos Aires derived from three distinct overlapping waves.

Open-couple dances were fading but still danced. One, the minuet, with its many little ceremonies and hierarchy-conscious courtesies, remained the standard first number at dances with any pretensions to social gravity. The first minuet would be danced by the man and woman perceived as most senior (by age and social status, with marked preference for the evening's hostess) or perhaps—a sticky moment averted!—by two couples of comparable seniority. The first couples were followed by others in strict descending order of social prestige. Interdependent-couple dances—contradance, quadrille, cotillion, and local variations—normally followed the minuet. Waltzing began later, when the dancers were warmed up, the minuet dancers had said goodnight, and everybody else had made a few trips to the punch bowl.[28]

The waltz retained its slightly risqué air, so unexpected today, well into the middle of the nineteenth century. Victor Hugo was known to have pronounced against the waltz, and his pronouncement clearly influenced José de Alencar, Brazil's principal romantic novelist and a leading figure of Rio's "best society" at mid-century. Alencar praises chaste women who refuse to waltz in several of his novels. In a poem with autobiographical tints, published only posthumously, Alencar describes a young man arriving at a dance. Suddenly, his lovely companion is snatched from his arms by an excellent waltzer and spiritually deflowered on the dance floor. "Offered to the eyes of the avid throng," she becomes damaged goods, and her beau cannot accept her afterward.[29]

Before 1850, many dances had an official master of ceremonies (called in Spanish the *bastonero* because of the staff he carried) who selected the partners for each dance. The bastonero's task was a delicate one. A miscalculation on his part might easily cause offense and send the insulted party stalking out the door in a huff—followed, in regretful solidarity, by family and friends.[30] The opposing, modern way to do it, in the mid nineteenth century, was for the young women to have dance cards with the names of their partners penciled in ahead of time for each number on the program. The names on their dance cards would not be chosen by a higher authority, but rather, decided by their responses to initiatives of young men who inquired, with a bow, "May I have the honor of the second quadrille?" This new system, like the closed-couple choreography of the waltz, was more individualistic and allegedly more in tune with the spirit of the age. Or at least, so we may divine from the remarks of an annoyed young sophisticate of Rio who wrote home, during an 1848 visit to distressingly old-fashioned São Paulo, that "they stubbornly insist on having the master of ceremonies pick the couples, and since such fellows are normally old guys . . . they keep the best partners for themselves and the other geezers. Then they saddle the boys with the venerable matrons, creating a kind of topsy-turvy world."[31]

The services of a master of ceremonies did minimize conflicts, of course, but our young whippersnapper actually seemed to relish the masculine competition over partners. He proudly narrated of another dance, one where the women had cards, the following events:

> Duarte, the district attorney, challenged João Maria Chichorro, saying he would bash his face in, Brusquinho dared Batistinha, and José Maria Gavião insulted Melo Franco. Then I had a bit of a tiff with Cándido Bueno. He was arguing with Olímpia about the date for the inscription of partners. So I went to see what the matter was. She said that Pinto had asked her for this quadrille but that Cándido insisted on dancing it with her. I told her to choose freely with whom she would dance, and she said with Pinto. I turned to Cándido and asked that he stop insisting because the lady had decided. He said he wasn't talking to me. "Well, my good sir," I replied, "he who argues with women should be ready to deal with a man."[32]

Here Otaviano (for that is our whippersnapper's name) shows how dances gave boys an occasion "to act like men," just as they gave women a chance to play the stylized feminine role.[33]

Dance is an intensely gendered activity. Almost all dances differentiate men's and women's moves, roles, styles. The elaborate courtesies of nineteenth-century ballroom deportment were transacted not so much between "people" as between "ladies and gentlemen." Dance fashions both responded to and shaped people's evolving understanding of themselves as women and men. The open-couple dances, with their stylized courtship, and the interdependent-couple dances, with their lines of men and women, were obviously gendered. The new closed-couple dances like the waltz and polka were certainly no less so. For one thing, they introduced the element of a "male lead" not present in earlier choreographical generations, when the dancers had moved independently or together followed a preordained pattern.[34]

The advent of polka in the 1840s exemplifies the internationally projected European dance fashion in action. Polka arrived simultaneously in Rio, Havana, and Buenos Aires amid blasts of hype only a year or two after the beginnings of its European vogue. Havana newspaper *El Faro Industrial* indicates the mood of apprehension created in 1844 when polka sheet music arrived ahead of people able to teach the dance: "There is no member of elegant society who has not heard speak of the polka, nor anyone who has not spoken of it. In our fashionable drawing rooms one hears the polka. In music stores, the polka. Women borrow the sheet music from each other to learn it. The dance will arrive to find itself already acclimated among us."[35] In 1845, the suspense ended. A Buenos Aires dancing master "dared to offer" the city's elegant set a chance to join "the furor of Europe."[36] In Rio, an evening of "constant polka" was advertised along with attendant consumer fashions such as polka scarves, polka hats, and no doubt (one guesses) polka dots.[37] Theatrical dancers were soon presenting polkas on stage.[38] All this polka dancing did not come without controversy, however. Novelist Machado de Assis was not alone in finding the new dance transgressively raucous and intimate. It is therefore hardly odd that polka was featured at Rio's first carnival costume balls, held in the late 1840s. Carnival balls were, after all, the natural habitat of "bosom-sniffing ties."

Sooner or later, people danced minuet, quadrille, waltz, and polka at all social levels. But waltzing at a society ball was not the same as waltzing at a tenement house party. Dance styles varied enormously from venue to venue.[39] Let us lend an ear to Charles Pepper, a late nineteenth-century visitor to Havana who makes the point with a sanctimonious spin typical of U.S. travel writing:

> [Havana's] immorality is worn on its sleeve. The American visitor may learn more of its vices in a week than he has known about the dark shadows of his home city in a lifetime. He may

> go without apology or without disguising his identity to one of the public balls during the carnival season. When he encounters there acquaintances whom he has met in other spheres, he need not be shamefaced and seek to explain that he is observing the customs of the country. No explanation will be expected.

Mr. Pepper noted that carnival dances involved the same ballroom repertoire as elite social functions, only "exaggerated and vulgarized in a manner that the good women at those social functions do not know to be possible."[40]

Let's start at the top, with the elite functions that Mr. Pepper mentioned. What venue could be more up-scale than Rio's Imperial Palace? Emperor Pedro II and Empress Teresa gave a dance there in August 1852, for example, at the end of the year's legislative session. There were about fifteen hundred guests, men outnumbering women roughly two to one. The program was conservative, including twenty quadrilles and nineteen contradances but only six waltzes and no polkas. (Pedro and Teresa were not too "Victorian" to waltz, at least occasionally. Their girls, the young Brazilian princesses, were also allowed to waltz, but only with visiting princes.) On that August 1852 night a social chronicler described the empress "seated in an arm chair on a low platform covered with crimson velvet, conversing with the Viscondessa de Abrantes and the Marqueza de Caxias." When she wished to dance, the empress let it be known to her prospective partner by means of a messenger. The Brazilian nobility dressed to impress. Near the Empress that night were "two lines of ladies seated to display, with spirit and grace, the ostentatious richness . . . of their vast *toilettes*."[41] An English traveler observed about a similar event years later: "No London or Parisian toilettes could have exceeded those present in taste or splendor, amongst which diamonds and Brussels lace figured conspicuously."[42]

Society women's clothing at a dance constituted a major status symbol, examined in detail for its resemblance to the most recent French fashion plate and often chronicled in detail by subsequent newspaper accounts of the fete. Here, for example, is the social chronicle of a gathering of Havana's elite society about ten years later:

> Behold, readers, the enchanting Rita Duquesne, wearing a lovely green dress trimmed with flowers a la Pompadour and a hair

> style of the same period; the beautiful Lola Herrera y Cárdenas in an exquisite white tulle dress adorned with ribbons and garlands of roses, with roses in her hair as well; the expressive Pilar de León y de Gregorio, also in a dress of white tulle with varied ornaments; that morning star known as Amelia Hamel, as graceful and elegant as always, coiffure and white dress adorned with pink; the lissome Domitila Bernebeu and her interesting sister, Paquita, the former in a dress of straw-colored chiffon with embroidered butterflies and birds . . .[43]

And so on. The rhetorical qualities of this genre are illuminated by the following account of the social chroniclers themselves: "These particular newspaper men are in their glory when one of the many important clubs in town gives a ball, which they attend to dance like marionettes with the prettiest girls in sight, whose names, in recompense, head a column-long list of those present." The toilettes described above, which graced the country house of Cuba's Spanish governor to celebrate the completion of important public works, were the stuff of dreams, realized only by a very few, but desired (and imitated, to a point) by many.[44]

The presence of a host and hostess personalized even the stiff official joy of government-sponsored dances. Argentine diplomacy in the era of Juan Manuel de Rosas (1829–1852) was much enhanced by the presence at "danceable" state functions of his daughter Manuelita, who received numerous proposals of marriage—both "diplomatic" and sincere—as a result. In Rio the imperial family rarely gave balls after mid-century. So the main dance on Rio's official calendar was the lavish fete at the Ministry of Foreign Relations to honor Nossa Senhora da Glória, the city's patron saint. Narrow streets became clogged with the carriages of arriving guests. Thousands filled the brightly lit and decorated second-story windows around the Catete Palace to watch their arrival. In 1876 Joaquim Machado de Assis, no dance enthusiast even leaving aside his aversion to polka, remarked on fatuous friends who saved their legs and practiced their French for weeks before the feast of Nossa Senhora da Glória.[45]

These elite balls were not public in the sense of admitting all comers. To the contrary, one attended them by invitation only. The guest lists for elite balls were the very definition of social distinction.

Just who got close enough to dance with the enchanting Rita, the expressive Pilar, or the interesting Paquita was a matter of large concern to their parents. Rita, Pilar, and Paquita most often danced at a social club frequented only by member families and their guests. Such clubs were extremely important in the social lives of elite Latin American families. In Rio, the Assambléia Estrangeira (a good place to pick up the latest steps in the 1830s) was surpassed by the Club Fluminense and the Cassino Fluminense as the city's social pinnacles, and there were many others: the Club da Floresta, the Sociedade de Dansa, the Cassino Americano, and the Assambléia Familiar Fluminense,* to mention some operating in 1850.[46] Families not invited to these bastions of "decency" still wanted to imitate what was danced there. "A brilliant waltz," available in locally printed sheet music in the early 1850s was advertised as "played at all dances and principally at the Cassino Fluminense." Another piece was a "Russian quadrille, with explanations in Portuguese, exactly as danced in Paris."[47] Havana and Buenos Aires were likewise well supplied with elite social clubs.

The mansions of the rich sometimes had ballrooms in the nineteenth century. People of all social classes often danced at home. "An evening party in Rio generally means a ball," wrote a British traveler of the 1860s,[48] and that is exactly what Julia Ward Howe (lyricist of *The Battle Hymn of the Republic*) found during her visit to Havana. She describes frequent, informal evening parties of music, games, and dancing:

> We all go round and round, and suddenly confront each other for a right and left, and look delighted, and then go round again. This dreamy performance goes on until we have just enough sense to remember that there is such a thing as bedtime. We break off, inquire the hour, find it late, say that we must go, which occasions no surprise. The piano ceases, the candles are put out. There is a general kissing and Buenas Noches, Hulita." [Howe thus represents the affectionate Cuban rendition of her name, *Julita.*] Doctor Hernández sees us home. We pass every evening at the house opposite, and all the evenings are like this.[49]

* Interestingly, *Assambléia* comes from the English word for dancing social club: Assembly. *Fluminense* is an old-fashioned adjective describing things and people of Rio.

Such evenings might be much more formal and salon-like, of course. But, overall, music and dance tended to predominate over literary and intellectual pursuits in the salons of all our Atlantic ports. In the *tertulias* (salon gatherings) of mid nineteenth-century Buenos Aires, normally held on Saturdays or Sundays, the guests danced from eight o'clock to at least midnight. Then they would be served Paraguayan tea and later, if they stayed until dawn, hot chocolate.[50] Tertulias, even more than other dances, were important to women because they were held in the home. Symptomatically, tertulias were often named by association with the hostess. Feliciana Ugalde de Maldonado, Toribia Escalada de Reyes Marín, Gertrudis Merlo de Llavallol, Damasa Caviedes, Juana Rodríguez de Carranza, Brígida Castellanos, Manuela Aguirre de García, Margarita Piñero de Rodríguez, and (the most famous) Mariquita Sánchez are only a few from the long lists of distinguished salon hostesses collected by a memorialist in Buenos Aires.[51] Their location in the home put tertulias squarely in women's sphere of action and authority. The story was told of a Spanish minister who refused to dance, one evening, at a party in Rio, because of the presence of another guest, a Cuban involved in the island's on-going anti-Spanish insurgency: "You haven't danced yet, sir minister?" inquired the hostess. "No, I cannot," he replied, "in the presence of a rebel, a bandit!" Her response was fulminating and irrefutable: "Why my good sir, what can you be saying? You'll never meet a bandit at *my* house! Come dance this waltz that I have reserved just for Your Excellency."[52]

Private dances held by people of modest means—less momentous, but no less important to our story—are much harder to document, the main form of evidence usually being some kind of "local color" writing. An unusually interesting description of "A Second-Class Dance" appeared in a Havana women's magazine *La Moda*, in 1830. The vignette is set in a one-story house, by which its nineteenth-century readers would know that the hosts were of modest means, since elite families always occupied a second story or higher. As always, at such parties, a crowd surrounds the open windows, gawking at the dancers and filling a good part of the street in front of the house. The harried bastonero, don Liborio, receives insistent entreaties from women on all sides: "Put me with that fellow wearing the starched collar," and "Remember, don Liborio, what I asked of you this afternoon." After the minuets come contradances and waltzes, with the accompanying threat to feminine chastity. "What fondlings! What liberties! What shamelessness! Are there really parents who bring their daughters to these dangerous gatherings, where innocence must fend off the perverse wiles of young strangers?" The neighbor women looking in at the windows gossip loudly about the women who dance and about the hostess, "respecting not even the ashes of her ancestors." The vignette concludes with the author's departure at 3 a.m., resolving to warn all who might consider opening their houses to such a dance.[53]

The women-out-of-control theme here strongly echoes late-eighteenth-century fears, and for good reason. The 1830s piece from *La Moda* was plagiarized from a much earlier periodical, *El Regañón de la Habana,* or *Havana Scold,* in 1800. This older version contains even more scenes of petty amorous intrigue. Over here: Aguedita, flirting with a young fellow to make her lover (with whom she had quarreled) jealous. Over there: Manuelita whispering behind her fan. In the air: "sweet words, born spontaneously and perhaps the beginning of other, bigger things." Meanwhile: people pack the room to see first the "serious dance" (minuet), and then, "all the dancers having put aside sanity and good judgement," contradance. (The depredations of the waltz were still unknown in 1800.) Another difference of the original vignette as it appeared in the *Havana Scold* was the "magic glass" through which its editor claimed to see everything that happened in Havana. The Scold's magic glass allowed him to relate minute details of a dance that a "decent" man could attend—but could not *admit* to attending, at least in print. The 1830 version dispenses with this fiction as quaint or unnecessary. The topic is still a "second-class dance," but even a writer for a women's magazine no longer needs to distance himself from it quite so much as had the *Havana Scold* in 1800.[54]

Many small details of fashion, language, and so on, were up-dated in 1830 to present a persuasive image of contemporary practice. The main message, however, remained the same as a generation earlier. Social dancing was an arena where feminine liberties threatened patriarchal sensibilities. The liberties enjoyed particularly by plebeian women constitute a secondary theme in both versions. Were those liberties exaggerated by the leering male "witness"? Probably. (And the whole question of "eyewitness testimony" is problematic here, to say the least.) But the general alarm about sexually transgressive behavior jibes with our overall picture of nineteenth-century social dance. In 1830, the patriarchs had lost some ground. The fuss about minor flirtations or someone's whispering behind a fan, for example, was deleted by the 1830 plagiarist as simply too old-fashioned to be credible anymore.

Further down the social heap, black people who could afford to follow Parisian fashion did so just as avidly as anyone else. Havana's black dancers continued to open their formal balls with minuets even after white dancers had abandoned the custom. Cirilo Villaverde describes a formal ball among black people of means (artisans, mostly) around 1840. The ballroom was draped patriotically in red damask and lit by crystal chandeliers. The women wore white silk; the men, black frock coats with silver buckles on their shoes in the best eighteenth-century style.[55] Villaverde emphasizes people's strict observation of formal deportment, precisely as does Buenos Aires chronicler Lucio Vicente López of a formal ball in that city's black community a few years later. "The quadrilles were danced with a rigid, almost Britannic seriousness. The etiquette of the waltzers left nothing to be desired." Interestingly, national colors—here, sky blue for Argentina—were in evidence at this dance as well.[56]

Any dance attracted attention. What happened on a dance floor was always public knowledge. In 1853, a Colombian visitor remarked of dances in Havana that "not just kids but even respectable people poked in their heads, even came walking right in, or climbed up on the window grills" to watch.[57] But the term *public dance* referred to dances with the very worst reputation, those requiring no invitation, those open to all comers, like the public carnival ball that scandalized Mr. Pepper. We have contemplated numerous carnival balls in our exploration of the transgressive maxixe, milonga, and danzón. A survey of nineteenth century social dance in our three Atlantic ports should include other public dances, as well. But yes, we will end up (as we always seem to do in this book) at carnival. First, though, a look at two other sorts of public dances: parish fairs and dance schools.

It is a bit surprising to encounter Catholic parish fairs alongside the dives and brothels so often cited in tango history. Angel Villoldo, "father of the tango criollo" and author of one of the first tangos to be danced in Paris, wrote his first tangos for the fairs of La Recoleta church, held in tents that remained set up for weeks each year in turn-of-the-century Buenos Aires. The word *public* was not applied to the dances of parish fairs, but anyone could attend them, and the crowd was notably diverse. The fair of La Recoleta attracted plenty of compadrito tough-guys who specialized in fancy cut-and-break dancing as well as knifeplay.[58] Tents set up for Rio's *Festa da Penha,* an exactly analogous parish fair, often figure in narratives of samba history. Penha church stood on the green mountains that rise behind Rio, and during the nineteenth century, penitents often climbed the steep road as a kind of penance. At Penha church they lit their candle, paid their *promessa,* and then stayed at the fair to eat a bite and shake a leg in the tents.[59] Both cities had many other parish fairs, too, of course—as many as they had parishes, though these two are by far the most celebrated in Buenos Aires and Rio, respectively. The parish fairs of Recoleta and Penha both reached their apogee in the early twentieth century, but they represent an old tradition. In 1846, for example, when the Emperor Pedro and the Empress Teresa returned safely to Rio after a dangerous trip, the parish of São José announced in the newspaper that it would sponsor a *tablado* (a raised dance floor set up for three days in a public square) and also provide music for any decently dressed group that wanted to dance there.[60] Such fairs introduced middle-class audiences to popular music and dance styles in Havana, as well as Buenos Aires and Rio.

Across the bay from Havana, at Regla, twelve nights of dancing attracted "decent people of elevated category," as well as lots of common folk, in 1831. We have a wonderful account from the successor of the *Havana Scold—El Nuevo Regañón,* or *New Scold.* According to the *New Scold,* parish fairs in Havana were "dances attended by all classes of people." Gambling was almost as central to the fair as dancing, though. Small gaming tables in the street attracted knots of gamblers, and alternating with these tables were others hawking fruit, sweets, and refreshments. The *New Scold* approved of the separate spaces arranged at the Regla fair for "decent people," but lamented that the same could not be said for Havana's parish fairs in general. As a consequence "many ladies go to stroll and look around at the fairs, but they make a rule not to degrade themselves by mixing with the low women, A RULE NOT FOLLOWED BY THE MEN," too stimulated, apparently, by "the painted figures who move among the tables set up outside."[61] A Scottish visitor of a few years earlier put like emphasis on the cross-class nature of the gathering: "A crowd of slaves and mulattoes moved back and forth, calling raucously to each other, while, now and then, a group of elegant Spanish ladies moved through the multitude on their way to the dance."[62] In the novel *Cecilia Valdez,* "bad boys from good families" arrive late at an elite ball because they have stopped first at three parish fairs to dance with pretty mulatas like the novel's eponymous protagonist.[63]

No matter how strenuously "proper" at any given moment, public dance venues always threatened to become settings for transgressive cross-class sexual encounters. Therefore, house parties open to paying guests normally required police permission, as did dance academies. Buenos Aires police reports enumerated a modest total of eight academies in 1856 and twenty in 1864.[64] Any business with a staff of women who taught on a pay-by-the-dance basis might be called an academy, so a fine line divided dance schools from dance halls. Another fine line divided dance halls from houses of prostitution, in Buenos Aires and elsewhere. That was precisely the point of two (almost simultaneous) complaints made by neighbors against a Buenos Aires dance "academy" in 1855. The complainants, who considered themselves "martyred by clarinet," alleged that the academy's two police watchmen often joined the dancing and shouted as loudly as any of the drunken "pupils." At 4 a.m. one morning a fight between the two watchmen over one of the teaching staff (a dark señorita disdainfully labeled *parduscа** by the complaining neighbors) scattered the instructors into the street vowing, at the top of their lungs, never to return unless paid double. Furious at the watchmen for disturbing the instructional atmosphere, several of the pupils attacked them with knives. Dawn founded the street splattered with blood and littered, if we are to believe the accounts of the irate neighbors, with shoes, ribbons, and underclothing.[65] Likewise, a formal 1870s police investigation of Havana's dance academies recommended that all be shut down as essentially bawdyhouses where the supposed students were "normally excellent dancers already" and the instructors were "of the class of pardos, in complete contravention to our laws against race mixing."[66] This evidence illuminates newspaper complaints about "an excessive number of dance schools" in Rio at the same time. Furthermore it explains why a

* *Parda* (indicating African descent) + the negative suffix "*–usca.*"

Rio woman required of her prospective husband in 1878 that, if she married him, he "take no dance lessons."[67]

The specter of transgressive dancing brings us back to the carnival balls that have already figured importantly in our story. In Rio, Buenos Aires, and Havana carnival dances played parallel roles, introducing middle-class dancers (men, especially) to the pleasures of maxixe, milonga, and danzón. Carnival dances also became the venue par excellence of cross-class sexual encounters—because they were public, because disguises hid faces and clothing, and because of the anything-goes carnival ethos itself. (Private clubs also held carnival masques, but when they did, the clubs' door committees reserved the right to make guests show their faces briefly upon arrival.) A disgusted Irene Wright was in agreement with Mr. Pepper on the subject of Havana's carnival balls: "Dust, noise, stale perfume, and the smell of cigarettes make the air fairly putrid." She found the men "approximately white." "On the other hand," she continued, "where gloves part from sleeves or the cotton lace on masks flies aside, one discovers that the women are mostly mulattoes and blacks." She saw a few beautiful "demimondaines too notorious to assume disguise." But most were "laundresses, scullery maids, and milliners' and modistes' apprentice girls," she thought.[68] Colombian Tanco Armero, on the other hand, detected the presence of "girls of decent family" disguised in hooded cape and mask, playing tricks on male friends and suitors who did not suspect their presence.[69]

Of a 1872 public carnival ball in Buenos Aires, *El nacional* reported that "the men there were not sufficiently well known, and the women too much so." It was a bit before the time of cortes y quebradas, but as for the prevailing dance style: "in the bouncy dances like polkas and mazurkas, the couples embrace so tightly that it is hard to separate them afterward."[70] Rio's elite male carnival societies reserved boxes and cut capers at public dances that were lavishly advertised in the newspapers. For example, in the advertisements for carnival masques at the city's theaters in 1864, Club X (its real name) announced that its box would be open to all women under the age of twenty-eight (and to all men over eighty), and the Club Cromático Carnavalesco pledged to enter the theater led by the god Bacchus himself. The rather conservative program included many more quadrilles than polkas or waltzes, but the management declared that this carnival dance would be "just like those of the Paris Opera."[71] Other advertisements for public carnival balls made the same claim. One Rio theater publicized the raffles and games it had organized for the dance, "as is the custom at carnival in French theaters." And the *Jornal do Comércio* helpfully reprinted a passage from a French novel describing the costume balls of Paris for the imitation of Rio's aspiring carnival revelers.[72]

The elite carnival activities of nineteenth-century Rio, Havana, Buenos Aires might be "Venetian-style," but their direct model was Paris, just as Paris was the center from which the century's international dance fashions emanated. This chapter has focused on those emanations, "laterally" across space and "vertically" down the social hierarchy. The influence of European dance fashions can be gauged by the similarities they produced in social dance in our three Latin American ports. The decline of minuet, the advent of waltz and polka, and so on—all happened synchronously in Rio, Havana, and Buenos Aires (and in Boston and Bremen, too, for that matter). People well-connected to the Atlantic economy were the first to embrace new dances, in which they were gradually followed by their less well-heeled and more rustic neighbors. Free blacks with sufficient resources held their own society balls and even reported on them in the same kinds of social chronicles. *La Broma* of Buenos Aires was full of these. Poor people's attempts to imitate their "betters" attracted withering scorn, of course, but scorn did not stop them from dancing.

On the other hand, this is only part of the story, and not the most important part for us. When poor people, especially poor black people, embraced international dance fashions, they inevitably changed them. Often, they transformed European dances into something more exciting, dances that their social "betters" eventually imitated, dances that might even return to Europe with a new name. Such dances are termed "rising transformations." The great mid-nineteenth-century example of a rising transformation that spread through the Atlantic world is habanera, which merits a bit of attention at this point.[72]

Because Cuba remained a Spanish colony until 1898, many Spaniards spent time in Cuba (especially Havana) and developed a taste for danza cubana—the same music that Gottschalk had adopted and composed, the same that would flow, eventually, into danzón. Touring Spanish musical theater companies learned the music and made it a staple of their performances. Around mid-century they carried it, traveling under the name *habanera,* to Spain (where it became so popular that Bizet wrote the world's most famous habanera as local color for his opera *Carmen,* set in Sevilla), and then throughout Spanish America. Interestingly, habanera is often mentioned as the music that inspired much maxixe and, especially, milonga dancing. In fact, some hyperbolic Cuban tellings of this tale make Argentine tango simply a branch sprouting from a Cuban trunk.[73] Argentine and Uruguayan versions, too, uniformly concede the musical importance of habanera in the development of both milonga and tango, especially melodically. Organ grinders were cranking out milonga versions of habanera melodies on Buenos Aires street corners as early as 1883.[74] In addition, habanera was true to Cuban danza in encouraging a close embrace and a swaying movement of the hips, and exotic stagings of habanera conveyed a transgressive mood, representing bodies supposedly exempt from European prudery. Habanera lent itself to maxixe or milonga technique because it was a kindred diasporic form.[75]

But traveling dances, like rising and descending ones, are always transformed en route. European actors would have failed to reproduce exactly the practice of Cuban social dance, even had that been the goal, which it was not. Stage habanera was stylized, theatrical, sometimes performed in blackface. By the time habanera got back to Cuba, the social dancers of Havana found it unrecognizable. "The great majority of dancers do not like the dance that they are trying to import from Madrid into Havana, calling it *habanera,* no less," reported a social chronicler of 1885. "These slow and graceless dances are falsifications." He goes on to report that at a ball he had recently attended, the orchestra had struck up one of these so-called habaneras, but that the couples had refused to dance it. Finally, the organizing committee had to tell the band to stop and play something Cuban.[76]

Rising transformations were always around in nineteenth-century Rio, Havana, and Buenos Aires, and the less pretentious the party, the more likely their presence. Peering through his "magic glass" in 1800, for example, the Havana Scold spotted a minuet transformation called *minué congó*. When Rio's parish of São José put a tablado in the street for its 1846 street fair, most who danced on it probably did open-couple transformations like *lundu* and *fado*. Even fashionable ballrooms in contemporary Buenos Aires or Montevideo might include the local contradance transformations, *cielito* or *pericón*. Such dances—the topic of the next chapter—were exact antecedents of closed-couple transformations like maxixe, milonga, and danzón. National rhythms were generated not at a particular moment, but constantly, at the interface between rising African influences and the top-down diffusion of European social dances.

Two hundred years ago, in other words, Latin America already had national rhythms. There has been a pronounced ebb and flow in their importance, however. Going backward (which the reader is perhaps getting used to by now) 1890–1950 was a flood tide for national rhythms, 1830–1890 an ebb, and 1800–1830 an earlier flood. Cuba is a bit out of synch with this chronology, admittedly— but only as the exception that proves the rule. That proof is the subject of the next chapter, and its basic message is unsurprising. What crystallized Latin America's national rhythms? Nationalism, of course.

Chapter Eight

"Dances of the Country" (Independence)

Nationalism made Latin America's "rising transformations" into national rhythms in the modern sense. Before that, they were just "dirty dancing," undeniably popular, linked to an American identity, but without redeeming social value in the eyes of both church and state. Take Mexico's *sonecitos del país.* These were *jarabes, jaranas, huapangos**—dances-of-two associated especially with mestizos. Readers may call to mind the *jarabe tapatío*—often called in English the "Mexican Hat Dance" and today performed mostly in corny, folkloric renditions. Back at the turn of the nineteenth century, the dancing of Mexico's sonecitos del país was often transgressive, eliciting "the most significant movements and signs of the carnal act" in the words of an 1803 denunciation. Sonecitos del país also sported satirical lyrics making fun of colonial authorities, who denounced them in turn. The sonecitos most often denounced were

* Sonecitos del país meant simply "music of the country." The other names do not have translations that would be helpful to the reader.

jarabes like the "indecent, dissolute, vulgar, and provocative" *jarabe gatuno,* banned by the viceroy from appearing on stage or anywhere else. Yet many sonecitos del país continued to enjoy wide popularity on the eve of independence. Popular virtuosos were brought from markets and taverns to perform them in the salons of aristocratic Criollos. Even the chimes of Mexican clocks were occasionally set to play snatches of sonecitos. They became standard theatrical fare. And they were a patriot symbol, predictably enough, during Mexico's long and hard-fought wars of independence.[1]

The independence-era rise of Mexican sonecitos is a significant but unremarkable story, a commonplace of dance history. "Dances of the country" were rising transformations with a local, often a rustic, flavor. Such dances, viewed as expressions of national authenticity, became associated with nationalist movements around the world in the nineteenth century. During Spain's own struggle to expel the occupying armies of Napoleon in the 1810s, Spanish national dances like fandango played a similar patriotic role among those gathered under the banner of Spanish resistance in Cádiz. Argentina's "dances of the country," *bailecitos del país,* offer further parallels, as do Brazilian lundu, Peruvian *zamacueca,* Cuban danza, and so on. Dances of the country were viewed as "mestizo dances" and associated with growing populations of mixed race on the middle rungs of the social ladder. During the crisis of independence, people of mixed race became a crucial swing group. Everywhere in Latin America, the independence movements adopted "mestizo dances" in a bid for the mestizos' political loyalty.[2] That, in a nutshell, is the story of this chapter.

A good starting point is what we might call a late-colonial crackdown against transgressive dancing. Mexico again provides key examples. The royal administration of Spain's richest and most populous colony became concerned in the eighteenth century about generally deteriorating moral standards. In the 1760s, when a transgressive dance-of-two called *chuchumbé* showed up in Veracruz, supposedly brought from Havana, the Inquisition soon opened a file on it. "The dancers' gestures and body movements [*meneos* and *sarandeos*] are entirely indecent and a very bad example to those who witness them," reported the investigator. He found that chuchumbé was danced in "dives," principally by "people of mixed color," especially "soldiers, sailors, and riffraff."[3] As the 1700s advanced, the

Inquisition launched an attack on various folk Catholic practices involving dance. Many cities and towns applied for routine permission to stage dances as part of their fiestas, only to find permission denied. This definitely represented a change. Burgeoning populations of mestizo plebeians appear to have invigorated Mexican popular culture in the late 1700s, giving it a more transgressive edge. But Spanish administrators were also on the offensive, trying to discipline colonial society in a number of ways—economically and socially, as well as culturally.[4]

More than a reaction to particular local conditions, it appears, the crackdown was systemic. Just as the Mexican Inquisition was investigating chuchumbé in Veracruz (1766), colonial administrators were issuing prohibitions against transgressive dancing in Buenos Aires. In 1765, they banned "indecent dances given by blacks" but also involving "mulatos, indios and mestizos." In 1770, they prescribed differential punishments for people apprehended at fandangos held in rented houses on the outskirts of town: for Spaniards, two years at public labor; for Indians, blacks, mulatos, and mestizos, two hundred lashes.[5] Late colonial authorities in Brazil also worried, but seemingly took less action, about "the scandalous contagion of deteriorating moral standards." The irreverent tone of certain lundu lyrics, like the following from Rio, gave Portuguese authorities understandable pause: "I'm gonna sing,/I'm gonna dance,/Shake my pants,/Give the girls a chance./And cool as I please,/I'll sing my lundu./To the mean old bishop,/I'll say uh! uh! uh!"[6] In sum, imperial repression and irrepressible popularity formed the context in which independence movements made dirty dancing into national rhythms. Let us get down to cases. First, Rio de Janeiro.

Brazilian bishops despised lundu. But like everyone else in late eighteenth-century Brazil, they knew lundu was not Portuguese or African but undeniably and unavoidably Brazilian. Lundu could not be Portuguese alone because its rhythms and its hip-driven undulations of the body showed the influence of Africa, yet it was played on the guitar and sung in Portuguese verse. In one of the earliest documentary references to the dance, the Portuguese governor of Pernambuco during 1768–69 is quite explicit about lundu's African influence. He says the dancing of "blacks divided into nations" had much in common with "the lundu of the whites and mixed-bloods."[7] Lundu is the paradigmatic *mestiço* (Portuguese for *mestizo*) dance. Mestizo dances of the country made persuasive symbols of new American identities precisely because they were so obviously products of a cultural encounter in the New World. One French traveler wrote of lundu that its charm "consists of a peculiar movement of the lower parts of the body which no European could ever imitate.[8]

Thomas Lindley's 1805 account of a visit to Bahia calls lundu "a mixture of the dances of Africa and the fandangos of Spain and Portugal." His description of wine-soaked banquets followed by lundu dancing is worth transcribing in full. He begins with references to the sound and look of lundu:

> It consists of an individual of each sex dancing to an insipid thrumming of the instrument, always to one measure, with scarcely any action of the legs, but with every licentious motion of the body, joining in contact during the dance in a manner strangely immodest. The spectators, aiding the music with an extemporary chorus and clapping of the hands, enjoy the scene with an indescribable zest. The orgies of the dancing girls in India never equaled the flagrancy of this diversion. It is not that minuets or country dances are not known and practiced by the higher circles; but this is the national dance, and all classes are happy when, throwing aside punctilio and reserve, and, I might add, decency, they can indulge in the interest and raptures it excites.[9]

In 1805, well before Brazilian independence, Lindley applied the term "national dance" matter-of-factly and without explanation. The notion that folk dances represented a distinctive national spirit was already widespread.

Lundu was a classic dance-of-two. A man and woman faced without touching, applying hip-driven requebros, Lindley's "licentious motion of the body." The man sometimes raised and arched his arms as in modern flamenco dancing, probably the reason that Lindley and others mention fandango, which uses the same position of the arms. Around the dancing couple, singing spectators formed a circle, completing the classic configuration. The dance-of-two had many other forms in Brazil, as well. The batuque of Brazil's black nations was generally a dance-of-two, and there were several other versions danced particularly by whites. In other words, all Brazilians danced basically the same choreography, but in widely differing styles.[10]

Especially popular among whites were *fofa* and *fado,* both of which caused a sensation in Portugal itself. "Long live the fofa of Bahia, that makes the black people dance!" cheered a Portuguese *Account of the Fofa* published in the mid eighteenth century, when the slave population of Lisbon was as large as that of many Brazilian cities. Fofas galore were promised by a 1730 pamphlet inviting the public to Lisbon's festival of Nossa Senhora do Rosário, who was the object of special black devotion in Portugal as in Brazil.[11] Once again, stage dancing provides evidence of dancing off stage. Most helpful are the *entremeses,* light comical-musical interludes performed between acts of a play. For example, in *The Stylish Bride and Groom* (1784) a male hair dresser approaches a street vendor saying that, because she is black she must know how to dance fofa. She challenges him instead to "shake his buttocks" in a lundu, a bit more hardcore than fofa—and then, lundu they do.[12]

As for fado, it eventually became so connected with Lisbon that its Brazilian beginnings are often forgotten today.* But numerous travelers' reports place fado first in Brazil. A Frenchman who circumnavigated the globe between 1817 and 1820 observed fado while in Rio. "The less educated classes almost always prefer the lascivious national dances, very like those of blacks in Africa," he opined. Lundu he thought "the most indecent" of all. A German traveler saw fado on Rio's Copacabana beach in 1825 when a black street vendor whom the German found dazzlingly beautiful, a seller of sweets like Tia Ciata, played a marimba for another woman who danced in the sand. According to him, fado was a dance "of young and old, black and white."[13]

Not in Rio, nor in Bahia, as we have seen, nor in Lisbon (where even aristocratic young eighteenth-century fops become fofa devotees) were these dances of the poor alone. To paraphrase Auguste St.Hilaire, who traveled so widely in independence-era Brazil, Africans had taught the Portuguese a thing or two about agriculture

* Today *fado* is not a dance but a song form, associated with Portugal, rather than Brazil.

and about panning gold, and more than a little about dancing.[14] "To judge the customs of countries by the theater one would compare the political tragedies of the English, the romantic dramas of the Germans, the sly comedies of the French, and the licentious entremeses of the Brazilians," declared a second French visitor.[15] Brazilian entremeses—like many other light theatrical forms we have seen—were all about popular dance, in this case lundu. Here, in the 1830s, is a transgressive national rhythm on stage:

> The demon of voluptuousness seizes the dancing woman. The rapid tremors of her hips reveal the fire burning within, and her delirium becomes convulsive. As the crisis of love overcomes her, she faints into the arms of her partner, pretending to hide with her handkerchief the flush of shame and pleasure. Her faint is the signal for great applause as the spectators, eyes bright with desire, demand an encore. And this spectacle fit for a brothel may be repeated twice more for audiences of this major, civilized city.[16]

The new nationalist spirit of independence-era politics clearly encouraged the theatrical airing of national dances in Brazil from the 1810s until the 1830s. "These days one sees only Brazilian actors, in general mulatos, unfortunately garnering the patriotic applause of the audience," complained a German spectator in Rio.[17]

An early historian of Brazilian theater describes a dance called *miudinho* that included elements of minuet, but also a moment when "the gentleman retreating, always retreating to the rhythm of castanets, suddenly charges toward the lady to deliver a powerful embigada." The reader may remember the embigada from our description of dancers in evening dress at the meeting house of Montevideo's Congo Nation in the 1870s. Dancers gave an embigada when they briefly—and scandalously, by Catholic standards—touched their bellies together. Mindful of new standards of respectability, the Congos had substituted a hand gesture ("Stop right there!") for the momentary contact. But in independence-era Rio de Janeiro, such was the prestige of Brazil's national dances that embigadas appeared on stage in lundus and miudinhos.[18]

Embigadas occurred, above all, in lundu, the most danced of Brazil's early national dances. As the independence-era vogue of Brazil's national dances evaporated in the middle years of the nineteenth century, when the former colonizing powers had disappeared from the scene and Brazil's emperor Pedro II turned the elite's attention to the goal of progress on a European model, the embigada became an embarrassing reminder of Brazilian backwardness. We can plainly feel this embarrassment in the most successful Brazilian comedy to play in mid-century Rio, *The Rural Justice of the Peace*, first staged in 1838. The main issue that the Justice of the Peace must resolve during the play is an accusation against a man who, as the clerk reads the charges, "had the temerity to give an embigada to the complainant's wife at the Big Stick Crossroads, which embigada knocked said woman on her tail, almost causing her to miscarry." Evidently, the victim and the accused were dancing lundu at the crossroads market. But the Justice of the Peace exhibits little interest in anything except self-aggrandizement, and much of the comic action reveals his scandalous venality. The play ends when, asked to perform a wedding, the Justice of the Peace instead invites the young bride to dance fado, his clerk picks up a guitar and sings, and the wedding party forms a circle to clap and respond with a chorus celebrating promiscuity: "If you give me some food,/If you give me some brew,/If you pay for the house,/Then I'll come live with you!" The over-excited Justice of the Peace, a picture of moral corruption, shouts *"Aferventa! Aferventa!"* (roughly, "Burn it down, Baby!") as the curtain descends.[19]

Typically of the late 1830s political mood in Brazil, the play invites Rio theater-goers to laugh at, and put themselves above, these unsavory rustic antics. It lampoons, rather than celebrating, what was rural and native to Brazil in the 1830s. A satirical newspaper story from the important northeastern city of Recife took similar aim, also in 1838. The story describes a street dance troupe of the kind so common in the Christmas/Epiphany season throughout Brazil. The young men and women of the troupe dance around their small town, then, "always to the beat of a most rigorous lundu, they enter the church and, inside, form a circle around their banner, shaking their thighs, wiggling their bottoms, and giving embigadas."[20]

These satirical views of Brazilian popular dance appeared in major cities at a moment when nativist political movements in the countryside threatened the unity and stability of the independent Brazilian state. These nativist movements were waving the banner of popular sovereignty that Brazilian patriots had used to justify separation from Portugal. Regional rebellions erupted all across

Brazil during the 1830s. In Rio, a period of conservative reaction set in, and dances of the country went entirely out of style with Brazil's ruling class. Only after the nativist movements had finally been defeated could elite literary representations of fado or lundu acquire a retrospective glow. Near the beginning of that process, *Memoirs of a Militia Sergeant,* a memorable local color novel published serially in a Rio newspaper during the 1850s, looked back fondly to the national rhythms of half a century earlier: "Now one person, a man or a woman, dances in the middle of the room for a time, executing the most difficult steps and assuming the most graceful poses," recalled the novelist. "Other times a man and woman dance together, following the rhythm exactly, moving in concert with steps fast or slow, separating and reuniting, he pursuing her, as she backs gently away with small movements of her arms and body, then she pursuing him, as he backs away in turn."[21] How different from the denunciations of the dance-of-two written while it was actually in style! Even given this benevolent nostalgia, however, some things were apparently better not remembered. When a later novel about colonial Brazil praised the dance-of-two for "showing off the native grace of the maidens of this country," for instance, the novelist completely forgot to mention embigadas.[22]

In Buenos Aires and Montevideo, the crisis of independence gave a parallel—and even stronger—boost to the dances of the country. Furthermore, the independence-era vogue of national dances lasted longer in the Río de la Plata than in Rio de Janeiro because of the rhetorically populist post-independence Argentine strongman Juan Manuel de Rosas, whose dictatorial rule filled nearby Montevideo with political exiles and kept the Río de la Plata region in turmoil. During the 1830s and 1840s, when the theater goers of Rio de Janeiro were already recoiling from satirical embigadas—and from Brazil's national rhythms, generally—Rosas was giving dances of the country a prominent place in the symbolism of his regime.

Even the dancing of the black nations acquired a patriotic glow amid this politically orchestrated surge of nativist pride in the Río de la Plata. Black fighters had helped repel the English invasions of the Río de la Plata in 1806–1807, and they had a major participation in the ensuing four decades of armed conflict. The populations of both Buenos Aires and Montevideo were roughly one quarter black at the time, but black men commonly numbered more than a quarter of any military force raised in those cities. The importance of black men as fighters was a dubious honor, of course, contributing ultimately to the decimation of their numbers, but it inspired solicitous treatment from the regimes they defended. Rosas systematically patronized the black nations of Buenos Aires and took his wife and daughter to make courtesy visits to the nation's meeting places, where he respectfully witnessed their candombes. At least once, the dictator's daughter Manuelita even joined in, creating such a scandal that a government newspaper hastened to defend her against wagging tongues: "Manuelita Rosas shows no reluctance to dance on certain occasions with the honest and hard-working mulatos, pardos, and morenos."[23] As part of the city's patriotic May celebrations in 1836, Rosas sponsored a candombe in the city's main square that, according to his furious enemies, attracted many thousands of dancers and spectators. A memoir recalls how the black dancers moved through the street to the sound of drums, the women in cotton dresses and head scarves, the men with white shirts and vests of bright red (the color of Rosas loyalists), the angry and overawed enemies of the regime watching silently from their balconies.[24] A Rosas verse propaganda sheet published in Buenos Aires during the 1830s exemplifies the nativist rhetoric of post-independence Buenos Aires. The sheet called itself *La Negrita* and a black woman was its verse narrator: "My name is Juana Peña/And as a point of pride/Let everyone understand/There's none more Federal than I." To be federalist was to support Rosas, so the first quality claimed for this nativist persona in her spirited self-introduction is political correctness. The second is steadfast loyalty. And the third? The third quality with which she introduces and qualifies herself as a true daughter of Argentina is her skill at dancing candombe: "In celebrations of my people/They give me pride of place/And they all make a space/When I step out to dance."[25]

The populist spirit of the Rosas years also maintained the political importance of Argentina's upbeat dances-of-two called bailecitos del país, danced throughout the interior of the country. The most important of these was zamacueca, which the reader may remember from Gottschalk's travels to Peru and Chile in the 1860s. In both

Peru and Chile, too, zamacueca had become a national dance during the independence era. Argentine *zamba* (a bailecito del país closely related to zamacueca) eventually took on importance as a national rhythm in its own right.[26]

But the *minué montonero,* or "montonero minuet," named for patriot guerrillas called montoneros, was the dance most closely associated with independence in the Río de la Plata. Dances like the montonero had existed at least since the 1750s, inspired by a European dance called *gavota.* Gavota's slow/fast structure permitted dancers to alternate the grave cadences and stately moves of the minuet with more sprightly interludes from the bailecitos del país. The result was a combination than occurred contemporaneously in both Brazil (where it was called *miudinho*) and Cuba (where it was called *minué congó*). After 1810, the montonero minuet was carried by the crusading armies of Buenos Aires throughout the former viceroyalty of the Río de la Plata and to Chile and Perú.[27]

The fighting of independence wars was a formative national experience, and music and dance were very much part of it. In 1827, the French naturalist Alcide d'Orbigny found montonero minuet "very much in style," danced even by Guaraníes (indigenous people) in remote Corrientes Province. D'Orbigny describes a band who—although playing on painfully "imperfect" homemade violin, harp, flute, guitar, triangle, and two drums—"with great precision, rendered various national airs," including the montonero minuet.[28] *Cuando,* another slow/fast gavota knock-off of the independence era, was carried to Chile by the Argentine patriot army that crossed the Andes to defeat the Spanish there in 1817. A Scottish sea captain who observed Chileans dancing cuando in 1820 described the strong influence of bailecitos del país in the fast section of the dance, "animated with drumbeats and shrill voices." Male dancers flourished handkerchiefs in cuando's fast section, just as they did in zamacueca. Frequently, they whirl the handkerchiefs over their heads. The sea captain found Chilean country people "more graceful and skilled" at this than city dwellers, which makes sense, since the bailecitos del país represented rustic traditions only recently reintroduced in urban settings by the independence-era vogue of nativism.[29] Maria Graham, who saw cuando danced in Chile a few years later (1822), indicates in her discussion of the dance that the nativist vogue had already begun to wane. She quotes a vulgar verse

("When I die let the aguardiente stills drop a tear for me!") sung with enthusiasm in the popular cafés called *chinganas,* a famous venue for Chile's national rhythms at the time. Such off-color ditties were "formerly accepted by all social classes," explains Graham. But after independence, she says, the opening of South American ports, bringing people into more intimate contact with Europeans, had "rendered the taste of the higher ranks more nice" and put them off such vulgar entertainments.[30] Once again, we can observe the familiar post-independence decline of national rhythms that occurred in most of Latin America.

Meanwhile, back in Buenos Aires where Rosas continued to harp on populist themes, national rhythms retained their political vitality. In the 1830s, the Rosas regime renamed the montonero minuet the *Federal* minuet. At dances given by the Rosas family, the Federal minuet was de rigueur. Meanwhile, Rosas's exiled enemies in Montevideo, under protracted siege by pro-Rosas forces through the 1840s, contested the dictator's exclusive claim to nativist pride by dancing montonero minuet themselves, though they called it the National minuet.[31]

These stormy politics strongly engaged popular culture, as one can see by looking at the contradance offshoots called *cielito, pericón,* and *media caña,* the most popular Argentine national dances of the period. Cielito, pericón, and media caña were similar, and their names were used somewhat interchangeably. All were interdependent-couple forms, basically square dances with line and circle variants. The interdependent-couple model, with its chains of set figures, provided the overall framework, but those figures included interludes of open-couple dancing (a gesture toward the bailecitos) as well as closed-couple waltzing.[32]

Singing was an important part of these national rhythms. The cielito, particularly, became the dominant lyric form of Argentine popular music in the first decades of independence. The name cielito comes from the playful repetition of the word *cielo,* "heaven," in the first line of each verse, as in the following tribute to "the defender of national glories": Cielo, cielito, cielo,/Cielo de los federales,/Que Rosas es defensor/De las glorias nacionales.* From the start, the

*Very roughly: "Heaven, heaven above,/Federalists, tell the story./Rosas is the defender/Of our national glory."

cielito lyrical form was closely associated with political conflict. The earliest documented example is a cielito sung by the patriot army of Buenos Aires in 1813. Argentine armies of independence seem to have produced cielitos by the fistful. Bartolomé Hidalgo, the first major poet of the gauchesque tradition, composed cielitos that Uruguayan patriots enjoyed singing within earshot of Spanish fortifications: "Skinny, mangy, and sad/The Huns [i.e., Spaniards] are all corralled," and so on.[33] In 1818, an Argentine officer with the patriot army in Chile complained to Gen. José de San Martin about an obscene cielito sung by an insubordinate officer who "visits the chinganas every night." The cielito in question (which survived in the national archives) accused an entire battalion of being (among many other things) a pack of cowards.[34]

The propagandists of the Rosas regime made particular use of cielito lyrics. For example, there was Pancho Lugares, the persona who supposedly composed the verse narratives appearing in the nativist sheet called *El Gaucho.* When this journalistic "gaucho" informed his readers that his wife Chanonga was soon to join him in Buenos Aires, his plans for a celebration were predictable. Lugares invited all his compatriots (a category that, for him, included only Federalists) to join him in dancing cielitos for a whole year. As for the enemies of Rosas, called Unitarians, Lugares invited them to sweep the streets for Chanonga's arrival. A few days later, the paper offered a tongue-in-cheek reply to itself, framed as a "Cielito Composed by a Unitarian Hag Drunk with Rage at Having Been Ordered to Sweep the Street for Chanonga." These upstarts—protested the embittered Unitarian character, her pride in tatters—*they* want to be served when we are the rightful masters. Where will the Federalists stop? Will they next try to dance with "decent" women?[35] The Lugares character talked colloquially, displayed local color, and used popular verse forms. Because everyone knew cielito melodies, topical cielito lyrics could easily be transmitted, remembered, and launched at their targets like musical missiles. When people read, then sang and even danced to political lyrics, the Rosas regime had managed to link print propaganda to popular culture, not merely by association, but in practice.

Singing cielitos was a practice involving women, as well as men. Meanwhile, another dance symbolized a practice strictly for men. Reference to this "dance of death" appears in the writing of the enemies of Rosas, especially exiled Unitarians. Unitarian propagandists were less nativist than Federalist ones but did not overlook the political potential of the popular lyric forms. Hilario Ascasubi, the most influential of the anti-Rosas lyricists, wrote many lyrics in forms corresponding to national dances during his long Montevidean exile. The politically engaged quality of this verse is evident in the lengthy title Ascasubi gave to one of his compositions, a media caña: "To the triumph of the patriots at Montevideo over the soldiers of Rosas in 1843,/To be danced by the Italians who bear arms in defense of Uruguayan and Argentine liberty." Media caña also had another name, *resbalosa,* that Ascasubi often used as a symbol of Federalist brutality. Resbalosa (also the corruption *refalosa*) means "slippery," and dancing "slippery," in the context of Rosas-era civil war, alluded gruesomely to the spasmodic kicking of a man whose throat had been sliced from ear to ear in the gaucho's customary form of execution. Ascasubi's wartime poem "La Refalosa" evoked the sadistic pleasure of a Federalist executioner who provides grisly details of the throat-cutting procedure.[36]

Esteban Echeverría, another exiled anti-Rosas propagandist, used media caña as mood music for his political horror story, "The Slaughterhouse,"[37] in which a young Unitarian opponent to Rosas is seized by a rabble and his form of execution quickly decided:

> "He has a nice neck for the violin."
> "Let's play him the violin!"
> "The best song is Resbalosa."

They drag their Unitarian victim to the slaughterhouse (Echeverría's metaphor for Buenos Aires under Rosas) and cut his throat as a guitarist sings a media caña. Throat cutting was also called "playing the violin." The Federalist gaucho character, Pancho Lugares, provocatively identifies himself, at one point, as "a violinist."[38]

Cielito, pericón, and media caña were danced everywhere from rustic festivities in thatched-roofed ranch houses lost on the pampa, at one social extreme, to the salons of the Buenos Aires elite, at the other. That, precisely, is why they functioned so well as emblems of a cross-class, nativist coalition. Imagine Rosas, his family, and powerful supporters dancing at his ranch in the 1820s, with Rosas as bastonero, personally calling the dance: "At his signal, the orchestra of fifty guitars struck up a pericón, danced by the couples that Rosas himself designated. The dance, which Rosas directed throughout, ended with the most enthusiastic applause and hurrahs." Outside, gauchos and chinas danced, too. And when gauchos and chinas danced on their own ground, at a corner wine shop, for example, national rhythms were what they chose. In the 1830s French traveler Arsene Isabelle was obviously discomfited by the "barbarous high spirits" of a wine shop "where a shiftless guitar player made the blacks and mestizos do an immoral dance called media caña."[39] Another French traveler to Buenos Aires in these years testifies to the pleasure that both humble and "decent" natives could take in a cultural form that freed them from their habitual feeling of inferiority vis-à-vis Europe: "They got me to dance a cielito," reports the traveler, "during which my problems at keeping my arms up and snapping my fingers caused the distinguished guests infinite delight. The good curate, laughing and holding his belly with both hands, did me the honor of assuring me that he had never enjoyed himself so much."[40]

National rhythms were featured in various popular spectacles. Once again, popular dance and light theater showed their natural affinity in Buenos Aires. The first documentary evidence of an Argentine square dance, clearly a proto-cielito, appears between 1780 and 1795 in stage directions for a sainete called (roughly) *Loves of a Ranching Lady.* A later sainete (1818) represents the homecoming of a young patriot volunteer, returning from Chile with triumphant news for the American cause. After the young man's ringing narrative of victory, his parents invite everyone to dance a cielito.[41] From an 1835 ad we read that a French play was followed by a sainete called *El Gaucho, or Chivico's Wedding,* which also promised a cielito.[42] A number of circus companies were based in the city and gave regular performances involving dance. For the most part, circus dancing was done by acrobats as part of their stunts—on a tight wire, on the top of a stack of chairs, and so on. For example, a January 1840 show of the Jardín del Retiro circus promised a media caña and a Federal minuet (danced with a flag in each hand). One circus proudly named its dancing daredevils Sons of the Country.[43]

Half a century later, the Podestá family drew on nativist circus traditions that we can now, perhaps, better appreciate. In 1889, the same season in which they added a milonga to their *Juan Moreira* melodrama, the Podestás also added a pericón. A few years later, in their *Fausto Criollo,* they began to dance cielitos. After the fall of Rosas, cielito, pericón, and media caña had finally gone out of style—along with Rosas-era nativism generally. By the time that the Podestás revived the pericón for their new version of the criollo circus (now half circus, half theater) pericón had mostly disappeared from dance floors. Pericón survived in the 1880s as a sentimental last number on an evening's program, a tribute to old times.[44] That made pericón a perfect focus for theatrical nostalgia, and nostalgia was the Podestá family's stock in trade. For *Juan Moreira,* the Podestás arranged the pericón so that the dancers held streamers of knotted handkerchiefs in the colors of the Argentine (or Uruguayan) flag—a sunny theatrical evocation of a rural fiesta that contrasted starkly, in mood, with the milonga of the melodrama's dark final scene. So, during the 1890s, the show's years of greatest impact, *Juan Moreira* used milonga and pericón to represent urban and rural dancing, respectively: the first, titillating and contemporary, but also vaguely menacing; the second, wistful, sunny, and safe. This staging in *Juan Moreira* began the reappropriation of pericón as a quasi-official national dance in both Argentina and Uruguay. And, long after they stopped performing in circus tents, the Podestás' various theatrical companies continued to dance a pericón as their habitual evening's finale.[45]

In 1900, the seventh of the Podestá brothers composed the pericón "Por María" for a one-act "national lyrical sketch." The composer was not Pepe, but Antonio Podestá, who had started dancing in his brothers' circuses at the age of six. Antonio wrote much of the Podestá family's music, including the milonga in Juan Moreira. Widely published piano arrangements of Antonio Podestá's pericón made it *the* pericón of the early twentieth century, the pericón best recognized and the one normally played when the dance was revived by traditionalists in the city's elite tertulias, as occurred in 1905–1906. For a season or two, in the tertulias of a few distinguished Buenos Aires families, pericón reappeared on dance cards, in a gesture of conservative nationalism. But it simply did not catch on. Without prior practice, perícon's many figures were too complicated for twentieth-century dancers who lacked experience with interdependent-couple dances. Then, too, some snobs recoiled in horror at "the hirsute visage of Juan Moreira emerging triumphantly from a tuxedo."[46]

Tango, not pericón, is what everybody now wanted to dance. During the 1910s and 1920s, tango's spontaneous popularity and international prestige overwhelmed all opposition and brought universal acclaim. The patriotic pericón never truly regained currency as a social dance. But, as the favored protégé of the Podestá brothers' circus, evoking a golden age before pimps and anarchists, pericón became the stuff of school assemblies and national holidays in the park, Argentina's (and Uruguay's) emblematic rural dance—a complement, more than a competitor, to the urban tango.

Cuba's national rhythms arose according to the general Latin American pattern, but with different timing. Independence movements invariably energized national rhythms, and Cuba is no exception, but the process happened in Cuba seventy years after it occurred in most of Latin America. Miguel Faílde was playing his danzones for "Cubans only" asaltos and for the patriotic Simpson Baseball Club not in the 1810s, but in the 1880s. Danzón was a precise analog of the montonero minuet, but of an entirely different choreographical generation.

As in Argentina, Mexico, and other countries where independence was hard fought, Cuban patriot armies marched (figuratively, at least) to the rhythm of popular music. "Whenever the encampment is established for even a few days," wrote U.S. war correspondent James J. O'Kelly in 1874, "this passion [for dance] must be satisfied." And he continues: "The families scattered about in the woods seem to know by instinct when a long halt is to be made and crowd in to meet parents, husbands, and lovers. The commander of the forces immediately organizes the *baile,* and while the troops remain, dancing takes place nightly."[47] O'Kelly reported that one general danced with his troops to celebrate the capture of some Spanish instruments. Normally officers and soldiers danced separately, sometimes on different nights, but blacks and whites danced together according to rank (and many officers were black). Of course, we should not place too much weight on this traveler's impressions. He also likened the spirit of the officer's dancing to "the craze of the opium eater" and called the soldiers' dancing "weird and well-nigh savage." But if O'Kelly is, like most U.S. travelers, unhelpful regarding the dances themselves, his account does show how closely popular music and dance accompanied the struggle for Cuban independence.

Back in the independence era of Latin America as a whole—the 1810s and 1820s—Havana had presented a picture of only mild political ferment inspired mostly by patriot movements elsewhere. Cuba's overwhelming dependence on slave labor dictated political conservatism among the island's dominant sugar planters, just as in Brazil. (Tiny Portugal could not forestall independence in the Brazilian sub-continent, but Brazilian slave owners chose the most conservative path, an independent monarchy.) Meanwhile, Cuba, a stronghold of Spanish military power, remained under direct control from Europe.[48] Patriot conspiracies were few, quickly extinguished, and came to nothing. Instead, particularly in the wake of Spain's 1824 comprehensive defeat on the continent, Cubans lived under Spanish martial law. Overt expressions of Cuban nationalism were not permitted, and the independence movement that might have encouraged them hardly existed—a situation that was to last for decades. Havana saw no official celebration of Cuban national dances in the early nineteenth century, no elite retreat from popular culture at mid-century.

The island's national rhythms quietly and steadily developed, nonetheless, gaining ground in the social dance repertoire with each passing decade. By mid nineteenth century Havana's reputation as a dancing town was well established. In neither Rio nor Buenos Aires did travelers rave so often or moralists worry so much about dance as in Havana. "Dancing, which they love madly, consumes their whole youth," wrote a French traveler about Cuban women in 1850, for example. "The whole year is one big dance, the island one big ballroom. When people don't dance at lyrical societies, at casinos, at private parties, or at country houses on the outskirts of the city, they dance at home, with their family members, sometimes [without more music than] the voices of the dancers themselves."[49]

And not just any music would do. Havana danced the entire gamut of nineteenth-century social dances, but the soul of the city's proverbial zest for dance was the island's own national rhythms. In the very early nineteenth century, the most natural candidates for national dance were various Cuban versions of the diasporic dance-of-two. "Fandango," wrote an English traveler (meaning the dance-of-two in general) "is really the national dance."[50] Old-fashioned Cuban *danzas del país*—precise analogs to Mexican *sonecitos del país* or Argentine *bailecitos del país*—were taught even by Spanish dance instructors in Havana, according to an 1842 newspaper ad.[51] The dances of the city's neo-African cabildos—from which twentieth-century *rumbas* descend—also tended to be dances-of-two, as we have seen.

When danced to string music, the dance-of-two became a *zapateo,* a name indicating a percussive action of the dancer's shoes. Zapateo was associated especially with the mestizo *guajiro* culture of the countryside.* Havana blacks danced zapateo, too.[52] But zapateo required shoes, and slaves, who usually went barefoot, rarely had them. So zapateo's associations were especially mestizo and white. Let us listen to the Countess of Merlin, who wrote beautifully about dance in mid 1800s Havana. Merlin was Cuban but had long lived in France when she returned home to Havana for a visit in the 1840s and published three volumes (in French) about what she saw. Her keen-eyed description of zapateo shows her value as a witness:

> Two people, man and woman, begin the dance with a gliding and energetic step, accentuated from time to time by stamping on the floor. These stamps mark the rhythm of the music, which is quite simple and never moves harmonically outside the tonic and relative seventh chords. But, what passion in the eye and aspect of the guajiro! What a sweet and provocative air of naivete in the guajira! Her hands lightly hold the sides of her dress, which she often pulls daintily back like a timid flower closing its petals to the heat of the sun. The man, his left wrist grasped behind his back in the fingers of his right hand, his eye bright, his attitude domineering, now advances toward his partner, who gradually retrenches and allows herself to be besieged again. New he pretends to retreat himself, and he soon receives the woman's counterattack. Finally, the two actors in this scene come together and the dance takes on an even more lively, ardent, and voluptuous character that lasts until the often delirious end. The dancers rarely

* In a feminine form, the word *guajira* (country woman), figures prominently in Cuba's twentieth-century patriotic classic "Guantanamera," dedicated to a country woman from Guantánamo, the *guajira guantanamera* of the song's refrain.

> change at the same time. Generally, the man is replaced various times in front of the woman, without the music stopping.[53]

In 1830s Cuba there were "low and adulterous offshoots" of the zapateo with sexually allusive "movements and pantomime," and there were more strait-laced ballroom variations, as well. Imagine the parlor game version in which "men and women alternate in a circle, each couple jumping inside, in turn, to do a figure that all the others then have to repeat."[54]

The most often danced national dance of these years was unquestionably *contradanza cubana.* Contradanza—later shortened to danza—was simply a national contradance variation. These were common in Europe. A Parisian compilation of 1811 included French, Polish, Russian, Spanish, German, and Italian versions of contradance.[55] Argentine cielito and pericón, two other contradance offshoots, have already come to our attention. Caribbean contradance variations abounded—among them, the Dominican variation that eventually became *merengue.*[56] Cuban musicians, especially black Cuban musicians, gave contradance a gently syncopated rhythm. Cuban dancers made their own variation by moving away from European bounciness, with more lateral movement to their hips. We can "see" this in the evidence because hip motion implies a lower center of gravity, and lowering one's center of gravity tends to produce a shuffling sound of the feet—the same sound we "heard" in Buenos Aires dance halls. Cubans called this sound *escobilleo* or *sopimpa.*[57] The novel *Cecilia Valdés* describes it this way: "Above the sound of the orchestra with its thunderous kettle drums, one could hear, in perfect time to the music, the monotonous and continuous shuffling sound of feet, without which Cuban people of color believe it impossible to follow exactly the rhythm of danza."[58]

By mid-century, Cubans (and Puerto Ricans, too) used the word *danza* for their national versions of contradanza, defined by a contemporary Cuban dictionary as "the favorite dance of this entire Island," practiced by all social classes. The dictionary was emphatic about the last point. Danza, it maintained, was "danced everywhere from the most solemn official occasion in the capital to the lowest *changüí* at the furthest corner of the Island." (A *changüí,* in turn, was defined as a gathering of Cuban blacks: "gente criolla de color.")[59] Colombian traveler Tanco Armero visited Havana on his way around the world in the 1850s: "Danza is the national dance, and a very simple thing it is—a sort of quadrille, with a half chain and frequent waltzing. Sometimes, a single danza can go on for hours. Cubans have an aversion to other dances, and when a waltz or polka is played, at most parties or salon gatherings few can dance it."[60]

Most people agreed that only Cubans could produce danza: "A European musician can play the notes," wrote the 1830s columnist who called himself El Lugareño (roughly, The Local Joe), "but he can never give them that air, that rhythm, that *flavor* that a Criollo musician gives them." Antonio de la Barra y Prado, a Spanish observer of Havana in the 1860s concurred, saying danza "can be played well only by musicians from here."[61]

Danza's syncopated rhythm, clearly, was what made it distinctively Cuban, and the syncopated rhythm, everybody knew, was an African influence on the music. "The rhythm is the same one the blacks play on their drums," declared de la Barra y Prado.[62] The observation was already commonplace in the 1830s: "Who can fail to recognize, in the way our young men and women dance," laments a private letter of 1837, "an imitation of the blacks in their *cabildos?* Who does not know that the bass notes of our danzas constitute the echo of African drums?"[63] Of course, no expression of African influence went unpunished. Danza's most vociferous critic was local color writer Luis Victoriano Betancourt, who called danza "a confused mélange of zapateo and tango."[64] Another of Betancourt's moralistic salvos, issued in the pages of *Cuban Garland (A Bi-Weekly Periodical of Literature, Morality, Art, Theater, Music, Fashion, Etc., with Etchings and Lithographs, Dedicated to the Fair Sex)* condemned danza as a "time-sanctioned moral travesty" that had unfortunately "gained front rank" among Cuban customs.[65]

African influence was not the only problem. Another problem with danza was the *cedazo* section. Many nineteenth-century contradance derivatives had a "swing your partner" figure in which the dancers formed closed couples and "waltzed" a few measures. Cubans called this figure the *cedazo*. By the 1830s, many young people joined the dance at the very end, merely for the cedazo. To keep the people dancing, a skillful dance band offered melodic variations as an opportunity for dancers to prolong their favorite part. Cedazo figures originally lasted eight measures, but by mid-century they might last sixteen or even thirty-two measures.[66] The reason for interest in the cedazo is not mysterious. It involved only a gentle swaying that some outsiders called "monotonous" and "boring." But sharp-eyed chaperones well knew how close the dancers held their bodies as they swayed, and they believed that "the vociferous preference for danza" showed precisely more on young minds than innocent diversion.[67]

At mid-century, there could be little doubt about this "vociferous preference." The elders of the 1860s decried the tendency for every party to become "an academy where men and women practice the current, simple danza."[68] In 1860, Felicia, a female author (or at least, female persona and journalistic pseudonym) provided a detailed history of Havana ballroom dancing for *The Cuban Album of Things Good and Beautiful.* The only dance that had ever threatened to eclipse danza, according to Felicia, had been polka in the 1840s. She repeated the general notion that danza dominated the Cuban salon repertory because it suited the climate, being slow—involving less striding and bouncing, more "delicate voluptuousness." As the Countess of Merlin had observed, Cuban danza was done "more with the body than with the feet." *Bailar sabroso,* the Cuban way of dancing, meant to savor the rhythm in the body by letting the hips express it. "Dancing with modesty, with reserve, with prudent restraint [now means] to dance the old-fashioned way," fretted Felicia. Refusing to "savor" meant "not knowing how to dance."[69] And only danzas—not polkas or lancers or schottisches—were really savory.

So, long before independence movements created a nationalist discourse in Cuba, being Cuban meant dancing in a distinctively Cuban way. Cirilo Villaverde, the author of *Cecilia Valdez,* who would eventually join the independence movement and help create that nationalist discourse, reported on dance for a Havana newspaper in the 1840s. One of Villaverde's newspaper chronicles describes a Criollo youth who had grown up in England and, on his return to Havana, was astonished to encounter the world of Havana social dance, with its complex practices and subtle codes, its semaphoric signals sent across the dance floor by fluttering fans. The bafflement of the young Criollo too-long-in-London confirmed Villaverde's sense of something satisfyingly and distinctively Cuban. It was pleasant to value something that a London education could not provide, as we can guess from his delighted tone.[70] Villaverde's famous descriptions of mid-century danza in *Cecilia Valdez* also communicate his excitement: "At about ten o'clock the dance was reaching a point of furor. Furor, I say, unable to find a term that better evokes the incessant movement of feet, shuffling gently with the bodies' movements to the beat of the music, the close crowd of dancers turning, jostling, and traveling back and forth between the onlookers without a moment's respite."[71]

Villaverde loved Cuban dance culture, but not all Cubans did. Luis Victoriano Betancourt, along with many others, thought that Cubans simply danced too much.

> Today we give a dance because it is Papa's birthday, tomorrow because it is Mama's, the day after, because it is Grandma's, and the day after that, because it is the birthday of the children's godmother. If big brother graduates from the university, a dance. For little brother's baptism, a dance. When Auntie's goiter gets better, a dance. Has the son of the children's teacher had a corn removed? A dance![72]

Nineteenth-century sources indicate that Cubans already danced with unusual frequency and fervor: the impressions of travelers, the prominence of dance in Cuban periodical and literary sources, and especially the frequency of social clubs devoted to dance. Cuban proclivity for dance—the common starting point of both Villaverde's appreciations and Betancourt's condemnations—was proverbial in Cuba by the 1840s and has remained, ever since, an important part of the story (to paraphrase Clifford Geertz) that Cubans tell themselves about themselves. "It's an undeniable fact that Cuba is the country par excellence for dancing," worried a Havana journalist in 1882. "We have a kind of delirium for the pastime. . . . It is a vice deeply rooted in our social customs."[73] Nicolás Tanco Amero's perspective as a Latin American world traveler seems especially valuable:

> [Cuba's] dominant passion, of course, is dancing. Everybody dances in Havana, people of whatever age, class, or condition, from toddlers to old women, from the Captain General to the least of the public employees. They dance the same dances in the palace and in the thatched-rooved huts of the blacks, and even cripples who cannot get up from their seats still move their

> bodies to the beat of the music. You can hear danzas playing all day long, both in people's houses and from organ grinders in the street, where even pedestrians go dancing by.

Tanco Armero recalled singing street vendors from other stops on his world tour, but only in Cuba had he ever seen street vendors dance.[74]

In Rio and Buenos Aires, stylish dance programs featured waltz, polka, lancers, schottische, quadrille—almost exclusively European styles—around 1850. But in Havana, it was not unusual for every other number in an evening's program, and sometimes more, to be danza cubana.[75] Havana elite's predilection for the beloved danza simply had no counterpart in these other cosmopolitan capitals—unless it was that itinerant version of danza itself, habanera. The early international projection of Cuban dance music seems significant. Touring Norwegian concert violinist Ole Bull wrote to his wife that Havana orchestras (besides being "composed, almost without exception, of blacks and mulatos") were "the best musicians in all America!"[76]

Did nineteenth-century Cubans like to dance so much simply because their music was better? All music is not aesthetically equal, and Cuban music is better than most. But aesthetic appreciation depends greatly on the context. The special conditions under which Cuba's national rhythms developed in the nineteenth century help account for their popularity at all social levels. In contrast to the situation in Rio and Buenos Aires, no independence movement gave public prominence to these dances in 1820s Havana. Yet the continuation of Spanish rule over Cuba produced serious tensions between Spaniards and Criollos, encouraging a strong binary opposition in the force field of Cuban identities. To embrace African-influenced music and dance was to distance oneself from Spain.[77] Is it merely coincidence that *patón,** a pejorative label used by Cubans to describe Spaniards during the late nineteenth century, also means someone who cannot dance well?[78]

In sum, when the "decent people" of Rio and Buenos Aires, no longer forced to differentiate themselves from colonial masters, turned their attention to "civilizing" Brazil and Argentina and redoubled their emphasis on European models in everything (including dance)—the same was not yet occurring in Havana. In

* *Pata* (foot or hoof) plus the augmentative suffix *–ón* means literally "big foot."

Havana, the politically emasculated sons of sugar planters were less mindful of a civilizing mission that was not theirs to control. In cultivating popular Cuban dance culture (instead of reacting against the vulgar throng) they drew a line between themselves and their Spanish overlords. That accounts for danza's long heyday in 1840s, 1850s, 1860s, and 1870s Havana, during the nadir of national dances in the salons of Rio and Buenos Aires. Eventually, this long experience helped danzón find quick acceptance among Havana's "decent people" in the 1880s and 1890s, while maxixe and milonga remained pariahs.

To this point, our "archeology" of Latin American national rhythms has uncovered substantial substrata beneath twentieth-century genres such as samba, tango, and salsa. Here are the main points succinctly stated. Latin America's contemporary national rhythms have multiple origins. They drew directly from maxixe, milonga, and danzón, the turn-of-the-century dances of the transgressive close embrace. Maxixe, milonga, and danzón themselves drew, in turn, on the dance heritage of the neo-African nations, refracted though a wider social dance culture. Finally, maxixe, milonga, and danzón had precise antecedents in an earlier generation of national dances, such as lundu, cielito, and danza cubana. These dances of the independence era mark an important point in our excavation, the point at which republican nationalism infused Latin America's mestizo dances with a new political meaning.

The national rhythms of the independence era (roughly 1800–1830, and later for Cuba) represented new national identities conceived as ethnic fusions of Europe, Africa, and indigenous America. It would be a long time, of course, before these new national identities were fleshed out in writing, explicitly elaborated, and officially proclaimed. It would be even longer before ethnic fusions actually took place, if they ever did. One must always consider the contrast between rhetoric and reality in the matter of Latin American race relations, a subject to which we will return. But, indisputably, the national rhythms of the independence era show the popular appeal of the idea of mestizo national identities in Latin America two hundred years ago. This is useful to know. The level of social engagement with republican ideologies back then is an open question. Dance history provides evidence for popular enthusiasm.

And there are a few more levels still to be excavated. Latin America's national rhythms had a public life even before independence and before nationalism. The region's earliest national rhythms did not yet symbolize mestizo identities. Instead, they symbolized the diverse ethnicities ruled over by a monarch. They also symbolized the diverse ethnicities gathered in bosom of the Catholic church. This association with state power and ideology reaches deep into the colonial period of Latin America and across the Atlantic to Spain and Portugal.

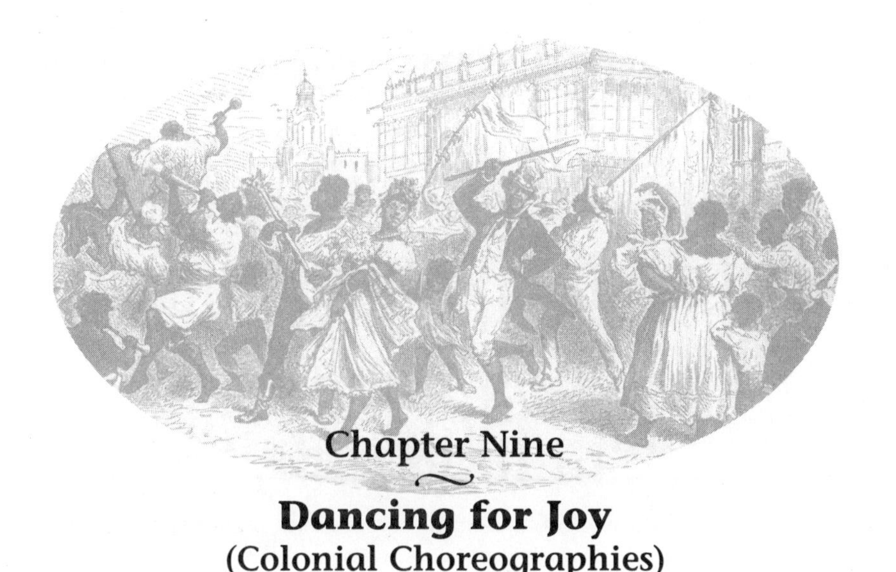

Chapter Nine

Dancing for Joy (Colonial Choreographies)

Recall the dancing Baianas of Tia Ciata's 1890s parade group, White Rose, that started out as an Epiphany pageant. Consider the duels of tango footwork and knife play between compadrito tough-guys in the tents of the Recoleta parish fair. Think of pre-Lenten carnival balls by the hundreds through the nineteenth century, and of the more personal occasions for dancing, like birthdays—or "saint's days"—baptisms, confirmations, and weddings. Somewhat mysteriously, in view of their frequent transgressiveness, Latin America's national rhythms have intermingled with, and been shaped by, the Catholic Church.

Dance expresses happiness perhaps above all other things. Socially, dance marks moments of collective joy. Church authorities understood dance to be a potent force, something to be strictly limited, carefully deployed. Secular authorities also paid heed to, and made use of, dance. They could neither permit the apogee of collective good feeling in illicit settings nor dispense with it on occasions of officially sanctioned gaiety. Indeed, sometimes *not* to dance for joy—as when the fortunate birth of a royal heir surmounted some vexatious dynastic impasse—was almost treasonous.[1]

Admittedly, public celebrations such as royal weddings and religious festivals do not seem a likely place to find transgressive dancing. Taverns, port districts—places where sailors, day laborers, petty traders, market women, and prostitutes from various corners of the Atlantic world mingled unsupervised—these were the natural habitats of dances that flaunted social norms. Hypothetically, to uncover the history of transgressive dancing in Latin America before 1800, we would consult the personal papers left by those sailors and market women, peruse guest lists and musicians' receipts from the private parties of the desperately poor, scan early newspaper features on table dancing at the local bawdy house, and examine other such nonexistent documents. Less than ideally, the evidence we have for the period 1500–1800 is, in fact, largely limited to descriptions of royal weddings and religious festivals, along with occasional edicts banning dance in this or that situation, and stray mention of popular dancing in the theatrical literature. In other words, we can see only a tiny slice of the dancing that went on, the slice that was promoted by church and state. Could religious or patriotic dancing be transgressive? Surely dancing that somehow "crossed the line" undermined both church and state. But, as the reader will see, despite the vigilance of the clerics, popular transgressiveness erupted spontaneously even in church dancing.[2]

Moreover, while it gives only vague indications about popular dance that happened "off-stage," so to speak, the existing evidence is ideal for something else. What could be better than elaborate descriptions of official celebrations, religious processions, and theatrical performances to reveal the public uses of popular dance? And public uses, after all, are what make dance and music into a national rhythm.

The idea of dancing in church may surprise contemporary Westerners, but spiritual dance is one of the most ancient and widespread kinds. Participants in the Candomblé ceremonies assisted by Tia Ciata in early twentieth-century Rio danced in ecstatic trances, and so did many Hebrew prophets and other Biblical figures, most notably King David.

Still, dancing and Christianity have had a somewhat troubled relationship. During centuries of medieval European history repeated church censures indicated concern about transgressive dancing. For example, during the entire first millennium of Christianity in Europe, church authorities worried occasionally about the persistence of pagan dance rites called (in Spanish and Portuguese) *calendas*. St. Augustine fretted about calendas in the late Roman Empire, and an encyclical of 1444 shows French prelates still fretting about them. Spanish and Portuguese churchmen had particular cause for alarm. Iberian dancers enjoyed a wide reputation already in Roman times, when they leapt particularly around funeral pyres. Cádiz dancing girls who accompanied themselves with castanet-like *crótalos* also became well known in the Roman world. Christian bishops of the sixth and seventh centuries had to issue multiple condemnations of uncontrolled dancing in Iberian churches.[3] Iberian Jews reportedly danced in their synagogues, too. Then came the eighth-century Moorish invasion of Iberia, bringing Islam and further varieties of dance to disconcert the bishops. Moorish dancers greeted princely visitors and took part in religious street pageantry, and their nocturnal diversions called *zambras* lasted until the Andalucian dawn. On the other hand, some Christians, such as Alfonso el Sabio, Spain's great thirteenth-century Christian law-giver, appreciated the highly cultivated arts of the African invaders. Moorish dancing continued in Spain and Portugal for centuries after the Christian Reconquest was completed.[4]

And so did royally mandated dancing for joy. For example, the nuptial celebrations of Holy Roman Emperor Frederick III and Portuguese Princess Leonor in 1451 brought a command performance of dances representing the diverse "nations" of multicultural Iberia. A member of Frederick's party described for his diary what he witnessed in the square in front of Leonor's palace in Portugal: "Before daybreak on the seventeenth of October, there came a party of Christians, another of Saracens, another of Savages, and yet another of Jews, and all sang, shouted, and frolicked in their own way." Three days later, more dancers appeared, women as well as men. And three days after that, more throngs "with horns and other musical instruments, divided into four groups, each dancing in its own way." This time the groups were Christians, Moors, Jews, and a fourth composite group of non-Iberian "Others," including "Ethiopians" and Canary Island "savages"—the first recorded occasion of African dance in Portugal.[5] The symbolism is unmistakable. Each dance signified the endorsement of a different "nation" subject to the Portuguese monarchy. Spontaneity played no part here. These dancers were not merely invited, they were contracted.

Christian monarchs displayed dancing Moors to show dominion over them. When Portuguese Prince Afonso was married a few decades later, a contemporary chronicle described the process by which Moorish dancers were recruited for the celebration at the walled city of Évora: "And so the order went out to all the Moorish quarters of the kingdom, summoning to the celebration all Moorish men and women able to sing, dance, or play a musical instrument. Plentiful provisions and fine garments were given them, and they even received money for the cost of the journey."[6] Later, during the reign of Sebastião, the Portuguese monarch whose crusading obsession drove him to the disastrous (and, for him, fatal) African expedition of 1578, Moorish dancers were nonetheless part of a royal welcome to Lisbon. Ecclesiastical dignitary Cardinal Alexandrino somewhat disapprovingly describes his arrival to that city by sea: "Ten barges floated up to us, variously painted and adorned, in which we saw flutes, horns, tambourines, and other instruments, with singers and dancers in Moorish dress. They danced with spirit, but their song sounded like what the Jews sing in their synagogues."[7]

Dancing at official wedding celebrations ratified the relationship between monarch and subjects by dramatizing the subjects' appropriately joyful response to the royal family's glad tidings. And even better than a hired spectacle was a spontaneous participatory celebration. So, when Prince João of Portugal was married in 1810, the people of Rio were invited to seven days of festivities in the Campo de Santana, the same commons area where Rio's black nations danced. Whether the black nations also danced to celebrate the prince's wedding is not a matter of record, but it would not be surprising. The police of Rio explicitly encouraged people to "put on costumes, arrange dances, present themselves publicly, and parade around in the streets" to manifest their pleasure.[8] Everybody's pleasure contributed to the show of joyous unanimity. In 1664, the birth of a Spanish prince inspired the town council of Buenos Aires to arrange a series of celebratory dances in a four-tiered arrangement to get the whole colony involved. There was a costume ball for the town's elite and another for the merchants and sea captains. There was a series of less formal dances for artisans and other town dwellers of middling status, and lastly, a series of rollicking, week-long hoedowns for the people of color at the bottom of the social hierarchy. Those who declined to attend the festivities were liable to pay a fifty-peso fine.[9]

By the 1700s, the presence of non-European subjects had become integral to the imperial pageantry of the Iberian monarchies. One more extended example will suffice. A royal marriage (quickly followed by a royal pregnancy and the birth of a male heir) in the early 1760s brought compulsory celebrants dancing into the streets throughout Portugal and Brazil. Local trade guilds put on many dances. In the Bahian town of Santo Amaro, the tailors put on a contradance, while the cutlers and carpenters put on a Moorish dance and the goldsmiths presented a Congo Embassy. There was nothing Moorish about these cutlers and carpenters, nothing Congo about the goldsmiths. Both the Moorish dance and the Congo dance were stylized representations, funded by guild members but probably put on by professionals. The members of the Congo Embassy were richly dressed, arrayed with gold and jewels, and, going largely on horseback, danced very little. On the other hand, a contemporary chronicle also mentions Cucumbys* who danced "to the sound of instruments appropriate to their use and rites." The ersatz Congo Embassy may have been played in blackface, but the Cucumbys were clearly of African descent and may even have been slaves.[10]

In Rio, the 1761 celebrations of the royal family's fecundity included a number of lavish floats upon which people danced. The carpenters, cabinet makers, and masons contributed a float showing Moors and Christians locked in choreographical mock combat. The shoemakers' float showed Brazilian Indians hunting—and then dancing with—wild beasts. There was also a King of Congos in the streets of Rio, but this time both the king and his entourage were mulatos, whom the chronicle identifies quite precisely as "mixed men, the natural combination of opposite colors." These mixed men were supposedly displaying "the gestures, music, instruments, and dance" of Africans.[11] Dances representing various ethnic or religious "Others"—Gypsies, Moors, and Jews, as well as Africans—were clearly familiar. Furthermore, to see non-Africans put on "African" dances seems to have been familiar, as well. Like other monarchical

* Remember the "African Indians" of Rio carnival in the 1880s?

fetes of this period, the 1761 celebrations were publicized far and wide. A pamphlet entitled *Enumeration of the Gracious Festivities Offered in the City of São Sebastião do Rio de Janeiro at the Felicitous News of the Birth of Our Serene Lord José, Prince of Beira* was only one of several descriptions to appear in 1763.[12]

Latin America's later national rhythms clearly have antecedents in these monarchical uses of popular dance, preserved for our consideration in the obsequious puffery of documents like the foregoing one. And not by accident have our examples been mostly Portuguese. To trace the genealogy of Latin America's national rhythms before independence, we must adopt a diasporic framework, which means looking more at Portugal than at Spain. After all, Portugal initiated the African slave trade and dominated it during its first century, establishing patterns followed by later slaving nations. The primary destination of African slaves at first was Portugal itself. By the mid 1500s, African slaves constituted around 10 percent of the population in cities such as Lisbon and Évora. Until the 1530s, even slaves on their way to Spanish territories passed through Portugal before being shipped to the Spanish Caribbean, or to Sevilla or Valencia, two Spanish cities with sizeable African populations.[13]

Enough royal weddings and birthdays! Dancing tributes to the monarchy were never so frequent as dancing on occasions sponsored by the Catholic Church. Religious dance flourished in Spain and Portugal during the initial colonization of America. Santa Teresa de Avila, who danced alone in her Spanish chapel, is merely the most famous ecstatic dancer in Iberian religious tradition. Overall, travelers found religious dance most pervasive in Portugal, where André Dias, Bishop of Megara, called the faithful to sing and dance before the altar in the early 1400s. In 1466, a Bohemian visitor remarked on frequent dancing in Portuguese churches. In 1500, "Gloria in excelsis Deo" was sung *and danced* for Christmas in the Portuguese royal chapel. In 1676, a French traveler registered his disapproval of such activities: "On the most solemn holidays, after mass is said, richly dressed women enter the church and dance in the presence of the Holy Eucharist, which remains exposed, and to the music of guitars and castanets they sing profane songs and adopt a thousand indelicate postures." Catholic mysticism in Portugal even included affectionate odes to a dancing Jesus—again, the Bishop of Megara: "I see my dear Jesus and feel his embrace/He frolics with me and does his dance."[14]

Portugal had a dancing reputation, at least in Spanish eyes. Furthermore, Spaniards saw the Portuguese as closely associated with people of African descent. Sevilla's 1587 Corpus Christi procession included a float on which five women did "a Portuguese dance," and Madrid's 1598 Corpus Christi procession had something similar. These dancers were mostly women, and frequently they were women of African descent. In 1605, a Portuguese observer at Valladolid, Spain, was dismayed at the dancing representations of Portugal:

> I cared not at all for an entertainment representing Portugal, though the Castilians enjoyed it immensely. It was a kind of tabernacle set up in the middle of the square. A Portuguese mulato and mulata couple climbed up there, and with them a court jester, and they all played and sang. Thinking this act was Portugal, the young people laughed no end.

Later, in the procession of Corpus Christi, the mortified visitor was treated to another "dance of Portuguese mulatas."[15]

São Gonçalo, a saint whose cult called specifically for dance, was an object of devotion mostly in Portugal and Brazil. São Gonçalo attracted especially the old and infirm, and he healed only those who danced to him. A traveler to Portugal saw people dance to São Gonçalo in public squares in the early 1700s.[16] In Brazil, São Gonçalo apparently developed a taste for lundu and a popular reputation as an amorous match-maker. The reader may recall from the last chapter a satirical description of dancing in a Brazilian church, complete with wiggling bottoms and embigadas. The dancers' inspiration, predictably, was São Gonçalo.[17] São Gonçalo's dancing cult seems to have been everywhere in the eighteenth century, far overshadowing devotion to São Guido and São Modesto, who also asked for dancing. In 1718, when a traveler to Bahia described "priests, monks, women, gentlemen, and slaves dancing and leaping together and shouting at the top of their lungs," the occasion "little known on theFrench calendar, but quite famous in Brazil," was, of course, São Gonçalo. The delighted crowd even persuaded the Brazilian viceroy to gyrate a bit in honor of the dancing saint. In 1758, a visiting bishop complained about the immoderate adoration of São Gonçalo in the Brazilian town (and future metropolis) of São Paulo, including batuque and African-style drumming at some of the ceremonies. "After dancing, they go on to other indecencies which everyone knows about but modesty forbids me to mention," wrote the bishop.[18]

Dancing to São Gonçalo was not religious at all by the bishop's definition. But religious dancing came in many varieties, not all of them Christian. Some of the most indisputably religious dancing in the Atlantic world was being done by non-Christian Africans, at home and in the diaspora. Drums were a help, not a hindrance, to their religious experience. Nor is it odd to find lundu danced to São Gonçalo. Though mostly a secular dance by 1800, lundu had a mystical past. Among the most probable origins of the name *lundu* is *calundu,* a word referring to Brazilian dance ceremonies with clear African roots, mentioned occasionally in documents of the 1600s and 1700s. Calundus seem, on occasion, to have involved spirit possession, and whites were not oblivious to their influence. In 1734 a Minas Gerais landowner was accused not only of permitting "the superstitious dances" in his house, but also of joining in himself.[19]

It is tempting to imagine calundu ceremonies through reference to the modern Afro-Brazilian religion Candomblé, but they were probably not identical. Religious dancing was preserved in secrecy by slaves, clearly, and calundus are an example. But we know virtually no details of calundu ceremonies. And we know that Candomblé has been shaped by ongoing contact with Africa, especially in late nineteenth and early twentieth centuries. What form African religious dancing took in Brazil before 1900, we can only guess. Modern Santería, the precise Cuban analog of Brazilian Candomblé, likewise differs from earlier religious dancing in Cuba—but just how, again, we cannot know for sure.[20]

In sum, both Africans and Iberians demonstrated a propensity for religious dancing. To some degree, their propensities flowed together in Latin America. For example, Catholic saints' days configured the dancing calendar, and many saints were associated with particular West African deities. In Brazilian Candomblé, the deity Xangô is represented by the figure of Santa Bárbara, and Iemanjá, by the figure of the Virgin of Rosário. In Cuban santería, the analogous deities Changó and Yemayá are represented by Santa Bárbara and the Virgin of Regla, respectively. On the January day sacred to Nosso Senhor do Bonfim, Brazilian worshipers of African descent go en masse to wash that saint's church in Bahia, something customarily required by the Yoruba deity, Oxalá. An Austrian visitor of the 1860s described the scene inside the church as "a large, mirthful dancing hall."[21]

Devotions to particular Catholic saints (whether or not they represented West African deities) gave African slaves a way to fit their own culture into the framework of Iberian religious practice. How religious their dancing was (or, to what religion it really pertained) is irrelevant to our inquiry. What counts is the framework that Catholic festivities created: free time in which to dance, approved settings, occasions, and associations for it, even access to resources. These are the reasons that Catholic festivities loom so large in the history of diasporic dance.

We have already seen how devotion to the black king of the Epiphany story (a saint, after all) became an excuse for collecting pious donations and electing kings at festive 6 January gatherings. We have seen how black nations existed within the framework of Catholic devotional brotherhoods. In Brazil, the most notable black devotion was to a manifestation of the virgin, Nossa Senhora do Rosário. A slave brotherhood devoted to Nossa Senhora do Rosário already existed in Lisbon by 1500, in Évora by 1518.[22] Sevilla had a black religious brotherhood by 1601, if not before. Interestingly, the meetings of Sevilla's black brotherhoods were called *cabildos,* the term later used in Havana for neo-African nations. The loyalty of these brotherhoods' members was proverbially strong. Legend tells of a free black man of Sevilla who, in a desperate attempt to raise money for the devotions of his brotherhood, offered to sell himself into slavery there in 1656.[23]

Did these black Catholic brotherhoods already "front" for neo-African nations in the first centuries of the diaspora? Evidence suggests so. Black kings were on the scene quite early. A late medieval chronicler of Portugal mentions a "King of Guinea" who appeared with two hundred dancing followers in the city of Évora. In 1567, a judicial official at Colares, near Lisbon, reported breaking up a festive gathering in which blacks had elected a king.[24] Whenever it started, the link between black nations and particular Catholic devotions was certainly durable. A Congo nation linked to Lisbon's brotherhood of Nossa Senhora do Rosário was still showing off its dancing in 1863, when a dispute between rival queens Sebastiana Júlia and Joana Ignácia da Conceição became the topic of a newspaper story. Just a bit later, Cucumbys parading at Rio carnival sang a verse that we can now better understand: "I'm the king of Congo/Raise your spirits all!/Because I've just arrived/From ye olde Portugal!"[25]

The reader may recall frequent references to Congo people among the neo-African nations who danced to the drums of Epiphany in Rio, Havana, and Buenos Aires. It makes sense that Congos in the diaspora were eager participants in church-sponsored dancing.[26] Congo was the area of Africa where Portuguese evangelizing had best succeeded. As in the earlier Christian evangelization of Europe, success came through the baptism of a king whose people converted along with him. In the early 1500s, Muemba Nzinga—baptized as Afonso I, King of Manicongo—sent his son Henrique to Portugal, where he became a Catholic priest and, eventually, a Catholic bishop. Afonso I of Manicongo even credited Santiago Matamoros (the sword-swinging patron saint of Spain and Portugal) for a miraculous victory against pagan enemies. The Catholic Congo monarchies remained powerful in central Africa for centuries. In Brazil, *congos* or *congadas* became the generic terms for street pageants associated with neo-African kingship, although dozens of different nations took part. So the Congos apparently initiated the practice or at least defined it in Portuguese eyes. The existence of Catholic Congo kings in Africa was a matter of Portuguese pride—which explains not only Portuguese toleration of Congo dancing, but also the occasional dramatization of Congo kingship by whites and mulatos.[27]

As early as the 1500s, African slaves in Portugal gathered to dance on Sundays and Catholic holidays, just as black nations throughout the Atlantic world did later. As usual, much of what we know about such gatherings comes from prohibitions. Dance gatherings were banned within a league of Lisbon, for example, in 1563.[28] The earliest description of a specifically black Catholic festivity that has so far come to light in Portugal dates from 1633. The participants wore what seemed to be African dress and marched through the streets playing

African instruments. A few of the men carried bows, as Brazilian Cucumbys did three hundred years later. The women carried baskets of wheat on their heads. After entering the church to hear mass, the group left its offering and danced away.[29]

Black participation in Epiphany pageants seems to have begun early, too, as we can see in Epiphany lyrics from the 1600s. The music and dance of these pageants was notably popular—not erudite and "churchy." Some vilancicos were written in mock black dialect.[30] The lyrics mention African-style dancing before images of the baby Jesus—precisely the tradition from which Tia Ciata's White Rose emerged. By the early 1700s, the dancing of slaves in devotions to Catholic saints was a well-established custom—but also the object of occasional ecclesiastical censure, and for the usual reason: "hip movements [*meneios*] that are too much to be imagined, let alone witnessed."[31]

Most dancing devotions were based on familiar popular dances and could easily slip toward a secular, even profane, mood. Seventeenth-century Bahian poet Gregório de Matos, a frequent source of social insights, satirized the celebration of one brotherhood with jocularly explicit references to the drunken antics and "wiggling asses" of the dancers.[32] A bit later (1707), the Archbishopric of Bahia found it necessary to prohibit, "on pain of excommunication and a fine of ten cruzados," indecent dances and improper songs in church. The prohibition waffled, however: Dancers could, of course, continue to take part in religious plays on the church steps. And those who danced decently in religious processions could naturally still dance into the church as part of the procession. They were simply asked not to do so during mass.[33]

In sum, the Catholic devotions of Portugal and Spain became an institutional framework within which Africans and their descendants, enslaved and free, born in Africa or in the diaspora, could dance. As several of our examples have already shown, many of these devotions involved a procession—another Portuguese specialty, one that merits further attention here.

Catholic processions of the 1500s and 1600s were not always somber, by any means. In Portugal and Spain, many were dancing processions. Because processions established the dancers' tacit claim to social participation and shared use of public space, they have particular importance in our archeology of Latin America's national rhythms. Dancing at private, nocturnal gatherings, defined neo-African nations as groups apart. Dancing in the street for thousands of spectators as part of an official celebration, on the other hand, gradually defined blacks as integral to the wider societies where they resided. That process of redefinition began, more or less, at Évora in 1451, when Christians, Moors, Jews, and "Ethiopians" danced together "for joy." It reached an apogee, one could say, in the street carnivals of twentieth-century Rio de Janeiro, when black and white Brazilians danced together for the same reason.[34]

"Today a procession is a party, even for the most sincerely religious," wrote Joaquim Maria Machado de Assis in the *Diario do Rio de Janeiro,* criticizing processions in 1869 Rio.[35] The party was older than Machado de Assis believed. A German traveler to Portugal in 1797 said the Portuguese "follow a procession with the same pleasure with which one attends the opera."[36] A Lisbon pamphlet of 1737 suggested that common people ("Manuel and Maria") joined processions mainly to dance:

> Is it not true that, feigning
> Devotion, Manuel and Maria
> Go out to the processions
> Saying they've promised a saint,
> And afterwards can't budge,
> They've danced so hard all night
> To guitars and tambourines,
> Which is why they went at all?[37]

The festive spirit of Portuguese processions became notable in the late middle ages. In the 1400s and 1500s, it was normal for a dancing procession to accompany a priest to and from church on the occasion of his first celebration of mass.[38] For hundreds of years, well into the 1800s in some provincial towns of Portugal, most processions had a dancing King David (oddly, a figure of fun, with false nose and beard, paper crown, and lyre) bringing up the rear or leading other dancers.[39] The procession itself was merely the centerpiece of an entire day of festivities that included a general holiday, public decorations, and abundant food and drink. Those festivities extended into the night, and sometimes the procession itself was nocturnal. Processions involved unusual freedom for women, and sharp-tongued commentators even professed to notice more pregnancies in the wake of Lisbon's major processions.[40]

Without question, the biggest procession of the year, in Spain as well as in Portugal, was Corpus Christi, "the feast of the triumph over heresy," which was added to the Catholic calendar in the 1300s. Corpus Christi celebrates the dogma of transubstantiation, whereby the consecrated host is believed to become physically the body and blood of Christ. That notion was challenged by various medieval heresies, and the Protestants of the 1500s challenged it again.[41] In reaction, Iberian monarchies, priding themselves on their militant counterreformation Catholicism, made Corpus into a state-sponsored show of civic and religious solidarity. Corpus processions became the standard by which all others were measured. Because the motif was triumph, with triumphal arches erected along the route of the procession, joy was the order of the day.[42] So Corpus naturally included plenty of dancing. Trade guilds and confraternities were more or less required to contribute to the Corpus procession. The presence of ethnic "Others" also dovetailed with the enactment of triumph over religious error. Moorish, Jewish, and Gypsy dancers (whether real or simulated) were often present to symbolize their political and religious submission to Iberia's state religion.[43]

Spain's Corpus Christi processions were, if anything, more splendid than Portugal's. And Sevilla, prosperous gateway to the Americas, had one of Europe's most extravagant Corpus processions, calling for large annual expenditures by both the church and the city government. Sevilla's Corpus celebration provides a welcome excuse to turn our attention to Spain. "Inside the cathedral, the music, the dances, and the trumpets blended in joyful clamor," according to an account of 1617. The cathedral of Sevilla was the second biggest in the world, and sometimes the procession took more than an hour merely to file out of it. Often the procession spent the better part of the day in the streets. The focal point of all Corpus processions was the sacrament of the Eucharist—the communion host itself, carried on an elaborate platform. Sevilla's famous procession became a model for other Spanish cities. Most Corpus processions included various of the elements standard in Sevilla, such as "giants" represented by large costumes twice the height of the man inside, and the *tarasca,* a large float representing a seven-headed dragon, operated by as many as a dozen men. Both the giants and the tarasca swayed along in time with the music, and there were anywhere from three to a dozen other dance troupes who performed at pauses in the procession. In addition, there were always several sacramental dramas mounted on floats.[44] About these dramas, which always included dancing, more in a minute.

A careful study of Sevilla's Corpus celebration shows two main varieties of dance in the procession. The first variety, "the *sarao* of the nations," consisted in courtly dances-of-two performed by a sequence of couples, each exhibiting a supposedly distinctive national style of the dance. For example, a 1640 "Sarao of the Nations" included couples characterized respectively as Spanish, French, Indian, African, Turkish, and Gypsy. The Africans might be people genuinely of African descent or, in the words of a helpfully explicit period description, "whites made into blacks."[45] Thus, choreographic representations of social identity were a standard aspect of Sevilla's Corpus procession. The second variety of processional dance at Sevilla, the *danzas de invenciones,* or "dramatic dances," had a more plebian character and more varied themes: anything from the infallible sword dance (often a Moors-versus-Christians mock battle) to "The Magi" (1540), "The Theft of Electra" (1627), or "King David and the Giant Goliath" (1636). And among the most common themes of the dramatic dances were those related to exotic "Others," especially Gypsies, indigenous Americans, and Africans: for example, "The Conquest of Guinea" (1627), "The Blacks and the Turks" (1637), and "The Marriage of King Bamba" (1645).[46]

Most dancers in Sevilla's Corpus procession were recruited locally. Those who put on "The Deceit of Guinea" in 1657, for example, were probably of the "whites-made-into-blacks" variety. The one black dancer clearly identified in the documentary evidence was a touring professional: "Juan Antonio Castro, black of color, director of the dance called Montezuma."[47] The choice of the Aztec motif suggests that Castro himself may have come to Spain from the Indies, but we do not know for sure. The important 1642 dance treatise by Juan de Esquivel Navarro, who includes a list of approved dance masters for various Spanish cities, fulminates against "blacks and others of low condition who try to win respect, make a living, and attract attention through Dance, discrediting the Art and those who teach it legitimately."[48] Esquivel Navarro's comment suggests that these black masters were numerous and that their fortunes were, in fact, not so low. One thing is sure. Corpus gave Sevilla's appreciable black population a regular opportunity to dance with official blessing. And official sanction created opportunities for sociability at practice sessions, too—an ancient tradition. "Pretending to rehearse a dance for the day of Corpus Christi" (in the words of a Spanish stage play) was a well-known excuse for a party in the seventeenth century.[49]

Unsurprisingly, Corpus Christi processions turn up, too, in the early evidence of African-influenced music and dance in Havana, Montevideo, and Rio de Janeiro. In 1573, for example, the Havana city council ordered the preparation of various Corpus dramatic dances by trade organizations (tailors, carpenters, cobblers, blacksmiths) and by the city's free blacks, who were to dance as a group.[50] Twenty-five years later, the Havana city council ordered a pension for four musicians who provided music at public celebrations, including Corpus. The musicians were two men from Málaga and Sevilla who played violin and bass viol, respectively, a clarinet player from Lisbon, and a free black Caribbean woman playing the guitar-like vihuela. This was Micaela Ginez, who was born in the present Dominican Republic and traveled with her sister Teodora to Santiago, Cuba, where the sisters performed together until Micaela left to form a band with the three Europeans. A contemporary Havana chronicler explains that Micaela's band often brought along two percussionists on güiro and castanets. As for Teodora, she stayed in Santiago and entered local folklore through the "Son de la Mamá Teodora," which was sung in eastern Cuba for more than two hundred years.[51]

Overall, Corpus Christi lost importance in the 1700s, as the counterreformation faded into irrelevance and church reformers gradually eliminated dance from religious services of all kinds. Late-developing colonial cities like Buenos Aires and Montevideo rarely sponsored lavish Corpus celebrations. Nonetheless, occasional news of processions in those cities suggests black participation. In 1760, for example, when a group of free pardos prepared an African-style dance for Corpus in Montevideo, certain soldiers refused to join a procession "with the aforementioned pardos doing their stuff."

Apparently the soldiers objected to the character of the dance more than to the color of the dancers, and they relented when the Montevideo city council arranged for the black dancers to be provided with shoes.[52]

In nineteenth-century Rio de Janeiro, where hardly a week went by without a procession of some description, Corpus retained its close link with state power. Corpus was Rio's Procession of the City. Warships in the harbor fired a salvo when it began. The national guard marched, troops in dress uniform lined the route, and the Emperor of Brazil himself helped transport the sacramental paraphernalia.[53] This military tone nicely complemented the Corpus Procession's perennially most popular attraction, the Man of Iron, a knight in armor, with lance and shield, mounted on a black horse, followed by the image of dragon-slaying São Jorge (St. George). Presumably, St. George and the Man of Iron might have come to slay the Corpus procession's traditional dragon. And by further extrapolation (or perhaps whimsy), the Three Wise Men of Epiphany also accompanied St. George, the dragon, and the Eucharist through Rio's streets at Corpus.[54] As these examples show, processions often took on a distinctive local character—yet another way that dance, and the pageantry surrounding it, helped define Latin American social identities well before the advent of nationalism.

Now let's see how processions like those of Corpus Christi helped make Rio's carnival what it is today.

The inclusion of the Man of Iron and the Three Wise Men in Rio's Corpus procession shows a creative process at work. Elements developed in one celebration were often transferred to another. Kings paraded especially at Epiphany, but they could tag along at Corpus, too . . . or at carnival, as began to happen in the 1880s. In fact, contrary to popular conception, Rio's distinctive modern carnival celebration, whatever its African inspirations, is built primarily on traditional Portuguese processional forms.[55] This does not mean, however, that Rio's carnival follows Portuguese models of carnival. Let me explain.

Scholars have written much about carnival's characteristics as a general European phenomenon. These include a tendency to allow social inversion (when servants, for example, might dress as masters) and a tendency to unleash the lower body (in sexual promiscuity, for instance). Our approach to the topic of carnival has concentrated, not on the universal essence of carnival, but on particularities of local practice.[56] To recap a bit, the local carnival practices of Rio, Havana, and Buenos Aires around 1860 followed the Venetian model—a big-city model, with parades of musical comparsas and costume balls held in theaters. This Venetian model was the starting point for the gradual popularization of the festival in the 1880s and 1890s.

In the early 1800s, however, carnival practices in all three of our Atlantic port cities followed a much older, more wide-spread model, one reflecting general European practices going back to medieval times. Traditional Iberian activities for the last days before Lent varied from locality to locality, but overall, they indulged "the flesh" in preparation for an extended period of self-denial and spiritual reflection. Carnival was often a general melee, a time to flirt, make noise, cross dress, play a prank, kick a dog, wear a disguise, humiliate a cripple, put up a swing, satirize the authorities, eat and drink to excess, engage in various sorts of sacrilege, throw ashes or flour or water on passersby, flaunt convention, and misbehave generally. Music and dance fit the spirit, but they were not the chief focus of Spanish or Portuguese carnival traditions. Nor did traditional Iberian carnival center on parades.[57]

Where, then, did the influence of religious processions enter in? It entered in the 1890s, when troupes like Tia Ciata's White Rose and Hilário Jovino's King of Diamonds transferred their street activities from Epiphany to carnival. Epiphany troupes were known in Portuguese as *ranchos de reis*—the *reis* in their name referring to the three kings, or Wise Men, who visited the baby Jesus in Bethlehem. When groups like White Rose and King of Diamonds left the Epiphany motif behind, which they did within a few years of beginning to parade at carnival rather than on 6 January, they became simply *ranchos*. At bottom, ranchos are the processional form from which the modern escolas de samba descend. The Portuguese word *rancho,* unlike Spanish *rancho* or English *ranch,* denotes primarily "a group of people on the march." Typically, ranchos were organized by a permanent association, such as a Catholic brotherhood or a trade guild. Ranchos had a theme linked to the Catholic calendar. They also had a banner, a characteristic costume, and a benevolent mission to accomplish. Usually, they had some kind of ceremonial leadership (often called a king) as well. In sum, ranchos were amateur festive associations devoted to sociability in a good cause.[58]

Now recall the dance groups that turned out for Corpus Christi processions in Portugal and Spain, Brazil and Spanish America, marching between city dignitaries and theatrical floats, presenting their dramatic dances at pauses in the procession. Professional dancers (such as the ones Juan Antonio Castro used for his "Montezuma" at 1693 Corpus in Sevilla) did not compose ranchos. They were doing a job for pay. But paid professionals were a minority in most processions. When the Havana city council called for tradesmen and free blacks to dance at Corpus in 1573, or when cities throughout Brazil called for devotional brotherhoods to do the same, over many generations, at holidays year round—amateur ranchos answered the call. And because most Portuguese and Brazilian processions—not just Corpus Christi, by any means—had dancing, ranchos had multiple opportunities to "go out." Sometimes, they moved through the streets independently of a procession. Epiphany was one such occasion.

Another occasion for free-roaming ranchos was the strictly Portuguese and Brazilian Festa do Divino, or Feast of the Divine Holy Spirit. On these occasions, celebrants organized "Empires," festive mock monarchies ruled by ten-to-twelve-year-old Emperors with paper crowns. The Feast of the Divine Holy Spirit was instituted in 1385 by Portuguese king João I in an effort to coopt the profane energies of popular *maias* (May celebrations of pagan origin, close relatives of January's calendas).[59] Raising money for Empires of the Divine Holy Spirit was itself an excuse for a party. Each Empire sent out three to six *bandeiras,** which amounted basically to ranchos on a fundraising mission. Bandeira members marched around carrying the banner of the Divine Holy Spirit, wearing hats adorned with long ribbons, and playing various noise makers, guitars, and drums. They announced the upcoming Empire by bringing the spirit of celebration. Along their route, bandeiras stopped at houses for a bit of music and dance, to enjoy the refreshments offered by their hosts, and of course, to collect donations.[60]

---

* *Bandeira* means literally "banner," in reference to the banner ranchos carried.

An Empire in progress was basically a parish fair. Vendors sold food and drink in tents, and there was a lot of music and dancing. *Barbeiros* ("barbershop" musicians), who were frequently slaves, often performed at these events. The city of Rio had four Empires operating annually in the nineteenth century. That of the Campo de Santana, its brightly lit tents shining in the night amid the excited crowd, seems to have been the most memorable. The Empire of the Campo de Santana had puppet shows and sometimes a circus.[61]

Gradually, as profane elements were eliminated from Brazilian religious *festas* after 1800, many such elements took refuge in carnival. Ranchos like White Rose become a standard modality of carnival parade group in Rio, as we have seen. The red devil costume worn by the Sons of the Flames at Rio carnival around 1900 had appeared in Catholic processions for centuries—especially at Corpus Christi, when devils represented the defeated adversaries of the holy sacrament. *Diabinhos** were included, too, in the Ash Wednesday procession, Rio's largest and most elaborate in the mid 1800s. Unfortunately for the authorities, the Ash Wednesday procession was also one of Rio's most profane, immediately following, as it did, the three main days of carnival. After struggling fruitlessly to purify the Ash Wednesday procession of its irreverent carnival spirit, frustrated authorities finally abolished the procession altogether in 1861.[62]

The Cucumbys who found a home in Rio's carnivals of the 1880s had likewise migrated from other dates on the calendar. This is the reason for the Cucumbys' puzzling characterization as Indians (wearing feathers, carrying bows and arrows, and so on), though they were clearly black. Dancing Indians (often played by black troupes like Juan Antonio Castro's) had been appearing in Iberian processions since the 1500s. No longer welcome in religious processions, black Indians found a nineteenth-century outlet at carnival. They still find an outlet there, not only in Rio but in also in Bahia, Trinidad, New Orleans, and elsewhere.[63] All in all, carnival in Rio's sambadrome today must resemble the nightmare visions of Portuguese and Brazilian churchmen who, over several centuries, tried in vain to banish dancing devils, King Davids, and Cucumbys from that most popular of religious events, the procession.

---

* *Diabinhos* are "little devils" in Portuguese.

Processions and royal birthdays were quite theatrical in their way. For one thing, both royal and religious celebrations included formal playmaking. Accounts of Spanish and Portuguese theater since medieval times linger particularly on religious dramas, especially the so-called *autos sacramentales** performed at Corpus Christi. This important tradition of Iberia and colonial Latin America is a rich source of evidence on dance.

Iberian Corpus processions of the 1500s and 1600s included rolling stages for dramas, which were sometimes performed inside the church itself. Autos sacramentales were related to the mystery plays performed in earlier centuries all over Europe, but an on-going emphasis on the conversion of non-Christians seems to have made the Spanish and Portuguese versions last longer.[64] Certainly, they were better funded. The autos sacramentales of Corpus Christi became an essential part of the lavish, state-sponsored demonstration of Counterreformation ideology. Autos sacramentales specifically celebrated the mystery of Eucharist (hence, their link to Corpus), but they were performed by professional actors, written by secular playwrights (such as Lope de Vega, Tirso de Molina, and Gil Vicente), and combined a profane with a religious spirit. In seventeenth-century Madrid, people waited in line all night to see the main dress rehearsal of the autos for the Corpus Christi procession.[65] After Corpus, a touring company might take the same dramas and the same rolling sets "on the road." The Spanish national theater was born from such tours.

This no place to attempt a history of the Spanish national theater (which also long dominated Portuguese stages) except to highlight its link to our topic. "Let faith dance!" proclaims an allegorical character representing Spain in a religious theatrical by master Spanish Golden Age dramatist Calderón de la Barca.[66] It may be hard to imagine the Virgin Mary dancing a fandango with the Holy Ghost, but autos regularly included comic relief in the form of popular dances, and many other kinds of dancing as well. Dance was more central to Spanish Golden Age Theater than to Elizabethan or

* Biblical plays that taught church doctrine.

later English theater.[67] In 1639, there were forty acting companies—more than a thousand full-time professional actors—at work on the Iberian peninsula, and most Spanish actors, as a rule, danced. A typical Spanish troupe of this time had six actors who only acted, twelve who acted and danced, twelve who only danced, and ten musicians.[68] The cast danced in the entremeses which occupied the time necessary for scene changes, and it danced at the end of the evening's program to send the audience home in a happy mood. Few Spanish Golden Age plays did not integrate some dancing into the dramatic action, as well. In fact, comedies sometimes became little more than vehicles for dancing, according to an 1804 treatise on *Spanish Comedies.* Despite criticisms, the treatise maintained that "the dances cannot be abolished for they are the spice of the comedies, which are worthless without them."[69]

The dance in question here was not ballet. To the contrary, the choreography of Spanish vernacular theater was based on popular dances like fandangos and *seguidillas*—even *zarabandas* and *chaconas,* the "dirtiest" dances of all, to which we shall return in the next chapter. From the Bufos Cubanos, to Rio's music halls, to the Podestá Brothers' gaucho melodrama *Juan Moreira,* we have made frequent use of theatrical evidence to probe the history of Latin America's national rhythms. We can now better appreciate the enduring link between theater and popular dance in Latin America. Theater, after all, could confer prestige on particular styles of music and dance. Touring companies could disseminate those styles far and wide. The mid nineteenth-century propagation of habanera by Spanish touring companies in Latin America offers a striking international example.

The connection between theater and popular dance was transferred directly from Spain to Latin America. In 1621, Mexico City had three full-time theatrical companies—but only two permanent theaters, which probably indicates touring activity. As in Spain, these companies offered performances free of charge for those who could not afford the normal price of admission. In the 1713–1714 Mexico City season, these free performances were more than a third of the total.[70] Rio, Havana, and Buenos Aires did not get started nearly so early, but there, too, popular music and dance were present from the beginning. By the late eighteenth century, Buenos Aires had a Corral Porteño located only a few blocks from the main square, and popular dance was a staple there. (The popular character of Spanish vernacular theater can be gauged from the fact that, when not performed in the patios of large houses, it was performed in structures called "corrals.") When progressive Viceroy Vértiz built a more imposing theater in 1783, hoping to make it a vehicle of social uplift, he soon had to open its doors to fandangos and carnival balls because the uplifting stuff alone failed to earn enough money to keep the theater open.[71] National music and dance, on the other hand, was a reliable crowd-pleaser. In Cuba, Francisco Covarrubias established the groundwork for the Bufos Cubanos genre by injecting Cuban "color," especially music and dance, into Spanish works, so that *Las tertulias de Madrid,* for example, became *Las tertulias de la Habana* (1814).[72]

Rio's first theater was the mid eighteenth-century Casa da Opera do Padre Ventura. It had a popular, sometimes strongly nativist tone, which, when the theater burned down one night, made some observers suggest the possibility of Portuguese arson. Rio's next theater was the Casa da Opera de Manuel Luís which had a much more elite tone. The Brazilian viceroy had his own luxuriously appointed box there. Nevertheless, one of its best remembered performers was an actress stage-named Rosinha, who specialized in national dances like lundu—the same dance that the coach drivers waiting outside in the theater danced to amuse themselves during the performance.[73] Rio's Empires of the Divine Holy Spirit featured comedies and puppet shows in tents. During the mid nineteenth-century retreat from popular dance in Rio's "serious" theaters, these tent spectacles continued to feature popular dance as their uproarious highpoint. Imagine a batuque danced by slave puppets, for example—or even, if you can, the startling final scene of *The Creation of the World,* a puppet show in which, after Cain kills Abel, the Eternal Father descends thorough cotton-ball clouds to settle matters and finally brings down the curtain by dancing with a character named Sinhá Rosa while another character shouts: "Shake it, Sinhá Rosa! Shake that thing!"[74]

The Creation of the World was surely a hard act to follow. Before announcing how we will attempt to follow it here, let us conclude this chapter without further ado. The written texts of theatrical productions provide rare evidence about the popular dances that, in other situations (as when poor people danced at their own gatherings) left no trace in the historical record. More importantly, popular dance held an important place in the public pageantry of Iberian church and state during Latin America's colonial period. Dancing for joy was basic to royal celebrations and church processions. When Christians, Moors, Jews, and "Savages" gathered (whether in person or by impersonation) at royal nuptials or in Corpus Christi processions, the dancers represented not a single national identity, but a collection of nations, united as subjects of the same Catholic monarchy. In sum, as a modality of collective self-definition, dancing one's national rhythm goes way back in the Latin American experience.

Official sponsorship gave popular dancers approved reasons to practice and approved venues in which to perform. Sometimes, official sponsors supplied resources to the dancers or allowed neo-African nations, doubling as devotional brotherhoods, to go door-to-door collecting contributions in the name of the church. True, official legitimation and sponsorship alternated, in an often tense relationship, with official condemnation and prohibition. Yet overall, sponsorship by the Catholic church (much more ritually inclined than Protestant churches) did much to promote the survival and dissemination of diasporic dance.

The peculiar combination of sacred and profane elements that we have just explored raises again that familiar riddle of inspiration, mood, and style: the oddly transgressive spirit of Latin America's national rhythms. The state has long harnessed the energies of popular dance in Latin America, it seems, at the cost of letting in that irrepressibly transgressive spirit. Where does the spirit come from? Here is the most fascinating, but also the most speculative, issue of all—a fitting end, or rather, *beginning* point for this backwards history of Latin America's national rhythms. The search for answers will take us back into the early years of the African diaspora and to the creation of another world, the Atlantic World.

Chapter Ten

Morena
(American Eve)

Before 1700, direct, descriptive evidence of Latin American dances virtually disappears. People did dance, of course. Mexico City dance masters (many of whom were black) taught the standard European dance repertory to Spaniards resident there. Mexico City's other inhabitants imitated these European models, surely, but they also had their own dances. As early as 1569, for another example, the Spanish viceroy of Mexico found it necessary to prohibit the dancing of slaves in Mexico City's main square anytime except for Sunday afternoons and church holidays.[1] In 1610, a French visitor to Bahia regarded it "a great pleasure on feast days and Sundays to see the slaves gather, men and women, dancing and enjoying themselves in public in the squares and streets, for on those days they are not subject to their masters."[2] One also finds mention of dances called *calenda, chica, chuchumbé, bamboula, mangana,* or *zarambeque,* all believed to have African influence, but these mentions do not get us very far without descriptive content. For example, a satirical song of the 1500s says Portuguese slave trader Fernão Gomes danced *mangana* skillfully. Other than that, we know the dance was popular, seems to have had African influence, and little else.[3]

The earliest reference with important descriptive content is by a 1698 French traveler to the Caribbean, Father Jean Batiste Labat. Labat saw black couples inside a circle facing, holding their arms up "as if playing castanets," moving together and apart, and finally meeting "as if bumping their bellies." The dance involved hugging and kissing and "quite lascivious gestures" of the lower body. Here—except for the kissing, a common element of European dances—we can easily recognize the dance-of-two, transgressiveness and all. Labat called this a calenda, a name he seems to have learned from the Spanish, who applied it, no doubt, by analogy with European pagan fertility rites. At any rate, Labat's early description suggests strong continuity in the basic elements of diasporic dance across at least three centuries.[4]

Diasporic dance was fluid and variegated. It was not a set of discrete dances, each defined by a unique name and specific steps. It had a thousand permutations. Diasporic dance was accompanied especially by percussion, but also by guitar, harp, and wind instruments. At times, it was accompanied merely by the voices and hand clapping of a circle of participant/spectators. Diasporic dance had sacred currents and profane ones. And it always had both European and African elements—most basically because all were couple dances with hip-driven undulations of the torso. Even without further direct evidence, if we focus our remaining inquiry on these basic characteristics, we can trace the genealogy of the national rhythms back into the 1500s, to the beginnings of Latin America itself.[5]

Before beginning that inquiry, a vital caveat. When searching for the deep history of African-influenced dancing in the Atlantic World, our thoughts go first to sacred African traditions, not to transgressive dances at all. Currents of sacred dance certainly ran deep in the African diaspora, deep both in the sense of being deeply meaningful and in the sense of being well hidden from prying eyes. Sacred dance within neo-African traditions offered a vital source of strength in any struggle to resist psychological absorption into the slave owners' world. Unfortunately, dances directly linked to neo-African religious belief are the least documented form of diasporic dance. In fact, written sources tell us next to nothing of sacred diasporic dance before the twentieth century.[6]

We know much more about the secular, profane forms of diasporic dance. Sexual transgressiveness threatened the colonial order much less than did neo-African religion, so profane dancing was not so carefully concealed from whites. Whites showed an avid interest and involved themselves from an early date. Labat declared that "the Spanish have learned to dance [calenda] like the blacks, and they do it all over America." Furthermore, Labat declared that calenda was even a part of Spanish American devotions, danced "in their churches and their processions."[7] Another rare early tidbit: poet Gregório de Matos indicates that white men and women went to calundus in 1600s Bahia seeking the resolution of amorous heartaches: "There is not a jilted woman/Nor a suitor unrequited/Who fails to join the dances/When they are feeling slighted."[8] It makes sense, therefore, that this second current of diasporic dance practice—the transgressive, profane sort—should loom large in historical sources created by whites, whether as spectators or occasional participants. The story of transgressive popular dance in Latin America, from its sixteenth-century inception, is a story of race mixing.

Admittedly, scattered sources from the 1500s and 1600s illuminate only the outward face of diasporic dance. In just this way, our examination of dance among the black nations of Rio, Havana, and Buenos Aires, circa 1700–1850, encountered mostly the face they presented to white society, showing little of their inner workings. Again here, however, an examination of that outward face offers valuable insight. It demonstrates a cultural exchange between blacks and whites far earlier than might otherwise be suspected. And, most significantly, it puts popular dance at the center of that exchange. Such evidence helps illuminate traditions of black showmanship exemplified perfectly by Miguel Faílde, the son of a Spaniard and a Cuban parda, whose music embodied the spirit of illicit 1870s "candle dances," then electrified the daring children of the Criollo planter class during the 1880s and 1890s. And such evidence helps illuminate ingrained patterns of sexual race relations. In sum, evidence of a deep history of race mixing around dance is just the thing to help explain the power of Latin America's national rhythms. Perhaps it will help solve, at last, the riddle of their jaunty transgressiveness, too.

Can we positively identify transgressive dances-of-two with "breaking" movements of the hips before Labat's 1698 description? The answer is yes. They surface a hundred fifty years earlier, in fact. The documentation comes from Europe, where these dances became quite popular. But there is little doubt about their American origin.

Chacona and zarabanda, dances-of-two performed to thrumming tambourines and bawdy couplets, were the most notable of these early trans-Atlantic forms. In Spain, at least, where these dances first took hold, the dancers commonly wore bells around their ankles. Little is known about the moves of the dance, except that they included, by all accounts, swaying hips and sometimes an explicit sexual pantomime.[9] Over the course of two centuries, chacona and zarabanda "rose" socially and, in much altered, more somber forms, entered the standard repertory of European courtly dances. Bach and Handel eventually composed music for these dances. At first, however, the transgressiveness of chacona and zarabanda was their most famous trait by far.[10]

Much of the earliest evidence on chacona and zarabanda is theatrical. For example, in 1583, Spanish moralist Father Juan de Mariana had inveighed against theatrical dancing and denounced zarabanda specifically for *meneos** of the hips that he judged "sufficient to enflame even quite well behaved people." A 1598 theatrical entertainment, *Satire Done by Mateo Rosas de Oquendo about Things that Happen in Pirú,* mentions the popularity of chacona and zarabanda among the Peruvian "lowlife." A 1599 Spanish entremés mentions chacona when, amid playful rhymes and occasional nonsense, the lyrics invite a morena to visit Tampico. The lyrics were probably sung and danced as a chacona on stage.[11] In 1593, zarabanda even appeared in Sevilla's Corpus Christi procession. Prohibitions and punishments abounded, of course. In the late 1500s, unauthorized zarabanda dancing potentially merited two hundred lashes or six years rowing in prison galleys for men, banishment for women. An official Spanish reproof to theatrical women in 1615 warns them away from the "lascivious meneos" of chacona and zarabanda, and further commands the players "not to invent similar dances with different names."[12]

The American origins of chacona and zarabanda can be established in various ways. Both chacona and zarabanda were consistently

* Meneo: swaying or wagging.

associated with the New World and with people of mixed European-African descent. Cervantes applies both associations when he calls chacona an *indiana amulatada.** The 1602 theatrical *Entremés de los negros* presented zarabanda in blackface with drums and other percussion instruments. An entremés by the great Spanish Golden Age playwright Lope de Vega says that zarabanda "arrived in Sevilla by post from the Indies." Chacona and zarabanda were originally known throughout Europe as inventions of "American savages" (a French reference of 1613) or as "twins from New Spain" (an Italian reference of 1623), and so on. Furthermore, the earliest identified reference to zarabanda comes, in fact, from New Spain (Mexico) itself. In 1572, when the Spanish Inquisition in Mexico investigated an unfortunate Pedro de Trejo for "heretical propositions," part of the inquisitorial file against Trejo was a manuscript of his works, including a "divine" zarabanda (*a lo divino*), intended for religious contexts like those discussed in the previous chapter. Trejo's zarabanda had been composed in 1556.[13] Therefore, 1556 can be our benchmark. Whatever the origins of the diasporic dance-of-two, they are earlier than 1556.

Let us consider the general progress of the African diaspora in Latin America around 1550. A Portuguese verse riddle of 1554 offers the following clue, really the answer to an unasked question:

A great lot come here every year
To Portugal and the islands.
They're always in demand
And will triple your investment
In Castile or her Antilles.

Sixteenth-century Portuguese readers knew that the question could only be: "What are African slaves?" Portugal had pioneered the Atlantic slave trade and still monopolized it in the mid 1500s. But the Portuguese had yet made little progress, in the mid 1500s, at colonizing Brazil. Therefore, the Spanish Caribbean (the Castilian Antilles mentioned in the verse riddle) was the main destination of the Atlantic slave trade in these years. At first, slaves bound for Spain, Mexico, or Peru passed through Portugal itself en route. Direct

---

* *Indiana amulatada* means something like "mulatified woman of the Indies."

exports from the Portuguese offshore bases on the African islands of São Tomé and Cape Verde ("the islands" of the verse riddle) were not authorized until around 1530.[14]

In other words, the African people who created the dance-of-two some time before 1556 had necessarily passed through the Portuguese system before landing in the Spanish one. Their numbers—only a few thousand slaves a year in the mid 1550s—were small, but they established a lasting pattern: the enduring primacy of the archetypal dance-of-two throughout the African diaspora of Spanish America and Brazil. The formative nature of these early developments must explain the powerful imprint of certain particularly Portuguese traits, such as processional dance, in disaporic dance culture. Only broadly shared, formative experiences, after all, can explain patterns of uniformity in diasporic culture. Particular elements can sometimes be traced to particular European or African sources—the dancing procession seemingly to Portugal, the embigada seemingly to Angola, for example. Particular American environments had an impact, too. But only the experience of the diaspora itself can explain the general outlines of diasporic culture.

The dance-of-two, our proxy for diasporic culture in general, exemplifies the formative process. The dance-of-two probably began in the early 1500s in various staging areas of the Portuguese slave trade, such as the islands of São Tomé and Cape Verde or around the fortress of São Jorge da Mina on the Gold Coast of West Africa. It was here, we know for sure, that race mixing started. Writes a historian of early Portuguese imperialism on the African coast: "Members of the garrison frequently took wives or mistresses from among the black villagers, and by the seventeenth century, São Jorge was filled with a mélange of women, mulatto children, African allies, slaves, and prisoners of war."[15] On the Cape Verde islands, hundreds of Portuguese and thousands of Africans developed a thoroughly mixed culture with its own dances-of-two and processional forms that have lasted to the present day.[16]

Still, there is little or no evidence of transgressive dances arriving in Iberia directly from Africa. Europeans always associated chacona and zarabanda with New World origins. Only in the New World, it seems, did the disaporic dance-of-two gain enough impetus and prestige to invade Europe. We can see this clearly in the differential timing with which transgressive, "mestizo" dances arrived in Spain and Portugal. Despite early Portuguese monopolization of the slave trade, chacona and zarabanda arrived in Sevilla more than a hundred and fifty years before Lisbon saw an analogous invasion of diasporic forms. African slaves were dancing among themselves in Portugal as early as the 1500s, but the Portuguese were not dancing with them yet—at least, not much.

The differential timing of the arrival of New World dances in Spain and Portugal corresponds to the different development of Spanish America and Brazil, respectively. Spain's profitable early exploitation of Caribbean gold (around 1500) and its rapid subjugation of numerous indigenous populations (1520s and 1530s) made Spanish America an early bloomer. Meanwhile, Portuguese imperial attentions were riveted on the Asian trade during the 1500s. Not until the 1600s did Brazilian sugar plantations begin to boom. Not until the 1700s, with the discovery of gold and diamonds in the Brazilian interior, did the wealth and prestige of Brazil (when viewed from the streets of Lisbon) approximate the wealth and prestige of Spanish America (when viewed from the streets of Sevilla). Chacona and zarabanda arrived in Sevilla in the late 1500s along with the *Peruleros* and *Indianos,** men who had made their fortunes in America and who often returned with black servants. Brasileiros with similar fortunes were a Portuguese phenomenon of more than a century later, in the 1700s—and so, therefore, were fofas and lundus a Lisbon phenomenon of the 1700s.[17]

When the Brazilian dances finally arrived in Portugal, they took hold with a vengeance, becoming so associated with Lisbon's plebeian population that foreign travelers to Portugal commonly viewed them as Portuguese national dances. The fofa craze began as early as the1720s. In Lisbon, fofa was a favorite of market women, and references to fofa frequently mention the city's mixed-race Alfama district near the waterfront. In fact, the first documented reference to fofa occurs in a 1730 invitation to Alfama's festa for Nossa Senhora do Rosário, patron saint of the city's black population. The invitation, written in mock black dialect, promises fofas at the festa. A verse description of Lisbon life, published in 1758, refers to music for guitar and tambourine arriving steadily from

* Both of these words, now archaic, referred to Spanish returnees from "Peru and the Indies."

Brazil, quickly picked up by the population of Alfama. A contemporaneous pamphlet, *Account of the Fofa, Recently Come from Bahia,* remarks that fofa "made a lot of people get married," and the Portuguese clergy found it unquestionably transgressive. Still, despite occasional bans, fofa was danced among both rich and poor.[18] Fofa showed up in Lisbon's Corpus processions, of course, and the city's poorest and least reputable women danced it in the ring before bullfights. *Account of the Fofa* also links the dance to the *casquilhos,* rich fops addicted to all things French. A traveler of 1774 called fofa "the dance particular to the Portuguese, as fandango is to the Spanish," and added "I never saw anything so indecent." Yet a traveler of 1797 reported that Portuguese nuns watched fofa dancers in their convents.[19]

The late timing of Lisbon's transgressive dance craze (when compared with Sevilla's in the 1500s) also suggests that urban environments were the most fertile grounds for early disaporic dance. Portugal's Brazilian colony was still a big sugar plantation with minimal urban development in the 1600s. There were plenty of African slaves there, but most slaves lived in barracks-like slave quarters, locked down at night, doing gang field labor by day—situations that limited their contact with free people. Despite the profits of sugar plantations, they exported no African-influenced dances to Portugal.

Spanish American cities were larger, more numerous, more diverse from very early on—particularly in Peru and Mexico, where chacona and zarabanda can first be detected. And, in the mid 1550s, when these dances emerged, places like Lima and Mexico City were already full of African slaves, who constituted prized allies in conquest and colonization, while the exploited workforce of mining and agriculture was mostly indigenous. Indeed, black slaves in early Spanish America resided particularly in cities, often working alongside whites. So chacona and zarabanda sprang, not from grim environments of plantation slavery, but among Africans, enslaved and free, and non-Africans—including Europeans, indigenous people, mestizos, and mulatos—who encountered each other in more fluid urban environments. It is a little hard, perhaps, to think of these encounters as opportunities for dancing. Nonetheless, some of them undoubtedly were. Otherwise the dance-of-two would not have arisen so early.

Europeans brought with them the basic dance-of-two choreography. Africans brought the characteristic "break" of the hips.[20] Combined, these elements charged the dance with erotic possibilities, calling attention to the dancers' bodies, presenting them as a couple, suggesting courtship, and sometimes, coitus. The result was a dance that would have been transgressive, no doubt, in any African or European society of the day. But colonial authorities in sixteenth-century Mexico or Peru, where the old order had been swept away and the new order was still emerging, could not afford to be strict disciplinarians. Therefore, Latin America's transgressive national rhythms had a quintessentially New World genesis. In the rowdy plebeian neighborhoods of early Mexico and Peru, people practiced their new entertainments, if not unmolested, at least undeterred. The dance-of-two gained momentum, spawned offshoots, acquired lyrics in Spanish. Gradually, the dance-of-two passed from servants and artisans to mule drivers, sailors, and others who moved around the Atlantic world. Soon chacona and zarabanda were on their way to Sevilla, and the rest is history—or rather, myth.

Today, in ten thousand liner notes, tourist brochures, school textbooks, and concert programs, Latin America's national rhythms persuasively represent a foundational myth basic to many nationalist ideologies. This is the "myth of mestizaje"* which may be summarized as follows: "We are a blend of Africa, Europe, and America, mixed into one people, and our special genius is the synthesis." One anthropologist refers to this "constantly reiterated" formula as "the founding myth of Colombian nationality." The same foundational myth enters, to one degree or another, into the official nationalist ideology of most Latin American countries. This is a story about overcoming difference, a myth of origin, explaining the creation of unified national identities from diverse ingredients. It is about ethnic fusion through cultural hybridity and merging gene pools. In the nineteenth century, long before it became official ideology anywhere, the myth of mestizaje ran rampant in romance novels—the foundational fictions of Latin American literary history.[21]

* Spanish *mestizaje* and Portuguese *mestiçagem*. Both usually imply complex processes of ethnic fusion.

What does it mean to call mestizaje a myth? Here we must specify several meaning of the word *myth*. In one sense, myths explain something important about the world, especially origins. Thus, the Greeks explained the winter season with a story of how the goddess Demeter grieved each year during the absence of her daughter in the underworld. All nature reflected her grief, supposedly, and the result was winter. In another sense, myths say something contrary to fact. The story of Demeter's grief is mythic in both senses. It explains the world *and* it is contrary to fact. One can say the same of the biblical story of Noah's ark. The story carries awesome lessons about a stern and omnipotent God, yet pairs of all living creatures obviously could not have fit into one ship or repopulated the earth after a flood covering all dry land. Documentary evidence makes the crucifixion of Jesus of Nazareth, to take a second example from the Bible, a historical fact. But the crucifixion story works as a kind of myth because of its transcendent promise of redemption. It is a myth "based on a true story." Any story with transcendent significance can be a myth in this second sense.

Now back to the myth of mestizaje: "We are a blend of Africa, Europe, and America . . ." Gene pools from these three continents did merge in Latin America after 1492. That is a historical fact, so here is another myth based on a true story. Such myths often use truths to imply falsities.[22] The broad outlines of the story are authentic, but the story is twisted in the telling—twisted, or perhaps simply "spun," told in a way that makes the teller's point. For example, nationalist tellings of the mestizaje myth imply a complete, all-embracing sort of ethnic fusion that really occurred almost nowhere in Latin America. Furthermore, indigenous and African elements usually appear only as origins, with no room left for them in the present. In the present, the myth implies, all Latin Americans define themselves as mestizo culturally if not biologically. These implications of the myth hinder attempts by some people of indigenous or African descent to maintain separate identities within Latin American nations. Finally, the mestizaje myth implies that race prejudice has vanished from Latin American societies. But that implication, too, is false. People of strongly African descent and indigenous people continue to be impoverished and downtrodden all over the region. Many recent studies by U.S. scholars have focused on these false implications of the myth of mestizaje, leading them to denounce it as an oppressive lie.[23] In a perceptive recent article on "Cuban Myths of Racial Democracy," Alejandro de la Fuente summarizes the recent scholarly critique:

> Mestizaje . . . rather than acting as an integrative force, has been characterized as a "powerful force of exclusion" articulated by predominantly white elites to keep blacks and Indians in a subordinated social position. Analysts assuming this perspective claim that the whole ideology has been constructed "at the expense" of blacks and other groups whose very existence is frequently denied, even in official and statistical records.[24]

This critique is a valuable one, founded on values of cultural pluralism that justly command our respect.

However, this critique itself falsifies the big picture of Latin American history by suggesting that mestizaje has not been a powerful integrative force in the development of Latin American societies. Mestizaje—not the myth, but the actual process of race mixing—made Latin America. That is the true story on which the foundational myth is based. Our backwards history of three national rhythms has afforded us a privileged, long-term view of that story. It is far from a complete view, but it reveals surprises. The sixteenth-century rise of the dance-of-two suggests that cross-racial socializing happened in Latin America very early. It shows that white elites used popular dance ideologically for their own ends, as when dance symbolized the integration of subjugated Africans and Moors into Catholic monarchies or when it symbolized the emergence of newly sovereign American "Peoples" in the independence era. But this elite manipulation was rarely cynical or one-sided. The deep history of Latin American popular dance reveals an unquestionable white attraction and even white participation going back centuries, despite pervasive racism. As Paul Gilroy puts it in *The Black Atlantic,* "the reflexive cultures and consciousness of the European settlers and those of the Africans they enslaved, the 'Indians' they slaughtered, and the Asians they indentured were not, even in situations of the most extreme brutality, sealed off hermetically from each other."[25] To trace the emergence of Latin America's national rhythms is to put flesh on Gilroy's abstraction. In the case of music and dance, this "lack of a hermetic seal" unleashed positive, creative forces. Latin

America's rich traditions of popular music and dance are undoubtedly a synthesis of the sort recently touted in academic circles as "transculturation" and "hybridity."[26] The history of the region's national rhythms also shows that black musicians and dancers enjoyed the attention and respect, not to mention the occasional material benefits, merited by their artistic endeavors. When independence-era elites first appropriated mestizo dances as national rhythms, they garnered crucial support from non-white non-elites, but they also made a sort of Faustian bargain, defining the new nations of Latin America as mestizo nations. In the nineteenth century, when only white nations could be "civilized nations" in European eyes, this was a major concession. Overall, the people of Latin America took that concession to heart and have never let the elites forget it.

This is not to deny the false implications of the myth, or even of the part played in it by music and dance. Tourist brochures that make Cuban music, for example, "a marriage of Spanish guitar and African drum" falsely imply a harmonious Spanish-African "marriage," obscuring a real history of bondage and exploitation. Likewise, the festive spirit of carnival samba implies a rose-tinted view of the Brazilian past. But the larger impact of this myth in Latin American history has been inclusion, not exclusion. Since the 1930s, when it became official or quasi-official national ideology throughout the hemisphere, the mestizaje myth has signaled a radical rejection of the hoary principle of white supremacy and a proud rhetorical and artistic embrace of indigenous or African heritage. Too often, this embrace is *merely* rhetorical or artistic. And sometimes, the rhetoric of "racial democracy" works *against* those at the bottom of the social heap. But, overall, I agree with Alejandro de la Fuente that "while social realities are not so pretty, the Latin American paradigms of racially mixed and integrated nations are not so ugly." The official myth often constrains overt racial oppression and supplies the oppressed with arguments for their own defense.[27] In sum, there are many worse versions of nationalism than those built on the idea of racial and cultural synthesis. With all its flaws, the mestizaje myth has been a valuable and distinctively Latin American contribution to the world's repertoire of national ideas.

I seem to have arrived at the brink of bombast and had better close. Good manners forbid that I do so, however, before saying what the Dark Woman, the Morena, has to do with the foundational myth of mestizaje, and why she is the (Latin) American Eve. Authors should always be held responsible for their titles.

Now, by *Morena* I mean not a person but a lyrical motif, a motif that includes Negra or Mulata or Morocha or China or any other name amounting to Dark Woman. This Dark Woman is the American Eve because she stands at the center of the imagery of popular music and dance, prime representations the region's foundational myth. When popular dance is put forward to symbolize the special genius of Latin America—attractively vital and spirited, a persuasive example of creative cultural hybridity—the dancer most easily imagined is, without question, the Morena. She represents a unanimous spirit of celebration and loyalty, as all the people of a particular place (nation, province, or city) pay tribute to what is distinctively theirs. Therefore song lyrics frequently address her by the name of the land she represents. Song after song praises the Dark Woman as the paradigmatic local beauty: "Brasileira" or "Venezolana," "Baiana" or "Chiapaneca," "Limeña" or "Caleña." Frequently, too, she is characterized with distinctive words indicating people of the countryside, like *la guajira* in the song "Guantanamera."* In sum, for over a century the Dark Woman has reigned lyrically over popular music and dance in Latin America. Her lyrical reign varies in intensity from place to place, of course, yet it is unquestionably a regional Latin American phenomenon.

The Dark Woman is part of the region's myth of origin. She exudes fertility, but, as with the biblical Eve, her motherhood is less salient in the collective imagination than her sensuality. One might even say that Eve's motherhood is not imagined at all but merely imposed by logic. And just as we imagine the biblical Eve not giving birth but offering Adam the apple, we imagine the Morena dancing. Who is she tempting? All red-blooded men of her country are tempted by her flashing dark eyes and her sinuous moves, of course. When the lyrical tradition of the Morena celebrates her charms, it implies a unanimous masculine response, a brotherhood of feeling: "The humble but beautiful women of our land are adored and protected by all." The Morena's conventionally haughty demeanor in

* The places alluded to in the list of examples are Brazil, Venezuela, Bahia, Chiapas, Lima, and Cali. On *la guajira guantanamera,* see the note on page 156.

the dance also implies a kind of equality with, of even superiority over, her partner. As with the foundational myth of mestizaje as a whole, the "feel-good" implications of social harmony surrounding the Morena derive some energy from truth, some from wishful thinking, and some from denial.[28]

The new scholarly critique of the myth of mestizaje has been applied, as well, to its star performer, especially in her incarnation as the Mulata, both in Brazil and Spanish America.[29] The Dark Woman is nothing, of course, if not a sex object. So the celebration of her charms can be a kind of trap, just as the celebration of mestizaje itself can also be. "Mulatas are glorified sex fetishes, tribute and proof of the white male's power," wrote Alma Guillermoprieto, reporting on Rio's carnival in the 1980s. Guillermoprieto found that, among the poor black residents of Rio's favela neighborhoods, a woman who "put on net stockings and a sequined bikini and danced for white foreigners at the Meridién Hotel" was said to be "working as a mulata." Guillermoprieto continues that the same, quite beautiful young woman "was probably a *mulata* when, folding up a costume and pushing away from the sewing machine," where she and other women prepared for a samba parade, "she adorned herself with lipstick and silver dangly earrings and went to meet her white boyfriend, a senior official in the Rio military police." "But in the favela," concludes Guillermoprieto, "she was simply a black woman with light skin."[30] While not herself an academic writer, Guillermoprieto here exemplifies the contemporary academic critique whereby the exaltation of the Dark Woman is just a hype that ultimately damages the very people it supposedly exalts.

Hype always distorts truth. The lyrical reign of the Morena is yet another myth "based on a true story." Its overall "feel-good" implications of social harmony are false, but the story does reflect a pervasive reality at the heart of the Latin American experience. White women of high social status were the very last Latin Americans to become involved in transgressive dancing. White men, on the other hand, were involved from the first, when the slave trader Fernão Gomes got his reputation for dancing mangana. "By mulato one means a child born of a black mother and white father, or vice versa," explained Father Labat around 1700, "but the second case is quite rare."[31] Labat was talking especially about male slave owners and enslaved women, but that (like the behavior of early conquistadors among indigenous people) is only the most extreme form of a more general phenomenon. Sometimes these encounters were nothing more (or less) than rape. Often, however, they were something else, and the history of popular dance helps us see that. The pretty, real-life counterparts of Cecilia Valdez went to dances hoping to improve their social standing by marrying "up," though they usually ended, like Cecilia herself, as mistresses. White customers of dark prostitutes learned transgressive dances in their visits to brothels. "Bad boys from good families" attended "candle dances" and launched slumming expeditions in Cartagena and Lima and Guadalajara, not to mention Rio, Havana, and Buenos Aires. One way or another, these asymmetrical encounters have been a commonplace of Latin American life for half a millennium, and the region's national rhythms have been closely linked to that experience from the very beginning.[32]

Myths gain influence when people's experience seems to confirm their truth. Perhaps the greatest strength of the mestizaje myth comes from its intersection with biology. Latin America's national rhythms stand for harmony in a multiracial society, partly by evoking the erotic pleasure of interracial union. People of different class and ethnicity who gathered at dances across the hemisphere over hundreds of years gained affinity for each other as they invented Latin American popular culture together. And while they were at it, they made mixed-race babies, lighter than one parent, darker than another. Mestizo children often suffered the stigma of illegitimacy and abandonment by white fathers unwilling to recognize their paternity, but not always. Sometimes the real-life counterparts of Cecilia Valdez bettered themselves socially. When, in 1879, "a phalanx" of Italian immigrants crashed a dance given by the black carnival troupe Las Bonitas in a Buenos Aires conventillo, for example, the eventual outcome was a number of interracial marriages later chronicled in the black newspaper, *La Broma*.[33]

Furthermore, some of the flesh-and-blood dark women of Latin America have experienced incessant lyrical tributes to them as an affirmation. It is dangerous, but also empowering, to be the object of desire. Overall, however, the interracial encounters associated with transgressive dance had little of the blissful unanimity implied by the great Latin American myth of origin. Relations characterized by vast inequalities of status, wealth, and power are inevitably exploitative, whether loveless or not.

José Ramos Tinhorão (whose many works on Brazilian popular music and dance have greatly influenced my ideas) found, to his surprise, that Brazilian novelists of the nineteenth century presented their own country's popular music and dance as exotically "Other," and they clearly found its exotic qualities appealing.[34] It is a common human tendency to perceive certain differences as erotic. People whose social status is defined by propriety and respectability may automatically experience a curiosity about, and a desire for, off-limits activities associated with the poor, whom they believe to lead emotionally less repressed lives.[35] Desire that crosses lines of race and class has always been transgressive in Latin America, as in most societies the world over. Those who benefit from a given social order make rules designed to maintain it, and these rules make line-crossing transgressive. Latin America's transgressive popular dances got their start in settings where such rules failed to operate. Colonial governments, dependent on Catholic doctrine for ideological legitimacy, condemned transgressive dances but failed to eliminate them. Then, the wars of independence made "dirty dances" into national rhythms. Despite their racial and sexual transgressiveness popular dances so compellingly reinforced the myth of mestizaje—the cornerstone of new national identities in the region—that Catholic objections were simply overruled. And who did the overruling? Powerful men, the sort who enjoyed privileged sexual access to poorer, darker women in popular dance venues, the sort who were, in a word, commonly transgressors themselves. Here at last is the full explanation of the riddle posed by transgressive national rhythms as a general Latin American phenomenon.

While liner notes, concert programs, and tourist brochures have bathed the region's dance history in a blissfully soft-focused glow, academic historians have ignored it altogether. Historians prefer written evidence, and dance produces fairly little. So diasporic music and dance, arguably Latin America's greatest cultural creation, have had almost no presence in a historiographical landscape dominated by the awesome spectacle of servitude and slavery. A truer picture of the deep history of Latin America's national rhythms dispels the blissful glow but also corrects one-sided critiques. Prejudice and exploitation are not the most important part of the story.

Glossary

Asalto (Spa.)—A dance arranged by guests rather than the host family

Autos sacramentales (Spa.)—Biblical plays that taught church doctrine

Bailes de candil (Spa.)—Hidden dances, scenes of cross-racial socializing

Bailecitos del país (Spa.)—Early 1800s Argentine dances-of-two

Bamboula (Spa.)—Dance of Caribbean slaves; also, piano composition that made Louis Moreau Gottschalk's reputation

Bambuco (Spa.)—Colombian dance-of-two

Bandeira (Port.)—Group that collected donations for religious celebrations

Batuque (Port.)—Dance of Brazilian slaves

Bossa nova (Port.)—Innovative samba music, harmonically complex and not for dancing, widely influential in the 1960s

Cabildo (Spa.)—Normally a town council, but in Cuba, the name for neo-African nations

Calenda (Spa.)—In Europe, ancient pagan fertility festivals involving dance; in the New World, a dance of Caribbean slaves

Calundu (Port., pronounced ka-loon-DOO)—Brazilian spiritual dance ceremony with clear African roots

Candombe (Spa.)—Dance of neo-African nations in the Río de la Plata

Candomberos (Spa.)—Carnival parade groups that mockingly imitated candombes

Candomblé (Port.)—Brazilian religion of West African origin, similar to Cuban ***Santería***

Casino (Spa.)—A contemporary style of Cuban salsa

Chacona (Spa.)—Early dance-of-two which became popular in Europe

Chica (Spa.)—Caribbean dance of African slaves

China (Spa., from Quechua) - Woman of indigenous descent

Chingana (Spa.)—Chilean tavern featuring popular music and dance

Choral dance—Dance in which men and women participate as groups, the most common sort of traditional dance worldwide (Cf. ***couple dance***)

Chuchumbé (Spa.)—Early Caribbean dance-of-two

Cielito (Spa.)—Modified contradance of the Río de la Plata (related to ***media caña*** and ***pericón***)

Cinquillo (Spa.)—Syncopated rhythm basic to modern Cuban dance music

Circo criollo (Spa.)—Circus featuring gaucho melodramas and popular music and dance of the Río de la Plata

Compadrito (Spa.)—An urban tough-guy of the Río de la Plata at the turn of the century, comparable to the Brazilian ***malandro***

Comparsa (Spa.)—Musical parade group such as those appearing at carnival

Congos/congadas (Port.)—Brazilian name for the dances performed by neo-African nations

Contradanza (Spa.)—Contradance in the original version of two facing lines

Contradanza cubana—Cuban contradance with a syncopated lilt, revealing African influence

Conventillo (Spa.)—A Río de la Plata tenement (Cf. ***Cortiço***)

Cortes (Spa.)—With ***quebradas,*** the basic choreography of the modern tango

Corte y quebrada (Spa.)—Formula describing tango choreography

Cortiço (Port., pronounced kor-CHEE-so)—A Brazilian tenement

Couple dance—Dance in which men and women form partners throughout, although the partners may change (Cf. ***choral dance***)

Open-couple dance—Dance in which the partners face but rarely touch, as in the dance-of-two

Interdependent couple dance—Dance in which partners change frequently and systematically, as in contradance

Closed-couple dance—Dance in which the partners embrace, as in waltz

Criollo (Spa.)—A product of Spanish colonization in America, whether black, white, or mixed race—most often used for whites ***not*** of recent immigrant origin

Cucumbys (Port., koo-koom-BEES)—Brazilian street dance groups who played black "Indians"

Cueca (Spa.)—Chilean dance-of-two, an abbreviation of ***zamacueca***

Cumbia (Spa.)—Colombian dance-of-two

Dance-of-two—Basic form of diasporic dance, characterized by open-couple choreography and mobility of the hips

Danza (Spa.)—Around 1860, a transformed version of ***contradanza cubana,*** with a lengthened closed-couple section

Danzas de invenciones (Spa.)—In Corpus Christi processions, choral dances with a dramatic element

Danzas del país (Spa.)—Early 1800s Cuban dances-of-two (Cf. ***bailecitos del pais, sonecitos del país***)

Danzón—Around 1880, a close-embrace versión of ***danza*** (see above)

Diabo (Port., pronounced ji-AH-bu)—Street dancer in a devil costume, a standard element of many religious processions and of carnival (diminutive form, ***diabinho;*** Spa. form, ***diablo***)

Embigada (Port.)—Moment in ***lundu*** and other dances-of-two when the dancers press their bellies together (other variants of the word are Port. ***umbigada*** and Spa. ***ombligada***)

Entremés (Spa. and Port.) Musical, comical, dramatic interlude, part of a larger evening of theatrical performance—much like later ***sainetes***

Escolas de samba—Rio's carnival parade groups from the 1920s to today

Fado (Port.)—Famously today, a Lisbon song form; historically, a Brazilian dance-of-two (diminutive, ***fadinho***)

Fandango (Spa.)—Spanish dance-of-two; also, a gathering centered on popular dance

Favela (Port.)—Poor hillside neighborhood in Rio de Janeiro

Festa (Port)/***fiesta*** (Spa.)—Church or state holiday

Fofa (Port.)—Brazilian dance-of-two, became quite popular in 1700s Portugal

Bastonero (Spa.)—Master of ceremonies at a dance

Guaracha (Spa.)—Cuban popular song form

Güiro (Spa.)—Cuban percussion instrument, "gourd scraper"

Habanera (Spa.)—Internationalized version of Cuban ***danza,*** a staple of Spanish musical theater

Jarabe (Spa.)—Mexican dance-of-two with many variations, such as ***jarabe tapatío*** and ***jarabe gatuno***

Joropo (Spa.)—Venezuelan dance-of-two

Lundu (Port., pronounced loon-DOO)—Brazilian dance-of-two

Mangana (Port.)—Early dance associated with Africans in Portugal and the Portuguese slave trade

Marinera (Spa.)—Peruvian dance-of-two closely related to ***zamacueca***

Maxixe (Port., pronounced ma-SHEE-shee)—Brazilian close-embrace social dance

Media caña (Spa.)—Modified contradance of the Río de la Plata (related to ***cielito*** and ***pericón***)

Meneo (Spa.)/***meneio*** (Port.)—"Wagging" of the hips, signals influence of African dance

Merengue (Spa.)—In the Dominican Republic, a closed-couple descendant of contradance

Mestizo (Spa.)—Person of mixed European/indigenous ancestry (Port. ***mestiço*** refers more often to European/African ancestry)

Milonga (Spa.)—Argentine and Uruguayan close-embrace social dance

Minué montonero (Spa.)—Argentine and Uruguayan minuet variation, analogous to Cuban ***minué congó***

Miudinho (Port., pronounced myu-JEE-nyu) Brazilian minuet variation with African influence, analogous to ***minué montonero*** or ***minué congó***

Morena (Spa. or Port.)—Dark woman, partly of either African or indigenous ancestry

Mulata (Spa. or Port.)—Dark woman, partly of African ancestry (a stronger term than ***morena***)

Nossa Senhora (Port.)— "Our Lady," the title of the Virgin Mary, equivalent to Spanish *Nuestra Señora.*

Ñáñigos (Spa.)—Members of a neo-African secret society in nineteenth-century Cuba

Pericón (Spa.)—Modified contradance of the Río de la Plata (related to ***cielito*** and ***media caña***)

Quebrada (Spa.)— From the verb ***quebrar,*** "to break," which may refer in all its conjugated forms to the effect of "wagging" hips (***meneo***), "breaking" the vertical line of the body

Rancho (Port., pronounced HAHN-shoo)—A group (often a musical group) on the march, especially with a festive mission

Rancho de reis (Port., pronounced HAHN-shoo jee HAYS)—a traditional Epiphany troupe which evolved, in Rio de Janeiro, into a modality of carnival parading

Reboleio (Port., pronounced heh-bo-LAY-oo)—Movement of hips ***and*** pelvis, more transgressive than ***meneio***

Requebrada (Port., pronounced heh-keh-BRA-da)—From the verb ***requebrar,*** "to break," which may refer in all its conjugated forms to the effect of "wagging" hips (meneio), "breaking" the vertical line of the body

Roda (Port., pronounced HO-da)—Circle formed around dancers

Rumba (Spa.)—Cuban dance-of-two, close to the dancing of the black cabildos

Sainete (Spa.)—Like ***entremés,*** but associated with the light musical theater of the 1800s

Salsa (Spa.)—An international descendant of Cuban ***son,*** performed by larger groups on electrified instruments

Samba (Port.)—Afro-Brazilian musical and dance form with many variations, today associated especially with carnival in Rio de Janeiro

Samba de roda (Port.)—Traditional Afro-Brazilian dance-of-two

Sapateado (Port.)—Percussive footwork requiring shoes (Cf. ***zapateo***)

Son (Spa.)—Musical antecedent of ***salsa,*** from eastern Cuba, performed by small groups on acoustic instruments

Sonecitos del país—Early 1800s Mexican dances-of-two

Tango (Spa.)—A wide range of historical meanings (see pp. 64–65), invariably associated with the culture of the African diaspora

Tertulia (Spa.)—Social gathering for conversation and, in the nineteenth century, dance

Tia (Port., pronounced CHEE-ah; Spa. ***tía***)—Literally "aunt," respectful term for matriarchs of African descent

Zamacueca (Spa.)—Dance-of-two prominent in Chile, Peru, and western Argentina, giving rise to both ***cueca*** and ***marinera***

Zamba (Spa.)—Argentine dance-of-two

Zapateo (Spa.)—Percussive footwork requiring shoes; a Cuban dance-of-two

Zarabanda (Spa.)—Early dance-of-two which became popular in Europe

Notes

Chapter One

1. Well-informed, judicious, and thorough, S. Fredrick Starr, *Bamboula!: The Life and Times of Louis Moreau Gottschalk* (New York: Oxford University Press, 1995) is by far the best of a long string of Gottschalk biographies and has strongly informed my discussion. On Gottschalk's 1854 visit to Cuba, see 170–94. A briefer and less expert, but still passable biography is Vernon Loggins, *Where the World Ends: The Life of Louis Moreau Gottschalk* (Baton Rouge: Louisiana State University Press [1958]).

2. Starr, *Bamboula,* 289–95.

3. Many episodes of Gottschalk's journey appear in his published journal, *Notes of a Pianist,* ed. Jeanne Behrend (New York: Alfred A. Knopf, 1964).

4. A sample of the best recent work in English would include Paul Austerlitz, *Merengue: Dominican Music and Dominican Identity.* Philadelphia: Temple University Press, 1997); Robin D. Moore, *Nationalizing Blackness: Afrocubanismo and Artistic Revolution in Havana, 1920–1940* (Pittsburgh: University of Pittsburgh Press, 1997); Hermano Vianna, *The Mystery of Samba: Popular Music and National Identity in Brazil,* trans. and ed. by John Charles Chasteen (Chapel Hill: University of North Carolina Press, 1999); and Peter Wade, *Music, Race, and Nation: Música Tropical in Colombia* (Chicago: University of Chicago Press, 2000).

5. For broad interpretations of the place of African culture within the Atlantic world, see Paul Gilroy, *The Black Atlantic: Modernity and Double Consciousness* (Cambridge: Harvard University Press, 1993) and Joseph R. Roach, *Cities of the Dead: Circum-Atlantic Performance* (New York: Columbia University Press, 1996). The mentioned reports from Brazil are in Delso Renault, *O Rio de Janeiro: A vida da cidade refletida nos jornais* (1850–1870) (Rio de Janeiro: Civilização Brasileira, 1978), 139, 150.

6. Oddly, however, dance does not figure importantly in the rich literature on the social function of carnival: Emmanuel Le Roy Ladurie, *Carnival in Romans,* trans. Mary Feeney (New York: Geogre Braziller, 1979); Julio Caro Baroja, *El carnaval* (Análisis histórico-cultural) (Madrid: Taurus, 1965); Samuel Kinser, *Carnival, American Style: Mardi Gras at New Orleans and Mobile* (Chicago and London: University of Chicago Press, 1990); Roberto da Mata, *Carnavais, malandros, e heróis: Para uma sociologia do dilema brasileiro* (Rio de Janeiro: Zahar Editores, 1979); Maria Isaura Pereira de Queiroz, *Carnaval brasileiro: o vivido e o mito* (São Paulo:

Editora Brasiliense, 1992); and Maria Clementina Pereira Cunha, *Ecos da folia: Uma história social do carnaval carioca entre 1800 e 1920* (São Paulo: Companhia das Letras, 2001).

7. At least stray reference in a Cuban memoir provides some evidence of Gottschalk's interest in black women: Dolores María de Ximeno y Cruz, *Aquellos tiempos* (Havana: Imp. El Universo, 1928) 1:126.

8. Louis Moreau Gottschalk, *Notes of a Pianist,* 358.

9. My view of transgressive dance was inspired by Peter Stallybrass and Allon White, *The Politics and Poetics of Transgression* (London: Methuen, 1986).

10. Starr, *Bamboula,* 185. For a survey of other early Latin American influences on U.S. popular music, see John Storm Roberts, *The Latin Tinge: The Impact of Latin American Music on the United States,* 2nd ed. (Oxford: Oxford University Press, 1999), 24–43.

11. Marta E. Savigliano, *Tango and the Political Economy of Passion* (Boulder: Westview Press, 1995) is an excellent guide to the historical evolution of tango dances styles.

12. In U.S. tango circles, the terms *leader* and *follower* are used to euphemize the situation. Because women outnumber men among U.S. tango aficionados, women often learn to lead but men never learn to follow. The power/gender dynamics of this situation have not passed without comment by feminist scholars, e.g. Julie Taylor, *Paper Tangos* (Durham: Duke University Press, 1998), 87.

13. An accessible introduction in English is Simon Collier and Susana Azzi, *Tango: The Dance, the Song, the Story* (London: Thames and Hudson, 1995).

14. See the vivid account of preparations for Rio carnival in the 1980s by Alma Guillermoprieto, *Samba* (New York: Vintage Books, 1990). See also Barbara Browning, *Samba: Resistance in Motion* (Bloomington and Indianapolis: Indiana University Press, 1995); and many richly informed essays by Nei Lopes (e.g., *O samba na realidade: A utopia da ascensão social do sambista,* Rio de Janeiro: CODECRI, 1981) and Muniz Sodré (e.g. Samba, o dono do corpo, Rio de Janeiro: CODECRI, 1979).

15. Lisa Shaw, *The Social History of the Brazilian Samba 1930–1945* (Aldershot, UK: Ashgate Publishing Ltd., 1999).

16. See C. McGowan and R. Pessanha, *The Brazilian Sound: Samba, Bossa Nova, and the Popular Music of Brazil* (Philadelphia: Temple University Press, 1998).

17. Vernon W. Boogs, *Salsiology: Afro-cuban Music and the Evolution of Salsa in New York City* (Westport, CN: Greenwood Press, 1992). Also see the chapter on salsa (72–96) in Peter Manuel, with Kenneth Bilby and

Michael Largey, *Caribbean Currents: Caribbean Music from Rumba to Reggae* (Philadelphia: Temple University Press, 1995), and Lisa A. Waxer's excellent description of salsa's diffusion in *The City of Musical Memory: Salsa, Record Grooves, and Popular Culture in Cali, Columbia* (Middleton, Conn.: Wesleyan University Press, 2002), 31-68.

18. While it focuses on music, rather than dance, Manuel, et. al., *Caribbean Currents,* provides the best introduction in English.

19. See the participant observation of Yvonne Daniel, *Rumba: Dance and Social Change in Contemporary Cuba* (Bloomington: Indiana University Press, 1995).

20. There is a significant literature on dance history, produced more by dancers than historians. The foundational work (outrageously out of date, but still not superseded) is Curt Sachs, *World History of the Dance* (London: Allen and Unwin, 1933). See also Frances Rust, *Dance in Society: An Analysis of the Relationship between Social Dance and Society in England from the Middle Ages to the Present Day* (London: Routledge & Kegan Paul, 1969); Katrina Hazzard-Gordon, *Jookin': The Rise of Social Dance Formations in African American Culture* (Philadelphia: Temple University Press, 1990); Linda J. Tomko, *Dancing Class: Gender, Ethnicity, and Social Divides in American Dance, 1890–1920* (Bloomington and Indianapolis: Indiana University Press, 1999); and a theoretical exploration, Susan Leigh Foster, ed. *Choreographing History* (Bloomington and Indianapolis: Indiana University Press, 1995). Of special relevance here is Ramiro Guerra's superbly informed *Calibán danzante: Procesos socioculturales de la danza en América Latina y la zona del Caribe* (Caracas: Monte Avila Editores Latinoamericana, 1998), the best introduction to dance history in the hemisphere. More narrow, but also excellent, are Maya Ramos Smith, *La danza en México durante la época colonial* (Habana: Ediciones Casa de las Americas, 1979) and Carlos Vega, *El origen de la danzas folklóricas* (Buenos Aires: Ricordi Americana, 1956). For practical discussions of dance history methodologies, see Janet Adshead-Lansdale and June Layson, *Dance History: An Introduction* (London and New York: Routledge, 1994).

21. Most of McNeill's evidence, in fact, concerns the efficacy of military drill in generating armies with a powerful esprit de corps: William H. McNeill, *Keeping Together in Time: Dance and Drill in Human History* (Cambridge: Harvard University Press, 1995). Though McNeill cannot really prove the physiological dimension in the social role of dance, the circumstantial case is a strong one. Peter Wade is much more cautious, but on the same track, when he suggests an embodying function, that makes dance "especially productive in the realm of constituting identities": *Music, Race, and Nation,* 238.

22. Very often, Latin America's regional and national dances are also "invented traditions," practices that have been officially instituted as part of a political movement. See Eric Hobsbawm and Terence Ranger, eds. *The Invention of Tradition* (Cambridge, Cambridge University Press, 1983). Ruben George Oliven, *Tradition Matters : Modern Gaúcho Identity in Brazil, translated by Carmen Chaves Tesser* (New York: Columbia University Press, 1996) applies the concept to a Latin American case.

23. Other examples: *rebolar* (Port.), as in *reboleio* (already mentioned), *gingar* (Port.), and *menear* (Spa.).

24. Mikhail Bakhtin, *Rabelais and His World,* trans. Helene Iswolsky (Cambridge: MIT Press, 1968) has argued that carnival celebrations also empower and unleash the lower body. If true, this would explain the notable affinity between carnival and Latin America's hip-driven national rhythms.

25. A classic in nineteenth-century Chilean literature offers another example: "*un joven hacía requiebros en voz alta a su companera*": Alberto Blest Gana, Maríin Rivas (*Novela de costumbres político-sociales*) (Mexico City: Rei Mexico, 1990), 127.

26. My term *dance-of-two* is based on one of the common Spanish names for this form, *baile de dos.* While fairly general, the term first came to my attention in Fernando O. Assunçao, *Origenes de los bailes tradicionales en el Uruguay* (Montevideo: n.p., 1968). There is no reason to doubt the undocumentable confluence of scholarly judgment and *vox populi* regarding the African and European provenance of the undulating torso and couple choreography, respectively. For example, see Guerra's judgment in *Calibán danzante,* 69.

27. While cultural hybridity and race mixing are completely separable processes, they have usually gone together in Latin American history. The idea of cultural hybridity has recently been highlighted by Néstor García Canclini, *Hybrid Cultures: Strategies for Entering and Leaving Modernity,* trans. Christopher L. Chiappari and Silvia L. López (Minneapolis: University of Minnesota Press, 1995). The starting point for the study of race mixing in Latin America is Magnus Mörner, *Race Mixture in the History of Latin America* (Boston: Little Brown, 1967). Since Mörner, few have attempted to map the region's historically merging of gene pools. A not-very-inspiring exception is Claudio Esteva-Fabregat, *Mestizaje in Ibero-America,* trans. John Wheat (Tucson and London: University of Arizona Press, 1995). The best recent work has instead studied the social construction of race. See, for example, Richard Graham, ed. *The Idea of Race in Latin America, 1870–1940* (Austin: University of Texas Press, 1990); Peter Wade, *Blackness and Race Mixture: The Dynamics of Racial Identity in*

Colombia (Baltimore: Johns Hopkins University Press, 1993); Howard Winant, *Racial Conditions: Politics, Theory, Comparisons* (Minneapolis: University of Minnesota Press, 1994); and Marisol de la Cadena, *Indigenous Mestizos: The Politics of Race and Culture in Cuzco, 1919–1991* (Durham: Duke University Press, 2000).

Chapter Two

1. "Os bailes." *Jornal do Brasil,* 5 January 1905, quoted in Jota Efegê (João Ferreira Gomes), *Maxixe: A dança excomugada* (Rio de Janeiro: Conquista, 1974), 53. This book is by far the best source on maxixe.

2. Description by Portuguese visitor João Chagas, *De bond* (1897) and lyrics from the 1902 musical review, "Cá e lá," quoted in Efegê, *Maxixe,* 51 and 80–81, respectively.

3. Efegê, Maxixe, 163. Useful context is provided by C. McGowan and R. Pessanha, *The Brazilian Sound: Samba, Bossa Nova, and the Popular Music of Brazil* (Philadelphia: Temple University Press, 1998). In Peru, military brass bands frequently play *marinera,* one of the country's national rhythms (along with the competing *huayno* of the Andean highlands). Marinera, the modern version of the zamacuecas that Gottschalk observed in 1860s Lima, represents the Peruvian coast, where African slaves worked on sugar plantations.

4. Vicente Rossi, *Cosas de negros* (Buenos Aires: Librería Hachette, 1958), 131, 136–37. The book was first published in 1926.

5. Carlos Octavio Bunge, *Nuestra América* (1906), quoted in Oscar Natale, *Buenos Aires, negros, y tango* (Buenos Aires: Peña Lillo editor, 1984), 230. Natale provides an excellent collection and synthesis of writing on the black roots of tango. See also Blas Matamoro, "Las raíces negras del tango" in *La historia del tango: Sus orígenes* (Buenos Aires: Ediciones Corregidor, 1976), 57–78.

6. Quoted by Natale from Carlos Vega, "La formación coreográfica del tango argentino," *Revista del Instituto de Investigación Musicológico Carlos Vega* 1 (1977):14.

7. Quotation from *La Nacion* 10, 16 de septiembre de 1896, cited in Vega, "La formación coreográfica del tango argentino," 15. An earlier newspaper notice about this "cut-and-break" dance also suggests that it was applied to all sorts of music: "Se va a bailar con corte, a lucirse con la niña A o B, y a hacer prodigios con ese quiebro danzante propio de los compadritos de las orillas": La Razón (Buenos Aires), 18 February 1887, quoted in *Antología del tango rioplatense* (Buenos Aires: Instituto de Musicología "Carlos Vega," 1986), 9.

8. Benjamín de Céspedes, *La prostitución en la Habana* (Havana: Tipografico O'Reilly, 1888), 140–42.

9. "Sobre el baile," *El triunfo* (Havana), 25 December 1878.

10. "Danzones," *El triunfo,* 13 May 1880.

11. "Bailes de invierno," *La voz de Cuba* (Havana), 22 November 1879.

12. For those familiar with the basic elements of Cuban dance music, it may be helpful to know that the *cinquillo* rhythm finds modern expression in the *clave:* Paul Austerlitz, *Merengue: Dominican Music and Dominican Identity* (Philadelphia: Temple University Press, 1997), 155n4.

13. The shift from danza to danzón was subtle enough to be described in one contemporary source as a simple shift from 2/4 to 6/8 time, a stylistic change applied to a widely shared repertory of dance music. Osvaldo Castillo Faílde, *Miguel Faílde, creador musical del danzón* (Havana: Editora del Consejo Nacional de Cultura, 1964), 124, 119–214.

14. John Miller Chernoff describes how African drummers modify their rhythms to follow dancers in *African Rhythm and African Sensibility: Aesthetics and Social Action in African Musical Idioms* (Chicago: University of Chicago Press, 1979), 110. Around 1900, Cuban musicians had a special name, "lemon," for dancers whose movements might lead them astray: Castillo Faílde, *Miguel Faílde,* 22.

15. The first one, in the Morro da Providencia, later called da Favela, was supposedly established in 1897 by soldiers returning from the destruction of Canudos: Ciro Flamarión Cardoso and Paulo Henrique Araujo, *Río de Janeiro* (Madrid: Editorial Mapfre, 1992).

16. Vivid (if unnecessarily lurid) descriptions of this social milieu appear in Luís Edmundo, *O Rio de Janeiro do meu tempo.* 2 ed. (Rio de Janeiro: Conquista, 1957), 355–403.

17. Natale, *Buenos Aires, negros, y tango,* 294.

18. James R. Scobie, *Buenos Aires: Plaza to Suburb, 1870–1910* (New York: Oxford University Press, 1974), 136, 235.

19. Natale, *Buenos Aires, negros, y tango,* 195.

20. Carretero, *Tango: testigo social* (Buenos Aires: Librería General de Tomás Pardo, 1995), 43.

21. André M. Carretero, *Tango: testigo social,* 35.

22. Céspedes, *La prostitución en la Habana,* 140–43.

23. A comprehensive overview of the history of Havana is available in Julio Le Riverend Brusone, *La Habana, espacio y vida* (Madrid: Editorial Mapfre, 1992).

24. Jota Efegê, *Maxixe,* 48.

25. First appearance of the word in "U.R. Primeira Sociedade do Catete," *Gazeta da tarde,* 29 November 1880. The phrase "num maxixe

requebrado a mulata vale tudo" comes from a Recife publication of 1901. The 1919 reference was by Augusto de Lima. All three quoted in Efegê, Maxixe, 21, 34, and 164.

26. Edmundo, *O Rio de Janeiro do meu tempo,* 483.

27. Edmundo, *O Rio de Janeiro do meu tempo,* 487–88.

28. Natale, *Buenos Aires, negros, y tango,* 133–34 (citing Ventura R. Lynch, *La Provincia de Buenos Aires hasta la definición de la cuestión Capital de la República*).

29. Natale, *Buenos Aires, negros, y tango,* 133.

30. The best overview is found in Fernando O. Assunçao, *El tango y sus circunstancias 1880–1920* (Buenos Aires: Librería "El Ateneo" Editorial, 1984), 45–83.

31. "Sobre el baile," *El triunfo* (Havana), 25 December 1878.

32. *El aprendiz* (Regla), 22 July 1881.

33. Pichardo's mid-nineteenth-century dictionary of Cuban terms defines *tango* as "a gathering of African slaves dancing to drums": Natalio Galán, *Cuba y sus sones* (Madrid: Pre-Textos, 1983), 234. In Brazil, Bruno Kiefer maintains that there were some subtle musical differences between maxixes and Brazilian tangos, but he concedes that the dance must have been identical. See his *Música e dança popular: sua influência na música erudita,* 3rd ed. (Porto Alegre: Editôra Movimento, 1990), 53.

34. "Concretando," *La aurora de Yurumí* (Matanzas), 30 July 1881.

35. "Os bailes," *Jornal do Brasil* (Rio de Janeiro), 5 January 1905.

36. Three examples from the magazine *Fon Fon:* "Na mascarada," 17 February 1917; "Arlequim," 16 February 1918; "Trepações," 21 February 1920.

37. Examples transcribed by Efegê, *Maxixe,* 106–7.

38. Aluísio Azevedo, *O Cortiço* (São Paulo: Editôra Scipione, 1994) has been nicely translated as *A Brazilian Tenement,* trans. Harry W. Brown (New York: H. Fertig, 1976), 98–99.

39. Azevedo, *A Brazilian Tenement,* 120. A penchant to woo mulatas was part of the image of Portuguese immigrants in the Brazilian *vox populi* of the period: Carlos Eugênio Líbano Soares, *A negrada instituição: Os capoeiras na corte imperial, 1850–1890* (Rio de Janeiro: Access Editora, 1999), 176–78.

40. See George Reid Andrews, *The Afro-Argentines of Buenos Aires, 1800–1900* (Madison: University of Wisconsin Press, 1980), 66.

41. Carretero, *Tango: testigo social,* 19–20.

42. A much shorter version of the novel had appeared in 1839. On mulatas in nineteenth-century Cuban popular culture, see Vera Kutzinski,

Sugar's Secrets: Race and the Erotics of Cuban Nationalism (Charlottesville: University of Virginia Press, 1993).

43. Cirilo Villaverde, *Cecilia Valdés o la loma del ángel,* ed. and notes by Esteban Rodríguez Herrera (Havana: Editorial Lex-Habana, 1953), 68.

44. "Oh tempora, oh mores!" *La voz de Cuba,* 13 August 1879. A note in the 1953 critical edition explains that in the early twentieth century such dances still occurred under the name *bailes de arroz con frijoles,* in reference to a common Cuban dish mixing black beans with rice: Villaverde, *Cecilia Valdés,* 66.

45. Another lyric from those years, which Ximeno y Cruz remembered as a particularly spirited tune: "Farewell, my Chinita,/Goodbye my fiery Negrita," it just won't work out!: Dolores María de Ximeno y Cruz. *Aquellos tiempos,* vol. 1 (Havana: Imp. El Universo, 1928), 290–93.

46. Ximeno y Cruz, *Aquellos tiempos,* 2:297.

47. Efegê, *Maxixe,* 75.

48. Héctor Bates y Luis Bates, *La historia del tango: sus autores* (Buenos Aires: Taller Gráfica de la Cía. Fabril Financiera, 1936), 238.

Chapter Three

1. Roberto Moura, *Tia Ciata e a pequena Africa no Rio de Janeiro* (Rio: FUNARTE, 1983), 64–65.

2. Moura, Tia Ciata, 65–66. On Candomblé and related religions, see Joseph M. Murphy, *Working the Spirit: Ceremonies of the African Diaspora* (Boston: Beacon Press, 1994).

3. Within that designation, however, much variation was possible. Tia Ciata "could spend half an hour dancing *miudinho* in the roda," someone recalled. This miudinho was a dance that combined requebros of the body with some choreography of minuet—a surprising combination not uncommon in Latin American folklore. Carmen Teixeira da Conceição, quoted in Moura, *Tia Ciata,* 66. Miudinho and its analogs will be discussed in chapter eight.

4. Vivaldo Coaracy, *Memórias da cidade do Rio de Janeiro* (Rio de Janeiro: Livraria José Olympio Editora, 1955), 420–23.

5. Maria Isaura Pereira de Queiroz, *Carnaval brasileiro: o vivido e o mito* (São Paulo: Editora Brasiliense, 1992), 45. Two scholars have more recently shown that Rio's carnival was never completely elite-dominated: Rachel Soihet, *Subversão pelo riso: Estudos sobre o carnaval carioca da belle époque ao tempo de Vargas* (Rio de Janeiro: Editora da FGV, 1998) and Maria Clementina Pareira Cunha, *Ecos da folia: Uma história do carnaval carioca entre 1800 e 1920* (São Paula: Companhia das Letras, 2001).

6. Early signs of change were perhaps the journalistic concern, expressed in 1876, of a general relaxamento dos costumes, or the journalistic celebration (1877) of more nightlife. For a close reading of the press, see Delso Renault, O dia-a-dia no Rio de Janeiro segundo os jornais, 1870–1889 (Rio de Janeiro: Civilização Brasileira, 1982), 92–93, 104.

7. Eneida de Moraes, *Historia do carnaval carioca.* Rev. Haroldo Costa. (Rio de Janeiro: Editôra Record, 1987), 39–43. See also, "Festejos carnavalescos," *Diário do Rio de Janeiro,* 16 February 1874.

8. See "O carnaval fluminense," *Gazeta de notícias,* 6 March 1905.

9. "Carnaval," *Gazeta de notícias,* 7 February 1883.

10. "Carnaval," *O paiz,* 10 March 1886.

11. "Carnaval," *Gazeta de notícias,* 21 February 1887. A Gazeta was not the only paper that used the term Zé Pereira this way. Another paper mentioned several Zé Pereiras that called themselves Cucumbys: "Carnaval," O paiz, 8 March 1886. Many studies of carnival too rigidly differentiate between the various kinds of groups. In fact the boundaries between them were quite fluid. See Maria Clementina Pereira Cunha, *Ecos da folia*), esp. 158–73.

12. A group of "*quicumbis*" appeared at a Recife celebration as early as 1745: Emanuel Araújo, *O teatro dos vícios: Transgressão e transigência na sociedade urbana colonial* (Rio de Janeiro: José Olympio, 1993), 135. Cunha, *Ecos da folia,* shows a photograph of Rio Cucumbys in the 1860s, and she indicates that they had never disappeared completely from Rio neighborhoods during the nineteenth century: 41–46. Rather, the desire for a progressive image seems to have banished Cucumbys from the capital city's collective celebrations during those decades.

13. "Carnaval: Os Cucumbys," *Gazeta de notícias,* 13 Februrary 1888. This article was substantially reproduced in Mello Moraes Filho, *Festas e tradições populares do Brazil.* (RJ/Paris: H. Garmier Livreiro, 1901), 55–65. Groups like "*Os Lanceiros Africanos,*" wearing feathers and possibly bearing spears, seem to have followed the Cucumbys model but without its customary script: "Mascaras avulsas," *O paiz,* 6 March 1889. On the thumb piano (lamellophone or marimba), see Peter Fryer, *Rhythms of Resistance: African Musical Heritage in Brazil* (Hanover, NH: Wesleyan University Press, 2000), 78–82.

14. "A.S.C. Triunfo dos Cucumbys," *O paiz,* 14 February 1889.

15. "A.S. Cucumby," *O paiz,* 14 February 1889.

16. "Carnaval," *O paiz,* 19 Feb. 1890.

17. See a wonderful description of late twentieth-century black Mardi Gras Indians practicing their street dance in Samuel Kinser, *Carnival,*

American Style: Mardi Gras at New Orleans and Mobile (Chicago and London: University of Chicago Press, 1990), 230.

18. From an oral deposition by Donga at the Museu da Imagem e do Som, quoted by Moura, *Tia Ciata,* 68–69.

19. Moura, *Tia Ciata,* 59, quotes *O Jornal do Brasil,* 18 January 1913. "O rancho da Bahia entrou no carnaval carioca com um rei de ouros": Efegê *Figuras e coisas,* 88–90.

20. "Tia Bebiana, a quem os ranchos reverenciavam": Efegê *Figuras e coisas,* 131–32.

21. "Garatujas," *Fon Fon,* 28 February 1925.

22. This transformation can be seen with great clarity in the 1906 carnival coverage by *Gazeta de notícias.* The groups led by *velhos* were called *cordões.* In comparison with the ranchos, cordões were remembered as turbulent and pugnacious: Jota Efegê *Figuras e coisas,* 175.

23. Epiphany troupes (called *ranchos* in Portuguese) are often described in recent studies as institutions of an incipient black "bourgeoisie." Nei Lopes, *A samba na realidade* (Rio de Janeiro: Codecri, 1981), 22–23. There is truth in this assessment, but the ranchos were not somehow alienated from Rio's majority of African descent.

24. Many scholars assert that it was. Maria Isaura Pereira de Queiroz makes that error in her otherwise excellent *Carnaval brasileiro: o vivido e o mito.* Soihet, *Subversão pelo riso,* and Cunha, *Ecos da folia,* both set the record straight on that point.

25. "O dia de hontem," *O Jornal do Brasil,* 26 February 1895. Also see "Ruas e Praças," *O Jornal do Brasil,* 11 February 1902.

26. "A entrada do carnaval," *O paiz,* 9 February 1902.

27. "Scenas da vida carioca no carnaval," A *Gazeta de notícias,* 23 February 1903.

28. Eneida, *História do carnaval carioca,* 93.

29. Eneida, *História do carnaval carioca,* 94–95. O Jornal do Brasil occasionally did neighborhood by neighborhood coverage of the 1901–1903 carnivals.

30. "Ideias de carnaval," *O paiz,* 3 February 1913.

31. Moura, *Tia Ciata,* 60, cites an interview with Ferreira in Diario Carioca, 7 February 1931.

32. Both Cucumbys and black *lanceiros* ("spinning men and women with brightly colored head feathers") visited the offices of *O paiz* in 1889: "Máscaras avulsos," *O paiz,* 6 March 1889.

33. *O paiz:* "Observações de um frade," 22 February 1898; and "Carnaval," 14 February 99. This praise of street dancers must be understood, of course, in the context of a larger, often quite racist,

journalistic discourse on popular carnival, amply documented by Cunha, *Ecos da folia,* 207 and passim.

34. "Grupos," *O Jornal do Brasil,* 28 February 1900.

35. "A entrada do carnaval," *O paiz,* 9 February 1902.

36. A *Gazeta de notícias,* February 1906, passim.

37. "Grupos carnavalescos," *O Jornal do Brasil,* 11 February 1902.

38. "Carnaval," *O paiz,* 14 February 1899.

39. "Carnaval," *O Jornal do Brasil,* 10 February 1902.

40. Ernesto de Souza's song "Quem inventou a mulata," performed at carnival in 1903 was an exceptional antecedent of later usage: Lisa Shaw, *The Social History of the Brazilian Samba 1930–1945* (Aldershot, UK: Ashgate Publishing Ltd., 1999), 174.

41. "Grupos Carnavalescos," *O Jornal do Brasil,* 24 February 1903.

42. "Os grupos," *O paiz,* 18 February 1896.

43. "Carnaval de 1906," A *Gazeta de notícias,* 13 February 1906.

44. "A arte nos cordões: a poesia," A *Gazeta de notícias,* 20 February 1906.

45. "Ranchos e blocos," *Jornal do Brasil,* 8 February 1920.

46. See "Carnaval," *O Jornal do Brasil,* 25 February 1895; "Os Grupos, *O paiz,* 17 February 1896; and "Os Grupos," *O paiz,* 21 February 1898.

47. *O Jornal do Brasil:* "Grupos," 28 February 1900; and "Carnaval," 10 February 1902.

48. *O paiz:* "Observações de um frade," 22 February 1898; and "Os Grupos," 15 February 1899.

49. The group was C.C. Yayá Tenha Paciencia. "Grupos e carros," A *Gazeta de notícias,* 23 February 1903. The translation attempts to capture the spirit of the phrase "quebrando-se e requebrando-se nuns maxixes dolientes."

50. "Pelas Ruas," *O paiz,* 25 February 1895.

51. "Grupos carnavalescos," *O Jornal do Brasil,* 19 February 1901. Interestingly, the term *lundu* appears not at all in this reportage. Lundu suggested something tame and old-fashioned, while *samba* had provocatively "African" resonances that some dancers wished to highlight.

52. On the major reforms carried out by Rio mayor Pereira Passos, see Jeffrey D. Needell, *A Tropical Belle Epoque: Elite Culture and Society in Turn-of-the-Century Rio de Janeiro* (Cambridge: Cambridge University Press, 1987), 33–51.

53. "Pelo telefone" was played even by military bands: Jota Efegê *Figuras e coisas,* 179.

54. Anonymous recollection in Moura's appendix "Lembranças, impressões, fantasias," 104.

Also on the dancing at Tia Ciata's house, see Muniz Sodré, *Samba, o dono do corpo* (Rio de Janeiro: CODECRI, 1979), 20.

55. Interview with João da Baiana: Moura, *Tia Ciata,* 63.

56. Quotation in Moura's appendix "Lembranças, impressões, fantasias," 104.

57. The trarnsition from ranchos to escolas is expertly discussed by Nei Lopes in *A samba na realidade: A utopia da ascensão social do sambista* (Rio: CODECRI, 1981), 22–32. See also Jota Efegê, Ameno Resedá: *O rancho que foi escola* (Rio de Janeiro: Editora Letras e Artes, 1965). On Rio's escolas de samba, see José Sávio Leopoldi, *Escola de samba, ritual e sociedade* (Petrópolis: Editôra Vozes, 1978); Ana Maria Rodrigues, *Samba negro, espoliação branca* (São Paulo: Editora Hucitec, 1984); and Alison Raphael, "Samba Schools in Brazil," *International Journal of Oral History* 10 (1989), 256–67.

58. "Carnaval," *Fon Fon,* 11 March 1922.

59. "Do meu diário," *Fon Fon,* 10 February 1923.

60. See Tulio Halperín Donghi, *The Contemporary History of Latin America,* ed. and trans. by John Charles Chasteen (Durham: Duke University Press, 1993), 231–34.

61. Dulce Tupi, *Carnavais de guerra: o nacionalismo no samba* (Rio de Janeiro: ASB Arte Gráfica e Editôra, 1985), 96–115.

62. The samba played at Tia Ciata's house was less percussive than later versions of the genre. One grandson of Ciata remembered tambourine, cavaquinho, guitar, flute, and clarinet, but no African drumming: "Não existia negócio de bumbo naquele tempo." Interview with Marinho da Costa Jumbeba, "Zinho," in the appendix to Nei Lopes, *O negro no Rio de Janeiro e sua tradição musical: partido-alto, calango, chulas, e outras cantorias* (Rio de Janeiro: Pallas, 1992), 105.

Chapter Four

1. José J. Podestá, *Medio siglo de farándula: memorias* (Buenos Aires: Rio de la Plata, 1930), 57.

2. "Originalidades sociales, Juan Moreira," *Sud América,* 11 November 1895. *La Ilustracón Sudamericana* (1 May 1899) immediately pronounced the show "a box office hit": *Antología del tango rioplatense* (Buenos Aires: Instituto de Musicología "Carlos Vega," 1986), 19.

3. By the same token, anything purely indigenous was *not* criollo. The application of the term criollo to American-born blacks had begun earlier than its application to whites. In fact, in independence-era Peru, some whites considered the term *criollo* offensive because of its original

association with blacks: Alberto Flores Galindo, *La ciudad sumergida: Aristocracia y plebe en Lima, 1760–1830,* 2nd ed. (Lima: Editorial Horizonte, 1991), 133.

4. On the criollista fiction, of which the novel *Juan Moreira* by Eduardo Gutiérrez is an important example, see Adolfo Prieto, *El discurso criollista en la formación de la Argentina moderna* (Buenos Aires: Sudamericana, 1988).

5. The criollo circus flourished in the early nineteenth century and then declined in popularity before rebounding in the 1890s. See Raúl H. Castagnino, *Centuria del circo criollo* (Buenos Aires: Editorial Perrot, 1959).

6. Still, foreign birth meant that "*Tanos*" (from *Napolitanos,* though applied to all Italians) could not become Criollos. The nativist club was, in that sense, exclusive and birthplace was destiny. On Cocoliche, see Ana Cara-Walker, "Cocoliche: The Art of Assimilation and Dissimulation among Italians and Argentines," *Latin American Research Review* 22 (1987): 37–68.

7. Podestá, *Memorias,* 9.

8. Podestá, *Memorias,* 14–33.

9. María Esther Podestá, *Desde ya y sin interrupciones (Memorias),* ed. Jorge Miguel Couselo (Buenos Aires: Corregidor, [1985]), 15.

10. The first piece was an estilo, the second, a gato con relaciones: Podestá, *Memorias,* 42–43.

11. Raúl H Castagnino, *Circo, teatro gauchesco, y tango* (Buenos Aires: Instituto Nacional de Estudios de Teatro, 1981), 20, lists other nativist circus theatricals (many created by Uruguayans) that followed on the success of "Juan Moreira": Eduardo Gutierrez, "Juan Cuello" (1890); Elias Regulas' adaptation of "Martin Fierro" (1890); Bernardo L. Peyret, "Idea de Patria" (1892); Abdon Arosteguy, "Julián Giménez" (1893); Elias Regules, "El entenao" (1891); Orosmán Moratoria, "Ña Toribia" (1894); a parody, "Fausto Criollo" (1894) and "Pollera y chiripá" (1894), both by Benjamín Fernández y Medina; and Francisco, "Nobleza criolla" (1894). On payadores, see Jorge B. Rivera, "Historias paralelas," in *La historia del tango: Sus orígenes* (Buenos Aires: Ediciones Corregidor, 1976), 13–16.

12. The name of the circus was actually Podestá-Scotti because of the brothers' brother-in-law and partner, Alejandro Scotti, who had worked with them since the 1870s: Castagnino, *Centuria del circo criollo,* 21.

13. Podestá, *Memorias,* 56–79.

14. "Gresca chistosa," *La Patria Argentina,* 27 September 1880.

15. Ibid.

16. Men clearly practiced tango with men fairly often, more often than they practiced other dances with each other. Probably, they did so because *corte y quebrada* technique requires the leader to understand the follower's moves in order to lead them.

17. "Uno de los parajes," *La Pampa,* 15 December 1881.

18. Archivo Histórico Municipal (Buenos Aires), Cultura 1882/41/1381 and 42/2694.

19. Archivo Histórico Municipal, Cultura 1886/109/4518.

20. *La broma,* passim, 1878–1882.

21. Héctor y Juan L. Bates, *La historia del tango* (Buenos Aires: Talleres Gráficos de la Compañía General Fabril Financiera, 1936), 22–23.

22. On Buenos Aires carnaval, see Enrique H. Puccia, *Breve historia del carnaval porteño* (Buenos Aires: Municipalidad de la Ciudad de Buenos Aires, 1974).

23. Buenos Aires carnival was, in fact, arguably a bigger event than Rio's in this period: Horace Rumbold, *The Great Silver River: Notes of a Residence in Buenos Ayres in 1880 and 1881* (London: John Murray, 1887), 311. The usual terminology for "blackface" in Buenos Aires was *con la cara tiznada o embetunada.*

24. "A nuestros lectores," *Los negros: Periódico semanal redactado por jóvenes de la sociedad de ese nombre,* 21 Mar. 1869; and "Los negros," *El nacional,* 26 February 1873.

25. Oscar Natale, *Buenos Aires, negros, y tango* (Buenos Aires: Peña Lillo editor, 1984) , 135.

26. Ortiz Odorico, Calunga, 64–67; and "Arte dramático popular americano," *El nacional,* 12 July 1869.

27. Las fiestas de carnaval," *El nacional,* 2 March 1881. At times in 1880s Buenos Aires carnival, most of the paraders seemed to be in blackface: Emilio Daireaux, *Vida y costumbres en el Plata* (Buenos Aires: Félix Lajouane, Ed., 1888), 1:263.

28. My view of blackface's contradictory meanings has been influenced by Eric Lott, *Love and Theft: Blackface Minstrelsy and the American Working Class* (Oxford: Oxford University Press, 1993).

29. "El carnaval antiguo: Los candomberos," *Caras y caretas,* 15 February 1902.

30. "Comparsas," *La broma,* 8 March 1878.

31. "Paseo a Montevideo," *La broma,* 30 December 1880.

32. Puccia, *Breve historia del carnaval porteño,* 49, 75–6. Vicente Rossi, *Cosas de negros* describes similar developments in Montevideo carnival, 106–9.

33. "Nuestras sociedades carnivalescas," *La broma,* 3 March 1882.

34. Fernando O. Assunçao, *El tango y sus circunstancias* (1880–1920) (Buenos Aires: Librería "El Ateneo" Editorial, 1984), 81–82.

35. Cited in Teodoro Klein, "Cultura negra y tangos: Las academias de baile," *Desmemoria* 2 (1995), 6:116.

36. "Mundele y Cagombo baila/La masucra e el choti ingré,/ Requebrando sintula solo/Y alastrando también los pies.": "Canciones carnavalescas," *La broma,* 6 March 1881.

37. In Cuba, this shuffling sound, called *sopimpa,* was a well-known characteristic of Afro-Cuban *danza:* Natalio Galán, *Cuba y sus sones* (Madrid: Pre-Textos, 1983), 135.

38. Rossi, *Cosas de negros,* 147. The first recorded reference to tango as a baile de corte y quebrada appears an 1892 review called "El año 92": Natale, *Buenos Aires, negros, y tango,* 162. "Bartolo" sheet music appeared as *milonga* in 1900, but three years later the same piece was listed as *tango*: *Antología del tango rioplatense,* 17–18.

39. Sergio Pujol, *Historia del baile: De la milonga a la disco* (Buenos Aires: Emecé, 1999), 61, has been one of the few to call attention this pattern.

40. Carlos María Santigosa, *El Río de la Plata: Montevideo, Buenos Aires* (Recuerdos de viaje) (Seville: Heraldo Sevillano, 1906), 198–99. Santigosa transcribes an undated article from *Caras y Caretas.*

41. Quoted from César Viale, *Estampas de mi tiempo* (1942) in Puccia, *Breve historia del carnaval porteño,* 91; and *La Tribuna,* 11 February 1903, cited in *Antología del tango rioplatense,* 1: 19.

42. "Bailes de carnaval," *Caras y caretas,* 20 February 1904.

43. Santigosa, *El Río de la Plata,* 198–99.

44. Bates and Bates, *La historia del tango,* 319; Horacio Salas, *El tango* (Buenos Aires: Planeta, 1995), 114–25.

45. On these changes in style, see Marta E. Savigliano, *Tango and the Political Economy of Passion* (Boulder: Westview Press, 1995), 119, 149–55.

46. See Carlos Vega, *El origen de la danzas folklóricas* (Buenos Aires: Ricordi Americana, 1956).

47. The division is a commonplace of Argentine history, see James R. Scobie, *Argentina: A City and a Nation,* 2nd. ed. (London: Oxford University Press, 1971).

48. In fact, gaucho comparsas had been around for a long time, and they had always been notably permeable to outsiders, one of the first being founded by an Englishman "with a criollo heart" back in 1870s.

49. Puccia, *Breve historia del carnaval porteño,* 82.

50. Podestá, *Desde ya y sin interrupciones,* 20–34.

51. Natale, *Buenos Aires, negros, y tango,* 165–67.

Chapter Five

1. "Asalto," *La aurora del Yumurí,* 24 October 1871.

2. A second purpose of *asaltos,* clearly, was to relieve the host family of expenses associated with the party. On the execution of the medical students and the accompanying political mood in Havana, see the useful collection of primary source materials in Gustavo Eguren, *La fidelísima Habana* (Havana: Editorial Letras Cubanas, 1986), particularly the account of traveler A. Gallenga, *The Pearl of the Antilles* (doc. 498).

3. For example: "Artistas y guarachas," *El triunfo,* 16 February 1881.

4. Alejo Carpentier, *La música en Cuba* (Mexico City: Fondo de Cultura Económica, 1972), 178–79, 252; and Ada Ferrer, *Insurgent Cuba: Race, Nation, and Revolution, 1868–1898* (Chapel Hill: University of North Carolina Press, 1999), 3.

5. Revolutionary nationalist movements—like Afro-Cuban musical forms—have always approached Havana from the east. On Havana during the war, see Anonymous, *The Book of Travels of a Doctor of Physic: Containing his Observations Made in Certain Portions of the Two Continents* (1871) excerpted in Eguren, *La fidelísima Habana,* doc. 487.

6. This is danzón defined musically by 1) the *cinquillo* rhythm, and 2) by a structure of successive development. See Osvaldo Castillo Faílde, *Miguel Faílde, creador musical del danzón* (Havana: Editora del Consejo Nacional de Cultura, 1964), 29–30.

7. Dolores María de Ximeno y Cruz, *Aquellos tiempos* (Havana: Imp. El Universo, 1928–1930), 2:294.

8. Castillo Faílde, *Miguel Faílde,* 40–41.

9. "Baile de color," *La aurora del Yumurí,* 5 November 1874.

10. "Serenata y baile," *La aurora del Yumurí,* 17 November 1874.

11. The first date seems reliable because it was recalled by Faílde's granddaughter Aurora, who could be expected to remember the occasion. The second date is a matter of record.

12. "El danzón," *El triunfo,* 25 July 1882.

13. Fredrika Bremer, *The Homes of the New World: Impressions of America* (New York: Harper and Brothers, 1853), 2:308.

14. Two examples from *La aurora del Yumurí:* "Danzón" and "Magnifica comparsa," 24 November and 2 December 1871.

15. "El danzón," *El diario de Matanzas,* 7 November 1878; and Castillo Faíde, *Miguel Faílde,* 85.

16. "El danzón," *El diario de Matanzas,* 7 November 1878.

17. Cinquillo is called a "rhythmic cell," a regular accentuation of

off-beats that can be applied to any melody. Faílde's friend Raimundo Valenzuela called the cinquillo rhythm danzón's "essential secret." Castillo Faílde, *Miguel Faílde,* 30. See also Eduardo Sánchez de Fuentes, *El Folk-lor en la música de Cuba* (Havana: El siglo XX, 1923), 29.

18. "Sobre el baile," *El triunfo,* 25 December 1878.

19. "El danzón," *La voz de Cuba* (Havana), 8 October 1879.

20. "El danzón," *La voz de Cuba,* 8 October and 20 November 1879.

21. The rival paper was *El diario de la marina,* quoted in "Y dijo el aquático," *El triunfo,* 17 May 1880.

22. Carpentier, *La música en Cuba,* 237.

23. "Baile en el Tacón," *El triunfo,* 5 Jan. 1883 and "Sobre el son," *Signos* [Havana], May–December 1975, 789.

24. "Ecos del carnaval," *El país,* 28 February 1887; and "Jueves 16," *El país,* 13 February 1888.

25. "Sectários del danzón," *El Fígaro,* 28 February 1892.

26. "Variedades," *La aurora de Yumurí,* 3 September 1882.

27. "Correo del Domingo," *El país,* 25 February 1888.

28. Castillo Faíde, *Miguel Faílde,* 69.

29. "El danzón," *La voz de Cuba,* 20 November 1879.

30. "El Carnaval," *El triunfo,* 1 March 1884

31. "Sobre bailes," *La Habana elegante,* 19 August 1888.

32. Quoted from *La unión* (Güines), 13 Aug. 1882 by Castillo Faílde, *Miguel Faílde,* 158.

33. "A Rosalía," reproduced by Castillo Faílde, *Miguel Faílde,* 141–42.

34. "El porvenir del baile en Cuba," *El almendares,* 7 September 1881. On ñáñigos, see Philip A. Howard, *Changing History: Afro-Cuban Cabildos and Societies of Color in the Nineteenth Century* (Baton Rouge: Louisiana State University Press, 1998), 68–72.

35. *La aurora de Yurumí:* "Por la tangente," 26 July 1881; and "Pobre Cuba," 3 August 1881.

36. Danzón's status as "baile nacional de Cuba" was not made official until the revolutionary government did that in 1960: Castillo Faílde, *Miguel Faílde,* 251–53. On Valenzuela see "Crónica," *El Fígaro,* 1 March 1903 and "Álbum de Salones," *El Nuevo Criollo* (Havana), 18 February 1905.

37. Early son, in contrast to danzón, had an explicitly rustic tone. Played by a small group featuring guitars, rather than a dance orchestra like Faílde's, son (more than danzón) is the *musical* analog of twentieth-century samba and tango. See Peter Manuel with Kenneth Bilby and Michael Largey, *Caribbean Currents: Caribbean Music from Rumba to Reggae* (Philadelphia: Temple University Press, 1995), 36–37.

38. "Culto a Euterpe y Terpsicore," *El triunfo,* 17 August 1878; "Eco y murmullos," *La Habana elegante,* 13 September 1885; and "Hoy," El Pais, 12 August 1893.

39. Castillo Faílde, *Miguel Faílde,* 49–50.

40. This overall interpretation of the rise of danzón contrasts somewhat with that offered by Robin D. Moore, *Nationalizing Blackness: Afrocubanismo and Artistic Revolution in Havana, 1920–1940* (Pittsburgh: University of Pittsburgh Press, 1997), 23–26.

41. "Placeres de la estacion," *El moro musa,* 15 February 1863.

42. Blackface comparsas were hardly unknown in Havana. A blackface comparsa is mentioned, for example, in 1893: "Comparsa de negros catedráticos," *El País,* 8 February 1893. The point is that the street carnival activities of the Havana elite had nothing like the importance, regularity, and institutionalization one finds in Rio or Buenos Aires.

43. "Carnaval," *El moro musa,* 7 February 1864.

44. "Habana, carnaval de 1864," *El moro musa,* 14 February 1864; and "Carnaval," El siglo, 17 February 1863.

45. "Comparsas," *El siglo,* 18 February 1863; and "El paseo de carnaval," *La Habana elegante,* 19 February 1893.

46. *El triunfo:* "Partes," 25 February 1884; and "El primer paseo de carnaval," 5 February 1883.

47. Fernando Ortiz, *Los bailes y el teatro de los negros en el folklore de Cuba* (Havana: Editorial de las Letras Cubanas, 1985), 442, 480.

48. "El paseo de carnaval," *La Habana elegante,* 19 February 1893.

49. "El paseo," *El Fígaro,* 8 February 1894.

50. Natalio Galán, *Cuba y sus sones* (Madrid: Pre-Textos, 1983), 328.

51. *El Fígaro,* 21–28 February 1908, passim.

52. "Crónica," *El Fígaro,* 12 March 1911.

53. For a good overview of the twentieth century, see Moore's chapter on "Comparsas and Carnival in the New Republic," in *Nationalizing Blackness,* 62–84.

Chapter Six

1. "Carnaval de 1886," *El país,* 6 March 1886.

2. See, for example, "Comparsas," *La broma,* 8 March 1878.

3. This term was used in 1973 by John Storm Roberts, *Black Music of Two Worlds,* and more recently by Peter Fryer, *Rhythms of Resistance: African Musical Heritage in Brazil* (Hanover, NH: Wesleyan University Press, 2000). Fryer's book is the best collection of source materials on its topic in any language. His abundant quotations are complete and well-translated.

4. See, for example, Emanuel Araújo, *O teatro dos vícios: Transgressão e transigência na sociedade urbana colonial* (Rio de Janeiro: José Olympio, 1993), 130–48.

5. William Ouseley, *Travels in Various Countries of the East (1819–1823)*, quoted in Fryer, *Rhythms of Resistance,* 88.

6. José RamosTinhorão, *Os negros em Portugal: Uma presença silenciosa* (Lisbon: Caminho, 1988, 147–53).

7. Fryer, *Rhythms of Resistance,* 86–87.

8. Samuel Kinser, *Carnival, American Style: Mardi Gras at New Orleans and Mobile* (Chicago and London: University of Chicago Press, 1990), 32–34.

9. S. Fredrick Starr, *Bamboula!: The Life and Times of Louis Moreau Gottschalk* (New York: Oxford University Press, 1995), 62–77.

10. John Thornton, *Africa and Africans in the Making of the Atlantic World.* 2nd ed. (Cambridge: Cambridge Univ. Press, 1998), 202–3, 320–24.

11. John Parish Robertson and William Parish Robertson, *Letters on Paraguay* (1838), quoted in Mary C. Karasch, *Slave Life in Rio de Janeiro, 1808–1850* (Princeton: Princeton University Press, 1987), 242.

12. Maria Dundas Graham, *Journal of a Voyage to Brazil and Residence There during Part of the Years 1821, 1822, 1823* (New York: Frederick A. Praeger, 1969), 199. Intermittent prohibitions characterize the long history of neo-African dance in Brazil, as in the rest of the New World, but black dancers were insistent about their right to dance, particularly in celebration of Catholic devotions. In 1796, black devotees of Nossa Senhora do Rosário in Bahia wrote directly to the queen of Portugal requesting permission to dance. See Pierre Verger, "Procissões e carnaval no Brasil," in *Estudos Afro-Orientais Ensaios/Pesquisas* 5 (1980), 2.

13. Karasch, *Slave Life in Rio,* 243.

14. Charles Samuel Stewart, a U.S. Protestant clergyman, saw Rio blacks dancing at Epiphany in 1852, but they were "within an enclosure by the wayside" in a peripheral part of town. C.S. Stewart, *Brazil and La Plata* (1856) quoted by Fryer, *Rhythms of Resistance,* 91.

15. Mello Moraes Filho, *Festas e tradições populares do Brazil* (Rio de Janeiro/Paris: H. Garmier Livreiro, 1901), 335, says that funeral banquets and wakes were the only functions of black nations in late nineteeth-century Rio.

16. Moraes Filho, *Festas e tradições,* 401–6. Much evidence on slavery in Rio was destroyed following abolition, yet indications from Bahia show a similar decline of neo-African nations after the slave trade to Brazil was finally ended in 1851: Meiko Nishida, "Gender, Ethnicity, and Kinship in the Urban African Diaspora: Salvador, Brazil, 1808–1888" (Ph.D. dissertation, Johns Hopkins University, 1991), 200–4.

17. Moraes Filho, *Festas e tradições,* 68. The close connection between black nations, lay brotherhoods, and coronation dances occurred throughout Brazil. See, for example, the history of the carnival groups called *maracatus* in the northeastern city of Recife: Fryer, *Rhythms of Resistance,* 66.

18. Moraes Filho, *Festas e tradições,* 372.

19. Moraes Filho, *Festas e tradições,* 369–73.

20. Luís Edmundo, *O Rio de Janeiro no tempo do vice-reis* (Rio de Janeiro: Conquista, 1956), 257–60.

21. For an authoritative survey of this family of dances, see Oneyda Alvarenga, *Música popular brasileña* (Mexico City: Fondo de Cultura Económica, 1947), 26–109.

22. "Los bienes de nuestros abuelos," *La broma,* 30 April 1881.

23. Rodríguez Molas, *La música y la danza de los negros en el Buenos Aires de los siglos XVIII y XIX* (Buenos Aires: Clío, 1957), 13–15.

24. "Varillazos," *La broma,* 27 January 1881.

25. For an excellent overview in English, see George Reid Andrews, *The Afro-Argentines of Buenos Aires, 1800–1900* (Madison: University of Wisconsin Press, 1980).

26. Rodríguez Molas, *La música y la danza de los negros,* 8.

27. Archivo General de la Nación (Buenos Aires, hereafter AGN). "Información hecha para esclarecer lo que expone Manuel Farías contra Pablo Aguero," IX 36.4.3.

28. AGN. "Información hecha para esclarecer lo que expone Manuel Farías contra Pablo Aguero," IX 36.4.3.

29. Rodríguez Molas, *La música y la danza de los negros,* 9.

30. See Oscar Chamosa, "To Honor the Ashes of their Forebears. "The Rise and Crisis of African Nations in the Post-Independence State of Buenos Aires, 1820-1860," *The Americas* 59:3 (2003).

31. AGN. "Hermandad de Morenos de Guinea," IX 12.9.13. *Tambo* was used in Lima, Peru, as a place of "música y diversiones de de tambores de los negros": Flores Galindo, *La ciudad sumergida,* 140.

32. "Representación del síndico procurador general sobre los bailes de negros," *Acuerdos del Extinguido Cabildo de Buenos Aires* (9 October 1788): ser. 3, vol. 8, bk. 49, 627–30.

33. "Se acuerda que se pase al Excelentísimo Señor Virrey," *Acuerdos del Extinguido Cabildo de Buenos Aires* (9 October 1788): ser. 3, vol. 8, bk. 49, 624–25.

34. The interest shown by white spectators, and the moral dangers that the spectacle posed to young white women, were commonplace of white discourse on black dance. See Fryer, *Rhythms of Resistance,* 91.

35. Quoted in Rodríguez Molas, *La música y la danza de los negros,* 9–11.

36. Alcide d'Orbigny, *Voyage dans l'Amérique Méridionale* (Paris, 1835), 1: 5.

37. Black soldiers had been important defenders of Montevideo against an external siege in the 1840s, while, in Buenos Aires, black involvement in internal partisan struggles inspired fear among the city's elite. See chapter 8.

38. Isidoro de María, *Montevideo antiguo* (Montevideo: Sociedad Amigos del Libro Rioplatense, 1938), 82–86.

39. Recollection of Domingo González in (no author) *La atalaya de Ulises* (Montevideo: Impr. y Casa Editorial "Renacimiento," 1922), 108–9.

40. Lauro Ayestarán, *La música en el Uruguay* (Montevideo: Servicio Oficial de Difusión Radio Electrónica, 1953), 71.

41. "Los reyes magos," reprinted from Montevideo in *La tribuna* [Buenos Aires], 10 January 1862.

42. Bottaro's chapter is called "Rituals and Candombes," in Nancy Cunard, *Negro* (London, 1934), 519–22.

43. Vicente Rossi, *Cosas de negros* (Buenos Aires: Librería Hachette, 1958). Rossi was born in Uruguay in 1871. He worked as a journalist both there and in Argentina, settling in Córdoba in 1898. Also wrote fiction and a *Historia del teatro nacional rioplatense* (1910).

44. San Benito in Portuguese is São Benedito, patron of many of Rio's nations. Rossi, *Cosas de negros,* 70–73.

45. Rossi, *Cosas de negros,* 62–63.

46. The meeting houses of the black nations of the Río de la Plata did have special rooms for religious rituals. In candombe, there is no explicit evidence of spirit possession, the essential culminating moment of *candomblé*—yet the two words are too close not to be somehow related. See Chamosa, "*To Honor the Ashes of their Forbears.*"

47. This kind of zigzagging was also characteristic of early street dancing in Rio carnival: Nei Lopes, *A samba na realidade* (Rio de Janeiro: Codecri, 1981), 37.

48. The omligada/umbigada appears to have Angolan origins. *Semba,* the most frequent guess for the etymological derivation of Brazilian *samba,* is an Angolan word for umbigada (Karasch, *Slave Life in Rio,* 244. Fryer, *Rhythms of Resistance,* supplies several descriptions of semba dancing in Angola, 1875–1881 (97–98).

49. The most influential of these reconstructions was done by Ayestaran, *La música en el Uruguay,* 84–86.

50. Eva Canél [sic], *De América* (2a serie) (Madrid, 1899), 56–58.

51. Ayestarán, *La música en el Uruguay,* 81.

52. Sketches from Figari's notebook are reproduced in Pedro Figari and Fernando Guibert, *Tango y candombe en el Río de la Plata, 1861–1979: Testimonio de un pasado histórico* (Montevideo: Librería Colonial, 1979), 25–35.

53. See Fernando Coronil, "Introduction to the Duke University Press Edition," in Fernando Ortiz, *Cuban Counterpoint: Tobacco and Sugar,* trans. by Harriet de Onís (Durham: Duke University Press, 1995), ix–lvi.

54. Fernando Ortiz, *Los cabilidos y la fiesta afrocubanos del Día de Reyes* (Havana: Editorial da Ciencias Sociales, 1992), 9–10. Howard, *Changing History: Afro-Cuban Cabildos and Societies of Color in the Nineteenth Century,* supersedes the work of Ortiz on this topic.

55. "Reloj de repetición," *El faro industrial de la Habana,* 6 January 1845.

56. "Día de los Santos Reyes," *La prensa,* 6 January 1843.

57. Leon Beauvallet, *Rachel and the New World,* trans. Colin Clair (London: Abelard-Schuman, 1967), 193.

58. "El Día de los Reyes en la Habana," *El abolicionista español,* 15 January 1866.

59. *La voz de Cuba:* "Día de Reyes," 7 January 1878; "La Fiesta de Reyes," 14 January 1878.

60. "La Festividad de Reyes," *La voz de Cuba,* 7 January 1880.

61. "El Día de Reyes," *La Habana elegante,* 9 January 1887. Like other neo-African nations, Havana's cabildos had many other officers besides the king and queen, too.

62. "El Día de Reyes," *La Habana elegante,* 9 January 1887.

63. "La Fiesta de Reyes," *La voz de Cuba,* 14 January 1878.

64. "La Festividad de Reyes," *La voz de Cuba,* 7 January 1880.

65. "El Día de Reyes," *El triunfo,* 7 January 1882. An early complaint was voiced in 1880: "Otra vez los tangos," *El triunfo,* 17 February 1880.

66. See Joan Casanovas, *Bread or Bullets! Urban Labor and Spanish Colonialism in Cuba, 1850–1898* (Pittsburgh: University of Pittsburgh Press, 1998), 131–34.

67. "El Día de Reyes," *La Prensa,* 6 January 1845.

68. "El Día de Reyes," *La Habana elegante,* 9 January 1887; Ximeno y Cruz, 2: 133–35.

69. "El Día de Reyes," *La Habana elegante,* 9 January 1887.

70. "El Día de Reyes en la Habana," *El Moro musa,* 23 February 1863.

71. "Los diablitos o el día infernal en la Habana," *Prensa de la Habana,* 6 January 1859.

72. "El Día de los Reyes en la Habana," *El abolicionista español,* 15 January 1866.

73. Beauvallet, *Rachel and the New World,* 193.

74. *La voz de Cuba*'s use of the word *bailarina,* in the original, indicates that these applauded dancers were women. "La Festividad de Reyes," *La voz de Cuba,* 7 January 1880.

75. These circles have a special name in Cuba, corro: "El Día de Reyes," *La Habana elegrante,* 9 January 1887.

76. Xavier Marmier, *Lettres sur l'Amerique.* In Pérez de Acevedo, *La Habana en el siglo XIX descrita por los viajeros.* Havana: Sociedad Editorial de Cuba Contemporanea, 1919, 34–35.

77. Fredrika Bremer, *The Homes of the New World: Impressions of America* (New York: Harper and Brothers, 1853), 2:348–49.

78. "El Día de los Reyes en la Habana," *El abolicionista español,* 15 January 1866.

Chapter Seven

1. Sachs, *World History of the Dance* (London: Allen and Unwin, 1933), 298–390.

2. A useful application of this standard rising-falling model can be found in Philip J. S. Richardson, *The Social Dances of the Nineteenth Century in England* (London: Herbert Jenkins, 1960), 18. The model usually involves a rise from peasant origins, acceptance as a courtly form, exportation to another location, and descent to the popular classes there. The most important Latin American application of this schema was done by Carlos Vega, who synthesized his ideas in *El origen de la danzas folklóricas* (Buenos Aires: Ricordi Americana, 1956). Vega sought to correct the fuzziness of the romantic "formula simplista" (p. 187) whereby Spanish folk culture, imported to America and subject to nebulous indigenous and African influences, became Latin American folk culture. Vega wanted to outline a much more specific set of processes of transmission and diffusion, operating in identifiable historical time and geographic space. Vega also downplayed the importance of cultural mestizaje, in favor of the more elitist, hispanicist Argentine nationalism of the 1930s. See especially his "Conclusions," 185–90.

3. In contrast to Latin America, early U.S. presses produced dozens of dance instruction books (and collections of dance music), at least thirty between 1794 and 1800 Blaustein, "Old-Time Fiddling and Country Dancing in North America: Some Reconsiderations," in Susan Eike Spalding and Janc Harris Woodside, eds., *Communities in Motion: Dance, Community, and Tradition in America's Southeast and Beyond,* Contributions to the Study of Music and Dancc no. 35 (Wcstport, CN: Greenwood Press, 1995), 195.

4. Luís Carlos Martins Pena, *Teatro de Martins Pena, Vol. 1: Comédias,* ed. Darcy Damasceno (Rio de Janeiro: Instituto Nacional do Livro, 1956). The examples come from separate plays: *Um sertanejo na Corte* (a fragment written between 1833 and 1837) and *A família e a Festa da Roça* (written in 1837), 65, 81.

5. W. S. W. Ruschenberg, *Three Years in the Pacific, including Notices of Brazil, Chile, Bolivia, and Peru* (Philadelphia: Carey, Lea & Blanchard, 1834), 43.

6. Maturin M. Ballou, *Due South, or Cuba Past and Present* (Boston: Houghton, Mifflin and Company, 1888), 152–53.

7. "Ortiz el músico" was a follower of Cortés who eventually opened an *escuela de danzar y de tañer* in Mexico City: Alejo Carpentier, *La música en Cuba* (Mexico City: Fondo de Cultura Económica, 1972), 22.

8. Wanderley Pinho, *Salões e damas do segundo reinado* (São Paulo: Livraria Martins, 1942), 15.

9. On Iberia see Daniel Tércio, *Dança e azulejaria no Teatro do Mundo* (Lisbon: Edições Inapa, 1999), 30–31; on Rio, Delso Renault, *O Rio antigo nos anúncios de jornais: 1808–1850* (Rio de Janeiro: José Olympio, 1969), 138, 322. (The manual was advertised in Rio's *Journal do Commercio* 22 Sept. 1836). On Cuba, see Natalio Galán, *Cuba y sus sones* (Madrid: Pre-Textos, 1983), 121. On Mexico Maya Ramos Smith, *La danza en México durante la época colonial* (Habana: Ediciones Casa de las Americas, 1979), 35.

10. Ruschenberg, *Three Years in the Pacific,* 43.

11. The remark was made by L. F. Tollenare in Pernambuco: Pinho, *Salões e damas,* 52.

12. Luís Joaquim dos Santos Marrocos, "Cartas escritas do Rio de Janeiro à sua família em Lisboa, de 1811 a 1821," in *Anais da Biblioteca Nacional* 56 (1934), quoted by Maria Beatriz Nizza da Silva, *Cultura e sociedade no Rio de Janeiro (1808–1821)* 2 ed. (Rio de Janeiro: Companhia Editôra Nacional, 1978), 97.

13. John Armitage, *The History of Brazil* (London: Smith, Elder and Co., 1836), 245.

14. Adolfo Morales de los Ríos Filho, *O Rio de Janeiro Imperial* (Rio de Janeiro: Editôra a Noite, 1946), 292–97.

15. Few travelers to Havana fail to mention this custom. See, for example, Nicolás Tanco Armero, Viaje de Nueva Granada a China y de China a Francia, (doc. 456) in Gustavo Eguren, *La fidelísima Habana* (Havana: Editorial Letras Cubanas, 1986).

16. No author. *Gan-Eden, or Pictures of Cuba* (Boston: John P. Jewitt and Co., 1854), 49.

17. Comtesse Merlin (María de las Mercedes Santa Cruz y Montalvo), *La Havane* (Paris: Aymot, 1844), 2:319.

18. Maturin M Ballou, *History of Cuba, or Notes of a Traveler in the Tropics, Being a Political, Historical, and Statistical Account of the Island, from its First Discovery to the Present Time* (Boston: Philips, Sampson, and Co., 1854), 78.

19. Juan Clemente Zenea to María Luisa Mas, quoted by Galán, *Cuba y sus sones,* 131.

20. Woodbine Parish, *Buenos Aires and the Provinces of the Río de la Plata* (London: John Murray, 1852), 118.

21. All cited by Lauro Ayestarán, whose work is essential to dance history in the Río de la Plata: *La música en el Uruguay* (Montevideo: Servicio Oficial de Difusión Radio Electrónica, 1953), 475–78.

22. Vega, *El origen de la danzas folklóricas,* 94–96.

23. Vega's account is based on José Torre Revello, "Un pleito sobre bailes entre el Cabildo y el Obispo de Buenos Aires (1746–1757), in *Boletín del Instituto de Investigaciones Históricas* 30 (October–December 1926). See also *Actas del cabildo de Buenos Aires,* série 3, vol. 1, corresponding to the sessions of 3 November 1752, 9 November 1752, 4 April 1753, 6 April 1753, and 10 July 1753.

24. Archivo General de la Nación (Buenos Aires):"Información sobre los Vayles de Máscara," 1773, IX 32.8.5. The episode in narrated is Enrique H. Puccia, *Breve historia del carnaval porteño* (Buenos Aires: Municipalidad de la Ciudad, 1974), 9–10.

25. "Idea de un buen baile," *Papel periódico de la Habana,* 25 November 1792.

26. "Señor don Joseph de la Havana," *Papel periódico de la Habana,* 9 December 1792.

27. Machado's verses ("E simples, quatro compassos/E muito sacaroteio;/Cinturas pressas nos brazos,/Gravatas cheirando o seio") appeared in the *Gazeta de noticias,* 20 January 1887. For the United States, the perceived moral threat of dance in this period is amply documented in Elizabeth Aldrich, *From the Ballroom to Hell: Grace and Folly in Nineteenth-Century Dance* (Evanston, IL: Northwestern University Press, 1991).

28. See, for example, José A. Wilde, *Buenos Aires desde setenta años atrás (1810–1880)* (Buenos Aires: Editorial Universitaria de Buenos Aires, 1960), 116.

29. The poem, which appeared in *A Revista Ilustrada,* 1881, is transcribed in Pinho, *Salões e damas,* 150.

30. Octavio C. Battolla, *La sociedad de antaño* (Buenos Aires: Emecé Editores, 2000), 193.

31. Pinho, *Salões e damas,* 77. Viewing the advent of closed-couple dances as symptomatic of a rising individualist ethic is commonplace in dance history. See, for example, Frances Rust, *Dance in Society: An Analysis of the*

Relationship between Social Dance and Society in England from the Middle Ages to the Present Day (London: Routledge & Kegan Paul, 1969).

32. Pinho, *Salões e damas,* 78.

33. Cuban evidence attests that such tiffs were a routine aspect of dances without a bastonero: "Intolerancia en los bailes," *La moda, o recreo semanal del bello sexo,* 5 March 1831.

34. The male lead, which had not been part of open-couple or interdependent couple dances, required specific comment in nineteenth-century dance manuals: "The lady should allow herself to be entirely guided by her partner, without in any case endeavoring to follow her own impulse of action": William B. DeGarmo, *The Dance of Society* (New York: William A. Pond & Co., 1875), 66.

35. "La Polka," *El faro industrial de la Habana,* 30 November 1844.

36. Ad from *El diario de la tarde* (Buenos Aires), quoted in Vega, *El origen de la danzas folklóricas,* 82.

37. See the newspaper discussed ads by Renault, *O Rio antigo (1808–1850),* 200–22.

38. "Teatro," *Diario do Rio de Janeiro,* 7 February 1846.

39. Important things are learned by not abstracting the dance from its social setting. For this reason, modern folkloric studies focus on "dance events": Susan Eike Spalding and Jane Harris Woodside, Eds. *Communities in Motion: Dance, Community, and Tradition in America's Southeast and Beyond* (Westport, CN: Greenwood Press, 1995).

40. Charles M. Pepper, *To-Morrow in Cuba* (New York: Harper & Brothers Publishers, 1899), 279–80.

41. Prince Adalbert of Prussia, *Travels in the South of Europe and in Brazil, with a Voyage up the Amazon and its Tributary, the Xingú* (London: David Bogue, Publisher, 1849).

42. William Hadfield, *Brazil and the River Plate, 1870–1876* (London: Edward Stanford, 1877), 41. The dance etiquette of the Brazilian imperial court included detailed prescriptions for dress: Nizza da Silva, *Cultura e sociedade,* 24.

43. "Baile en la Quinta de los Molinos," *El Moro Musa,* 16 August 1863.

44. Irene A. Wright, *Cuba* (New York: Macmillan Co., 1900), 73.

45. Mello Moraes Filho, *Festas e tradições populares do Brazil* (Rio de JaneiroJ/Paris: H. Garmier Livreiro, 1901), 227–36; Pinho, *Salões e damas,* 133–34.

46. Ríos Filho, *O Rio de Janeiro Imperial,* 165; Delso Renault, *O Rio de Janeiro: A vida da cidade refletida nos jornais 1850–1870* (Rio de Janeiro: Civilização Brasileira, 1978), 22.

47. Renault, *O Rio de Janeiro 1850–1870,* 75.

48. James C. Fletcher, *Brazil and the Brazilians Portrayed in Historical and Descriptive Sketches* (Boston: Little, Brown, and Company, 1868), 173.

49. Julia Ward Howe, *A Trip to Cuba* (New York: Frederick A. Praeger Publishers, 1969), 188–89.

50. Formal balls, on the other hand, began well after midnight in Buenos Aires, just as the city's nightlife does today: Thomas Woodbine Hinchliff, *South American Sketches, Or a Visit to Rio de Janeiro, the Organ Mountains, La Plata, and the Paraná* (London: Longman, Green, Roberts, & Green, 1863), 84.

51. Battolla, *La sociedad de antaño,* 195–99.

52. Pinho, *Salões e damas,* 227–28.

53. "Bailes de segundo orden," *La moda, o recreo semanal del bello sexo,* 26 June 1830.

54. "Señor público," *El Regañón de la Habana,* 23 December 1800.

55. In 1790, Lima blacks protested legally against a theater owner's attempt to keep them from dancing the minuet because "el uso de estos Bayles es improprio de su Baxa Calidad": Vega, *El origen de la danzas folklóricas,* 30. On Havana, see Fredrika Bremer, *The Homes of the New World: Impressions of America,* 2:308; Cirilo Villaverde, *Cecilia Valdés,* 440–42.

56. Héctor Vivaca, "El baile de la Alegría," *Todo es historia* 39 (1985), 80-89.

57. Tanco Armero, *Viaje de Nueva Granada a China y de China a Francia, in Eguren, La fidelísima Habana,* doc. 456.

58. Héctor y Juan L. Bates, *La historia del tango* (Buenos Aires: Talleres Gráficos de la Compañía General Fabril Financiera, 1936), 355–57.

59. Mello Moraes Filho, *Festas e tradições,* 141–53.

60. Announcement appeared 9 April 1846 in the *Diario do Rio de Janeiro:* Renault, *O Rio antigo nos anúncios de jornais: 1808–1850,* 204.

61. "Ferias," *El nuevo regañón,* 27 September 1831.

62. John Howison, *Foreign Scenes and Travelling Recreations* (1825), in Eguren, *La fidelísima Habana,* doc. 403.

63. Villaverde, *Cecilia Valdés,* 259.

64. AGN (Buenos Aires). "Expediente sobre academias de baile," 19 January 1856; "Solicitudes despachadas para establecer academias de bailes," and related papers dated around 1864: X 32-7-2.

65. "Bailes públicos," *El nacional,* 1 and 6 June 1855.

66. Archivo Nacional de Cuba (Havana). "Expediente formado sobre las adademias de baile" (1872), Fondo GG 352/16917.

67. Quoted from *O Globo* (15/9/1877) and *A gazeta de notícias* (7/3/78) by Delso Renault, *O dia-a-dia no Rio de Janeiro segundo os jornais,* 103. Two months earlier (*Jornal do Comércio,* 4/7/1877), one of these schools had advertised its wish to hire "seis moças pardas ou brancas de família para acompanhar os discípulos na arte de dança."(101) The association with

prositution was noted by *Gazeta de notícias* less than a year later (17/2/1878), 123.

68. Irene Wright, *Cuba* (New York: Macmillan, 1910), 70–71.

69. Nicolás Tanco Armero, *Viaje de Nueva Granada a China y de China a Francia,* in Eguren, *La fidelísima Habana,* doc. 456.

70. "Los bailes públicos degeneran," *El nacional,* 14 February 1872.

71. "Teatro Lyrico," *Jornal do Comércio,* 7 February and 28 February 1864.

72. "Baile mascarado," *Diario do Rio de Janeiro,* 15 February 1847; "Variedades," *O Jornal do Comércio,* 20 February 1855.

72. The terminology "rising transformation" draws on Paul Austerlitz, Merengue: *Dominican Music and Dominican Identity* (Philadelphia: Temple University Press, 1997), 15–29 and Vega, Vega, *El origen de la danzas folklóricas,* passim.

73. Carpentier, *La música en Cuba,* 62–64.

74. Ventura R. Lynch, La provincia de Buenos Aires hasta la definición *de la cuestión Capital de la república* (1883), cited by Fernando O. Assunçao *El tango y sus circunstancias*, 133–34.

75. An 1885 description of habanera dancers: "ambos unidos como un solo cuerpo seguian las ondulaciones ritmicas de la musica," from *Antología del tango rioplatense* (Buenos Aires: Instituto de Musicología "Carlos Vega," 1986), 8; and another from the Argentine countryside:"en un rancho de campana las parejas se abrazan estrechamente, las piernas se rozan sin que el pudor se resienta, los alientos caldeados se confenden, y la bailarina con su cabeza reclinada sobre el hombo de su companero, baila, completamente entregado a este . . . "Los bailes de mi pago" *Caras y Caretas,* 21 January 1899. On habanera in the creation of modern samba, see Muniz Sodré, *Samba, o dono do corpo*, 20.

76. "Ecos y murmullos," *La Habana elegrante,* 22 February 1885.

Chapter Eight

1. Maya Ramos Smith, *La danza en México durante la época colonial* (Habana: Ediciones Casa de las Americas, 1979), 43–46, 166.

2. See, for example, Carlos Vega, *El origen de la danzas folklóricas* (Buenos Aires: Ricordi Americana, 1956), 46; and. Fernando O. Assunçao, *Origenes de los bailes tradicionales en el Uruguay* (Montevideo: n.p., 1968), 131.

3. Ramos Smith, *La danza en México,* 43–44.

4. Ramos Smith, *La danza en México,* 44–45. On the interpretive problem of how, and how much, colonial morays were really changing, see Juan Pedro Viqueira Albán, *Relajados o reprimidos?: Diversiones públicas y*

vida social en la Ciudad de México durante el Siglo de las Luces (México: Fondo de Cultura Económica, 1987).

5. Archivo General de la Nación (Buenos Aires), Bandos, IX.8.10.3.

6. Mary del Priore, *Festas e utopias no Brasil colonial* (São Paulo: Editora Brasiliense, 1994), 95. The quoted lyrics are from Joaquim Manuel de Macedo, *As mulheres de mantilha* (Rio: Oficinas Graficas do Jornal do Brasil, 1931) 1: 9. Written in the 1870s but set in 1760s, this novel contains some lyrics of a lundu that Macedo (who knew) says was widely sung and applauded: "E hei de cantar/E hei de dançar/Saracotear/Com as moças brincar/E impunemente/Cantando o lundu/Ao bispo furente/Direi uh! uh! uh!" In his 1780 satire *Cartas Chilenas,* the poet Tomás Antônio Gonzaga comments on the rise of lundu in Vila Rica, saying that the dance had gone from bare feet on the ground to treading the polished floors of mansions: "Agora ja consegues ter entrada/nas casas mas honestas e palacios": quoted by José Ramos Tinhorão, *Fado: dança do Brasil, cantar de Lisboa* (Lisbon: Caminho, 1994), 41.

7. Priore quotes the Conde de Pavloide, *Festas e utopias,* 56–57.

8. The traveler (writing of Bahia in the 1830s) was Ferdinand Denis: Fryer, *Rhythms of Resistance,* 123.

9. Thomas Lindley, *Narrative of a Voyage to Brasil* (London: J. Johnson, 1805), 276–77.

10. A traveler's 1814–1815 description of what he calls "batuco" reveals the similarity with lundu: "Os dançadores formam roda, e ao compasso de uma viola move-se o dançador no centro, avança, e bate com a barriga na barriga do outro da roda, de ordinário pessoa de outro sexo. No começo, o compasso da música é lento, porém, pouco a pouco aumenta e o dançador do centro é substituído cada vez que dá uma embigada; e assim passam noites inteiras." G.W. Freireyss, "Viagem ao interior do Brasil nos anos de 1814–1815," *Revista do Institututo histórico e Geográfico de São Paulo* vol. 11, quoted by Beatriz Nizza da Silva, *Cultura e sociedade no Rio de Janeiro (1808–1821),* 80.

11. The interesting pamphlet *Relação da fofa que veio agora da Bahia* (circa 1750, author: "CMMB") is further discussed in chapter ten. Peter Fryer, *Rhythms of Resistance,* 127, provides a full translation of the key passage. See José Ramos Tinhorão, *Música popular de índios, negros, e mestiços* (Petrópolis: Editôra Vozes, 1972), 126. On the *Folheto de ambas Lisboas* (1730), see his *Fado,* 23.

12. *Os Casadinhos da Moda* (1784) is quoted at length by Tinhorão, *Fado,* 40.

13. Louis Claude Desaulces de Freycinet and Carl Schlichthorst quoted in Tinhorão, *Fado,* 50, 53–54.

14. Júlio Dantas, *Lisboa dos nossos avós* (Lisbon: Câmara Municipal de Lisboa, 1966), 182; Fryer, *Rhythms of Resistance,* 101.

15. L. F. Tollenare, *Notas dominicais,* trad. Alfredo de Carvalho (Recife: Secretaria de Educação e Cultura de Pernambuco, 1978) was in Bahia in 1817. Cited in Tinhorão, *Música popular,* 141.

16. Tollenare, *Notas dominicais,* cited in Emanuel Araújo, *O teatro dos vícios,* 129.

17. Tinhorão, *Música popular,* 143. Finally, one more of Tinhorão's works is essential on Brazil's early national dances: *A música popular no romance brasileiro,* vol. 1: *Século XVIII–Século XIX* (Belo Horizonte: Oficina de Livros, 1992).

18. Tinhorão, *Música popular,* 139.

19. Luís Carlos Martins Pena, *Teatro de Martins Pena, Vol. 1,* 35–36 and 44–45.

20. From O Carapuceiro (17 February 1838), quoted in Baptista Siqueira, *Origem do termo samba* (Brasilia: Instituto Nacional do Livro, 1978), 101.

21. Manuel Antônio de Almeida, *Memórias de um sargento de milícias* (Rio: Imprensa Nacional, 1944), 40.

22. Jose Maria Velho da Silva, *Gabriella, chrónica dos tempos coloniais* (Rio de Janeiro, 1875), 24–25.

23. Andrews, *The Afro-Argentines of Buenos Aire,* 97; see also Puccia, *Breve historia del carnaval porteño,* 34. On Uruguay, see *Descripción de las fiestas cívicas celebradas en la capital de los pueblos orientales el veinte y cinco de mayo de 1816* (Montevideo, 1816), 11.

24. Vicente Quesada, *Memorias de un viejo* (1942), quoted in Hugo E Ratier, "Candombes porteños," in *Arqueología, Antropología cultural, Etnología* (VICUS Cuadernos) 1 (1977), 129.

25. "Yo me llamo Juana Peña," *La negrita,* 21 July 1833.

26. The zamacueca, like the other bailecitos del país, had originally developed on the Pacific coast of South America and had gradually disseminated throughout the Andean region, including western Argentina, by the early 1700s. But nearer the eastern coast of the continent, zamacueca and other bailecitos del país had been eclipsed, in the late 1700s, by newer dances (like contradance) arriving from the Atlantic side. On the bailecitos del país, see the articles collected in Carlos Vega, *Danzas populares,* vol. 2 (Buenos Aires: Ministerio de Educación y Justicia, 1986), reprint of a 1952 original.

27. Vega, *Danzas populares,* 1:375–76.

28. Vega, *Danzas populares,* 1:378.

29. Vega, *Danzas populares,* 1:296, quoting Basil Hall, *Extracts from a*

Journal Written on the Coasts of Chili, Peru, and Mexico in the Years 1820, 1821, 1822 (1824).

30. Maria Graham, *Journal of a Residence in Chile during the Year 1822 and Voyage from Chile to Brazil in 1823* (New York: Frederick A. Praeger, 1969), 216–17. In Chile, post-independence politics would mostly abandon the populist themes upon which the Argentine dictator Rosas continued to harp through the 1830s and 1840s.

31. Lauro Ayestarán y Flor de María Rodríguez de Ayestarán, *El minué montonero* (Montevideo: Ediciones de la Banda Oriental, 1965); and Assunçao, *El origen de los bailes folklóricos,* 131.

32. Vega, *Danzas populares,* 1:149–290.

33. In fact, the first published cielito on record is entitled "Cielitos que con acompañamiento de guitarra cantaban los soldados del ejército patriota frente a las murallas de Montevideo": Francisco Acuña de Figueroa, *Diario histórico del sitio de Montevideo en los años 1812, 1813, 1814* (Montevideo, 1890), 2:218; quotation is from Lauro Ayestarán, "El cielito," *El día,* suplemento dominical, 23 mayo 1948.

34. Vega, citing a Legajo del Ejército de los Andes in the Archivo General de la Nación: *Danzas populares,* 1:177–78.

35. *El gaucho* (Buenos Aires), written largely by Luis Pérez: "Invitación del Gaucho a sus compatriotas" and "Cielito compuesto por el Gaucho para cantar en la fiesta de Chanonga," 11 Dec. 1830; and "Cielito compuesto por una vieja unitaria que se emborrachó de la rabia cuando le dieron la orden de barrer la calle para que pasase la Changonga," 15 December 1830.

36. Vega, *Danzas populares,* 1:259–60, 277.

37. Esteban Echeverría, "El matadero," in *Orígenes de la novela argentina* (Buenos Aires: Instituto de Literatura Argentina, 1926).

38. *El gaucho,* 31 July 1830–29 December 1831, passim.

39. Manuel Bilbao, *Tradiciones y recuerdos de Buenos Aires* (1934), cited by Vega, *Las danza populares argentinas,* 1:213. Arsene quoted 2:269.

40. Alcide D'Orbigny (1827), quoted by Vega in *Las danza populares argentinas,* 1:156.

41. Vega, *Las danza populares argentinas,* 1:151–54.

42. "Teatro," *El diario de la tarde,* 17 February 1835.

43. "Jardín del Retiro" and "Circo Olímpico," *El diario de la tarde,* 23 January 1840 and 1 April 1844.

44. An alternative last number was another oldie, a cielito, recalled an 1881 memoir: José A. Wilde, *Buenos Aires desde setenta años atrás 1810–1880* (Buenos Aires: Editorial Universitaria de Buenos Aires, 1960), 116.

45. María Esther Podestá, *Desde ya y sin interrupciones (Memorias),* ed.

Jorge Miguel Couselo (Buenos Aires: Corregidor, [1985]), 37.

46. Vega, *Las danza populares argentinas,* 1:220–26. The quotation is from a 1906 article by Juan Pablo Echagüe.

47. James J. O'Kelly, *The Mambi-Land, or Adventures of a Herald Correspondent in Cuba* (Philadelphia: J.B.Lippincot and Co., 1874), 221–22.

48. Louis A. Pérez, Jr., *Cuba: Between Reform and Revoluion* (Oxford: Oxford University Press, 1988), 100–4.

49. Fernando Ortiz, *Los bailes y el teatro de los negros en el folklore de Cuba* (Havana: Editorial de las Letras Cubanas, 1985), 266, quoting G. D'Harponville D'Hespel, *La Reine des Antilles* (1850).

50. Francis Robert Jameson, "Cartas habaneras," doc. 394 in Eguren, *La fidelísima Habana.*

51. "Academia de baile," *Faro industrial de la Habana,* 29 Sept. 1842.

52. The evidence on this point is abundant. See, for example: "Crónica," *El moro musa,* 5 February 1860.

53. Comtesse Merlin (María de las Mercedes Santa Cruz y Montalvo), *La Havane.* 3 vols. (Paris: Aymot, 1844), 2:59–60.

54. "El Lugareño," 1838, and the entry for bolanchera in Pichardo's dictionary are quoted by Natalio Galán, *Cuba y sus sones* (Madrid: Pre-Textos, 1983), 47, 165.

55. Madame Angiolini, *Divertisement dansant formant six contradances des diferentes nations avec figures caracteristiques* (Paris, 1811) cited by Galán, 116–17.

56. Paul Austerlitz uses the term Afro-Caribbean contradance transformations for these homologous forms that arise from African influence on contradance. See his highly informed *Merengue: Dominican Music and Dominican Identity* (Philadelphia: Temple University Press, 1997), 15–29.

57. Only lateral movements (driven by the hips) and not vertical movement (driven by the knees) created friction on the floor to make this noise. Galán, *Cuba y sus sones,* does an excellent, detailed study of the transformation in the chapter "Contradanza sin contra," 119–214. See also Alejo Carpentier, *La música en Cuba.*

58. Cited by Galán, *Cuba y sus sones,* 135.

59. Cited by Galán, *Cuba y sus sones,* 126.

60. Tanco Armero, Viaje de Nueva Granada a China, doc. 456 in Eguren, *La fidelísima Habana.*

61. Quoted by Galán, *Cuba y sus sones,* 128.

62. Antonio de la Barra y Prado, *La Habana a mediados del Siglo XIX* (Madrid, 1926).

63. The last phrase is "el eco del tambor de los Tangos" in the original. Felix Tanco to Domingo del Monte, 1837, cited by Galán, *Cuba y sus sones.*

64. Luis Victoriano Betancourt, "El baile," in *Costumbristas cubanos del siglo XIX* (Caracas: Biblioteca Ayacucho, 1985), 364.

65. "Las bodas," *Guirnalda cubana: Periódico quincenal de literatura, moral, artes, teatros, música, modas, etc., con grabados y litografías, dedicado al bello secso,* 1854: 89–91.

66. Galán, *Cuba y sus sones,* 125–50.

67. "Sobre el baile," *Revista habanera,* 1861: 15–27.

68. Ibid.

69. "El baile," *Album cubano de lo bueno y lo bello,* 1860: 370–73.

70. "De las bailadoras y de los bailadores," *Faro Industrial de la Habana,* 1 December 1842.

71. Cirilo Villaverde, *Cecilia Valdés o la loma del ángel,* ed. and notes by Esteban Rodríguez Herrera (Havana: Editorial Lex-Habana, 1953), 84.

72. Betancourt, "El baile," in *Costumbristas cubanos,* 368.

73. "No hay virilidad?" *El palenque literário* (1882), 3:473-74.

74. Tanco Armero, *Viaje de Nueva Granada* (doc. 456) in Eguren, *La fidelísima Habana.*

75. See, for example, the program listed for "Grande Pavilhão Fluminense," *Jornal do Comércio* (Rio de Janeiro), 15 February 1863. Montonero minuets and cielitos had their day in Buenos Aires under Rosas, but they never dominated dance programs as utterly as danza did in Havana. See the routine social chronicle "Remitido: Gran Baile del miercoles," *El Liceo de la Habana,* 17 November 1857, that gave the program as "six danzas, two polkas, and a series of lancers."

76. Galán, *Cuba y sus sones,* 158.

77. So strong was the rejection of Spain, in fact, that U.S. culture was more easily elided into "Cuban." See Louis A. Pérez, Jr., *On Becoming Cuban: Identity, Nationality, and Culture* (Chapel Hill: University of North Carolina Press, 1999).

78. Ada Ferrer, *Insurgent Cuba: Race, Nation, and Revolution, 1868–1898* (Chapel Hill: University of North Carolina Press, 1999), 31.

Chapter Nine

1. The "Introduction" by Paul Spencer, ed. *Society and the Dance: The Social Anthropology of Process and Performance* (Cambridge: Cambridge University Press, 1985), 1–39, surveys diverse social functions of dance. He finds the study of dance still undeveloped even within anthropology. For

a world-historical view of dance, see William H. McNeill, *Keeping Together in Time: Dance and Drill in Human History* (Cambridge: Harvard University Press, 1995).

2. Susan Leigh Foster, ed., theorizes the importance of dance in the historical study of the body (from Norbert Elias and Bakhtin to Barthes and Foucault) and concludes that "dance, more than any other body-centered endeavor, cultivates a body that initiates as well as responds": *Choreographing History* (Bloomington and Indianapolis: Indiana University Press, 1995), 15. No matter how refracted by the character of the evidence, the study of dance history offers a privileged view of popular agency.

3. Frances George Very, *The Spanish Corpus Christi Procession: A Literary and Folkloric Study* (Valencia [Spain]: Tipografía Moderna, 1962), 7–8.

4. Anna Ivanova, *The Dance in Spain* (New York: Praeger Publishers, 1970), 35–45.

5. José Sasportes, *História da dança em Portugal* (Lisboa: Fundação Calouste Gulbenkian, 1970), 48.

6. Quoted from Garcia de Resende, *Crónica de D. João II,* in Sasportes, *História da dança em Portugal,* 63.

7. Sasportes, *História da dança em Portugal,* 65.

8. Adolfo Morales de los Ríos Filho, *O Rio de Janeiro Imperial* (Rio de Janeiro: Editôra *A Noite,* 1946), 29.

9. Puccia, *Breve historia del carnaval porteño,* 7.

10. Francisco Calmon, *Relacão das faustissimas festas que celebrou a Câmara da Vila de Nossa Senhora da Purificação e Santo Amaro da comarca da Bahia pelos augustíssimos desponsórios da Sereníssima senhora dona Maria , princesa do Brasil com o Sereníssima senhor dom Pedro, infante do Portugal* (Lisboa, 1762) is an excellent example of the written commemorations that extended the reach of public rituals. It has been republished as *Relação das Faustissimas Festas (reprodução Fac-similar da edição de 1762),* Introduction and notes by Oneyda Alvarenga (Rio de Janeiro: FUNARTE/INF, 1982).

11. *Pregão para as Reaes Festas do Feliz Nascimento do Sereníssimo Príncipe da Beira, que faz celebrar nesta Cidade Sua Alteza o Sereníssimo Senhor D. Gaspar. Portugal velho representa a Farsa trajado, e vestido à antiga, a cavalo no Drago, timbre de suas Armas, acompanhamento de arcabuzeiros, e caixas militares* (Lisbon: Na Offic. De Antonio Vicente da Silva, 1761) and *Epanáfora festiva, ou relação sumária das Festas, com que na Cidade do Rio de Janeiro Capital do Brasil se celebra o Feliz Nascimento do Sereníssimo Príncipe da Beira Nosso Senhor* (Lisbon: Offic. de Manoel Rodríguez, 1763) are discussed in Daniel Tércio, *Dança e azulejaria no Teatro do Mundo* (Lisbon: Edições Inapa, 1999), 68–69.

12. *Relação dos obsequiosos festejos que se firmou na cidade de S. Sebastião do Rio de Janeiro pela plausível notícia do nascimento do Sereníssimo Senhor Principe da Beira o Senhor D. José,* (Oficina de Francisco Luiz Ameno, 1763), quoted by del Priore, *Festas e utopias no Brasil colonial,* 50–51.

13. A. C. de C. M. Saunders, *A Social History of Black Slaves and Freedmen in Portugal, 1441–1555* (Cambridge: Cambridge University Press, 1982), 22–33.

14. José Sasportes argues that this tendency carried over from pre-Christian Iberian customs: Sasportes, *História da dança,* 61–75.

15. The occasion was Valladolid's birthday celebrations for the future Spanish sovereign Felipe IV: Sasportes, *História da dança,* 136–37.

16. The traveler reported the following lyrics: "Quem com o santo quiser sarar/Ao santo ha-de bailar." Sasportes, *História da dança,* 171–72.

17. The setting was a town in Pernambuco, 1838: Tinhorão, *Música popular de indios, negros, e mestiços,* 144.

18. Pierre Verger, "Procissões e carnaval no Brasil," in *Estudos Afro-Orientais Ensaios/Pesquisas* 5 (1980), 8–9. Mary del Priore, *Festas e utopias no Brasil colonial,* 100–1.

19. Cordeiro da Matta's Ensaio de Dicionario Kimbundu-Portugués identifies kilundu as a secondary divinity responsible for a person's destiny. Tinhorão believes this to be the origin of calundu: José Ramos Tinhorão, *Fado,* 27.

20. For an overview, see Joseph M. Murphy, *Working the Spirit: Ceremonies of the African Diaspora* (Boston: Beacon Press, 1994).

21. João José Reis, *Slave Rebellion in Brazil: The Muslim Uprising of 1835 in Bahia,* trans. by Arthur Brakel (Baltimore: Johns Hopkins University Press, 1993), 126. Fryer, *Rhythms of Resistance,* 59–60, transcribes at length the fascinating mid-1860s description by the cited traveler, who was none other than the soon-to-be Emperor of Mexico, Maximilian.

22. Saunders, *A Social History of Black Slaves and Freedmen,* 152.

23. Ortiz, *Los cabilidos y la fiesta afrocubanos del Día de Reyes,* 67.

24. Sasportes, *História da dança,* 58; Saunders, *A Social History of Black Slaves and Freedmen,* 106.

25. "O baile dos pretos legítimos," *Jornal do Comercio* (Lisbon), 24 January 1863; and Luís Edmundo, *O Rio de Janeiro do meu tempo.* 2 ed. (Rio de Janeiro: Conquista, 1957), 262.

26. Congo nations were notably numerous and vigorous throughout the diaspora. Interestingly, when an umbrella organization for Cuban cabildos functioned briefly in the 1890s, it requested permission to use the Congo flag, a gold star on a blue field, as recognized by an 1885 treaty between Spain and the Congo. Ortiz, *Los cabildos y la fiesta*

afrocubanos, 15–16.

27. John K. Thornton, *The Kongolese Saint Anthony: Dona Beatriz Kimpa Vita and the Antonian Movement, 1684–1706* (Cambridge: Cambridge University Press, 1998), 33–35, 62–63.

28. Saunders, *A Social History of Black Slaves and Freedmen,* 106.

29. Saunders, *A Social History of Black Slaves and Freedmen,* 150. The *Anatómico Jocoso of Friar Lucas de Santa Catarina (1660–1740)* describes a later celebration for Nossa Senhora do Cabo in which blacks do a "dança das flechas." Tinhorão, *Os negros em Portugal: Uma presença silenciosa* (Lisbon: Caminho, 1988), 159.

30. The vilancicos in question are from the Diogo Barbosa Machado collection, quoted by Tinhorão, *Os negros em Portugal,* 151.

31. The censure came from Bernardes, *Exercicios espirituais* (Lisbon, 1731), quoted by Priore, *Festas e utopias,* 93.

32. Matos describes a dance-of-two, apparently in the third quarter of the seventeenth century, in which all the dancers are mulatas: "No grande dia do Amparo/Estando as mulatas todas/Entre festas e entre bodas/Un caso sucedeu raro: /Macotinha a foliana/Bailou rebolando o cu/Duas horas com Jelu, /Mulata tambem bailona. /Se não quando outra putona/Tomou posse do terreiro/E porque ao seu pandeiro/Não quis Macota sair/Outra saiu a renhir . . .": Priore, *Festas e utopias,* 112.

33. *Constituições primeiras do Arcebispado da Bahia* (1720), cited by Priore, *Festas e utopias,* 93.

34. On the general importance of processions in public festivities, see Emanuel Araújo, *O teatro dos vícios: Transgressão e transigência na sociedade urbana colonial* (Rio de Janeiro: José Olympio, 1993), 130–37. By Araujo's estimate, about a quarter of the days of the year were given over to Catholic festas in colonial Brazil (32).

35. Machado wrote in the *Diário do Rio de Janeiro,* 16 February 1869, quoted by Delso Renault, *O Rio de Janeiro: A vida da cidade refletida nos jornais 1850–1870* (Rio de Janeiro: Civilização Brasileira, 1978).

36. A German visitor of 1797 (Link) said that the Portuguese "follow a procession with the same pleasure with which one attends the opera." See Júlio Dantas, *Lisboa dos nossos avós* (Lisbon: Câmara Municipal de Lisboa, 1966), 265.

37. Tinhorão quotes this folheto de cordel in *Fado,* 32.

38. Sasportes, *História da dança,* 71.

39. Dantas, *Lisboa dos nossos avós,* 35–36.

40. Tinhorão, *Os negros em Portugal,* 162.

41. Nina Epton, *Spanish Fiestas (Including Romerías, Excluding Bullfights)* (London: Cassell & Co., 1968), 92.

42. Antonio del Rocío Romero Abao, "Las fiestas de Sevilla en el Siglo XV," in *Las fiestas de Sevilla en el Siglo XV y otros estudios,* Centro de Estudios e Investigación de la Religiosidad Andaluza (Madrid: Editorial Deimos, 1991), 83.

43. Sasportes, *História da dança,* 67.

44. See Very, *The Spanish Corpus Christi Procession,* 23–50; and Antonio del Rocío Romero Abao, "Las fiestas de Sevilla en el Siglo XV," 84.

45. Lynn Matluck Brooks, *The Dances of the Processions of Seville in Spain's Golden Age,* Teatro del Siglo de Oro/ Estudios de literatura 4 (Kassel: Edition Reichenberger, 1988), 156–61, (quotation) 188. Brooks meticulous work has informed my entire discussion of Corpus.

46. Brooks, *Dances of the Processions,* 189. Substantial monetary prizes were sometimes awarded to the best invenciones: Romero Abao, "Las fiestas de Sevilla en el Siglo XV," 97.

47. Brooks, *Dances of the Processions,* 186.

48. Juan de Navarro Esquivel, *Discursos sobre el arte del danzado* (Madrid: Patronato del Instituto Nacional del Libro Español, 1947), 24.

49. From Lope de Vega's *Entremés del letrado,* quoted in Very, *The Spanish Corpus Christi Procession,* 85.

50. " . . . se acordó que el dias de Corpus Christi biene presto e que para aquel día e cosas conbinientes al servicio de Dios nuestro Señor que en la procesión e fiesta que se ficiere que aya algunos regocijos e fiesta mandaron que para lo susodicho todos los oficiales como con sastres carpinteros sapateros ferreros e calafates saquen invenciones e juegos para aquel dia e que para ello se junten con pedro castilla el qual les dará la horden de como lo an de façer e repartir e ansi mismo acordaron que los negros horros se junten a ayudar a la dicha fiesta conforme a como les mandare el dicho pedro castilla con su invension lo qual se mandó se pregone por que venga a noticia de todos e ninguno pretenda ynorancia." Extract from a Havana cabildo session of 10 April 1573, doc. 121 in Gustavo Eguren, *La fidelísima Habana* (Havana: Editorial Letras Cubanas, 1986).

51. The band was so busy that its services had to be arranged far in advance and were quite costly. See doc. 262 in Eguren, *La fidelísima Habana.* The source is a contemporary chronicle whose source Eguren identifies incompletely as H. de la Parra, *Protocolo de antiguedades,* 1:219.

52. Libro de Acuerdos del Cabildo de Montevideo, 7 May 1760, published in *La revista del archivo general administrativo* (1887), 3:51 quoted by Lauro Ayestarán, *La música en el Uruguay* (Montevideo: Servicio Oficial de Difusión Radio Electrónica, 1953), 65.

53. Delso Renault, *O Rio antigo nos anúncios de jornais: 1808–1850* (Rio

de Janeiro: José Olympio, 1969), 22; and Vivaldo Coaracy, *Memórias da cidade do Rio de Janeiro* (Rio de Janeiro: Livraria José Olympio Editora, 1955), 440.

54. Mello Moraes Filho, *Festas e tradições populares do Brazil,* (Rio de Janeiro: H. Garmier Livreiro, 1901), 247–54.; Jean-Batist Debret, *Viagem pitoresca e histórica ao Brasil* (São Paulo, 1949), 2:39.

55. See Araújo, *O teatro dos vícios,* 133; and Tinhorão, *Música popular de indios, negros, e mestiços,* 152.

56. For a critique of the normal emphasis on carnivalesque inversion, see Samuel Kinser, *Carnival, American Style: Mardi Gras at New Orleans and Mobile* (Chicago and London: University of Chicago Press, 1990), 6–7. On the lower body, see Mikhail Bakhtin, *Rabelais and His World,* trans. Helene Iswolsky (Cambridge: MIT Press, 1968), 395. Maria Isaura Pereira de Queiroz, *Carnaval brasileiro: o vivido e o mito* (São Paulo: Editora Brasiliense, 1992), 212–15, suggests a move away from emphasis on carnival's supposedly universal characteristics to concentrate on local particularities.

57. See chapter 3, "Actos propios del carnaval," in Julio Caro Baroja, *El carnaval (Análisis histórico-cultural)(Madrid: Taurus, 1965),* 47–66. In Portugal and Brazil, these pre-Lenten activities were called entrudo rather than *carnaval.*

58. While no direct link can be detected, the phenomenon of Beni dancing suggests the possibility of African inspirations for this modality of festive organization. See T[erence] O. Ranger, *Dance and Society in Eastern Africa, 1890–1970* (Berkeley and Los Angeles: University of California Press, 1975).

59. Priore, *Festas e utopias,* 13–14; and Luís Edmundo, *O Rio de Janeiro no tempo do vice-reis* (Rio de Janeiro: Conquista, 1956), 280–90.

60. On the *festa do divino* in Rio province, see Mello Moraes Filho, *Festas e tradições,* 45–57. This sort of activity was also used to raise money for celebrations in Spanish America. A late example is described in Elena Poniatowska, *Todo empezó el domingo,* illus. Alberto Bertrán (Mexico City: Editorial Oceano, 1997), 190.

61. Mello Moraes Filho, *Festas e tradições,* 167–84.

62. Coaracy, *Memórias da cidade do Rio de Janeiro,* 420–23.

63. Caro Baroja found "Indians" clearing the way for a carnival procession in seventeenth-century Spain, just as they still did in Rio de Janeiro, ca. 1900: *El carnaval,* 122.

64. Various sorts of evangelical theater were employed by Spanish and Portuguese missionaries among indigenous Americans in the 1500s and thereafter. See Smith, *La danza en México durante la época colonial,* 16; and

Tércio, *Dança e azulejaria no Teatro do Mundo*, 28.

65. Nieves de Hoyos Sancho, *Las fiestas del Corpus Christi,* Temas Españoles no. 429 (Madrid: Publicaciones Españolas, 1963), 6–7; and Very, *The Spanish Corpus Christi Procession,* 11.

66. Very, *The Spanish Corpus Christi Procession,* 14; and Tércio, *Dança e azulejaria,* highlights theatrical evidence throughout.

67. Ivanova, *The Dance in Spain,* 60–61.

68. Ramos Smith, *La danza en México,* 47–48.

69. Ivanova, *The Dance in Spain,* 77.

70. Ramos Smith, *La danza en México,* 82.

71. Puccia, *Breve historia del carnaval porteño,* 9–10.

72. Carpentier, *La música en Cuba*, 228–30.

73. Edmundo, *O Rio de Janeiro no tempo do vice-reis,* 525–29.

74. Mello Moraes Filho, *Festas e tradições populares,* 175–81.

Chapter Ten

1. Maya Ramos Smith, *La danza en México durante la época colonial* (Habana: Ediciones Casa de las Americas, 1979, 28–35. In the mid 1600s, it was common for both musicians and dance masters in Mexico City to be black men.

2. From Peter Fryer, *Rhythms of Resistance: African Musican Heritage in Brazil* (Hanover, NH: University Press of New England, 2000), 86.

3. A.C. de C. M. Saunders, *A Social History of Black Slaves and Freedmen in Portugal, 1441–1555* (Cambridge: Cambridge University Press, 1982), 105. Many names were applied more or less generically to the dancing of African slaves during this period. Calenda and chica, for example, seem to have been identical. On overlapping names, see Guerra, *Calibán danzante,* 116.

4. See Jean-Baptiste Labat, *Voyage aux Iles de lÁmerique (Antilles), 1693–1705* (Paris: Seghers, 1979), 206–7. (The description here has been slightly abridged. A good translation of the full passage is available in Fryer, *Rhythms of Resistance,* 113–14.) Kissing is a clear evidence of European influence. "A kiss before and after the dance was the usual custom in the fifteenth and sixteenth-century Europe": See Curt Sachs, *World History of the Dance* (New York: W. W. Norton, 1937), 89.

5. We proceed now largely through inferences leveraged by evidence in earlier chapters. The most important, enabling argument, advanced over the course of the book, is that a Latin American tradition of transgressive dance can be identified by the presence of these two elements: European couple choreography and African-influenced

movement of the lower body.

6. For well-informed speculation about African religious belief in early Latin America, see John Thornton, *Africa and Africans in the Making of the Atlantic World*. 2nd ed. (Cambridge: Cambridge Univ. Press, 1998), 228.

7. Labat, *Voyage aux Iles de lÁmerique,* 206; Fryer, *Rhythms of Resistance,* 113–14.

8. Quoted in José Ramos Tinhorão, *Fado: dança do Brasil, cantar de Lisboa* (Lisbon: Caminho, 1994), 27.

9. The "meneos" mentioned by Mariana were noticed by many others. In fact, meneos defined *zarabanda* in the seventeenth-century Covarrubias *Tesoro de la lengua castellanda o española.* See Lynn Matluck Brooks, *The Dances of the Processions of Seville*, 34, 199.

10. Ramos Smith, *La danza en México,* 40.

11. Quoth Juan de Mariana: "Entre otros ha salido estos años un baile o cantar, tan lascivo en las palabras, tan feo en los meneos, que basta para pegar fuego a las personas muy honestas," from "Del baile y cantar llamado Zarabanda," in Mariana's *Tratado contra los juegos públicos.* See Ramos Smith, *La danza en México,* 37–39, 54; and "Sátira hecha por Mateo Rosas de Oquendo a las Cosas que Pasan en el Pirú. Año de 1598," cited by Robert Morell Stevenson in *Music in Aztec and Inca Territory* (Berkeley: University of California Press, 1968).

12. Emilio Cotarelo y Mori, *Colección de entremeses, loas, bailes, jacaras, y mojigangas desde fines del siglo XVI a mediados del XVIII, facsimile* (Granada: Universidad de Granada, 2000), 1:229; and Matluck Brooks, *The Dances of the Processions of Seville,* 199–200, 298–99.

13. Ramos Smith, *La danza en México,* 38–40.

14. G. de Resende, *Miscellanea,* stanza six (1554), quoted in Saunders, *A Social History of Black Slaves and Freedmen in Portugal,* 4. An official Portuguese commercial monopoly on the West African coast was granted by Pope Nicholas V in 1455. Reexport of slaves from Portugal to Spain began as early as 1462. In the early 1500s, about as many were re-exported to Sevilla and Valencia—very roughly 1000 yearly—as stayed in Portugal. (Direct imports to Spain were prohibited.) Around 1550, roughly 3000 a year were arriving in the Antilles, tiny numbers compared with the 1700s. See Saunders, 22–23; and Thornton, *Africa and Africans in the Making of the Atlantic World,* 155.

15. Vogt, *Portuguese Rule on the Gold Coast, 1469–1682* (Athens, GA: University of Georgia Press, 1979), 182.

16. José Maria Semedo and Maria R. Turano, *Cabo Verde: O ciclo ritual das festividades da tabanca* (Praia: Spleen Edições, 1997), 59–74: and Richard A. Lobban, Jr. *Cape Verde: Crioulo Colony to Independent Nation*

(Boulder: Westview Press, 1995), 58–59, 76–77.

17. Tinhorão links the arrival of these dances in Portugal to slaves brought from Brazil by gold-rich Brazilian families. Previously almost all black slaves in Portugal were brought from Africa: *Fado,* 26–35.

18. On the *Account of the Fofa (Relação da fofa que veio agora da Bahia,* circa 1750, author: "CMMB"), in addition to José Ramos Tinhorão, *Música popular de índios, negros, e mestiços* (Petrópolis: Editôra Vozes, 1972), 126, see *Fado,* 22–23, 39; and Júlio Dantas, *Lisboa dos nossos avós* (Lisbon: Câmara Municipal de Lisboa, 1966), 182.

19. Daniel Tércio, *Dança e azulejaria no Teatro do Mundo,* 47–48; and Dantas, *Lisboa dos nossos avós,* 261–65.

20. Open couple courtship dances did probably exist in 1500s Africa (they exist now), and dance movement of the hips was probably not unknown in Europe. An open-couple dance of Chad's Sara people is depicted in Michel Huet, *The Dances of Africa* (New York: Harry N. Abrams, 1996), 104. The point is not the absolute uniqueness of couple dance to Europe or an undulating torso to Africa, but rather, that couple dance was characteristic Europe and rare in Africa, just as the undulating torso was characteristic in Africa and rare in Europe.

21. Wade, *Music, Race, and Nation,* especially chapter three, "Origin Myths: The Historiography of Costeño Music," 53–66; Richard Parker, *Bodies, Pleasures, Passions* (Beacon Press, 1992), esp. "Myths of Origin" 7–29.

22. This aspect of the discussion draws on Roland Barthes, *Mythologies* (Hill and Wang, New York, 1972).

23. For example, see Michael George Hanchard, *Orpheus and Power: The Movimento Negro of Rio de Janeiro and Sao Paulo, 1945–1988* (Princeton: Princeton University Press, 1994) or Jeffrey L. Gould, *To Die in This Way: Nicaraguan Indians & the Myth of the Mestizaje, 1880–1960* (Durham: Duke University Press, 1998).

24. Alejandro de la Fuente, "Myths of Racial Democracy: Cuba, 1900–1912," *Latin American Research Review* 34 (1999):43. Note that de la Fuente is describing a position that he does not himself endorse.

25. Paul Gilroy, *The Black Atlantic: Modernity and Double Consciousness* (Cambridge: Harvard University Press, 1993), 2. Gilroy's overarching emphasis on the constant transmutation of diasporic culture, in contrast to a supposed primordial African purity, is fully consonant with the view presented here. See especially his chapter three, on "Black Music and the Politics of Authenticity," 72–110.

26. See Néstor García Canclini, *Hybrid Cultures: Strategies for Entering and Leaving Modernity,* trans. Christopher L. Chiappari and Silvia L.

López (Minneapolis: University of Minnesota Press, 1995) and (for discussion of "transculturation" in this context) Fernando Coronil, "Introduction to the Duke University Press Edition," in *Cuban Counterpoint: Tobacco and Sugar* (Durham and London: Duke University Press, 1995).

27. Alejandro de la Fuente, "Myths of Racial Democracy," 46–47.

28. Examples abound in Latin America. The samba lyrics of Ari Barroso constitute a particularly salient and influential case: Lisa Shaw, *The Social History of the Brazilian Samba 1930–1945* (Aldershot, UK: Ashgate Publishing Ltd., 1999), 168–79.

29. See, for example, Vera Kutzinski, *Sugar's Secrets: Race and the Erotics of Cuban Nationalism* (Charlottesville: University of Virginia Press, 1993), 21.

30. Alma Guillermoprieto, *Samba* (New York: Vintage Departures, 1991), 180.

31. Jean-Baptiste Labat, *Voyage aux Iles de l'Amérique (Antilles) 1693–1705,* 155.

32. Rarely can such matters be quantified statistically. An exception is Sueann Caulfield's study of early twentieth-century deflowering trials in Rio, where she found that men reluctant to marry women they had deflowered were of lighter skin color in two thirds of the cases: *In Defense of Honor: Sexual Morality, Modernity, and Nation in Twentieth-Century Brazil* (Durham, NC: Duke University Press, 2000), 162. For an interesting discussion of the phenomenon in contemporary Brazil, see Robin E. Sheriff, *Dreaming Equality: Color, Race, and Racism in Urban Brazil* (New Brunswick: Rutgers University Press, 2001), 135-43.

33. Héctor Vivaca, "El baile de la Alegría," quotes *La broma,* 3 Sept. 1879, in *Todo es historia* 39 (1985), 88.

34. José Ramos Tinhorão, *A música popular no romance brasileiro,* vol. 1: *Século XVIII–Século XIX* (Belo Horizonte: Oficina de Livros, 1992).

35. Peter Stallybrass and Allon White, *The Politics and Poetics of Transgression* (London: Methuen, 1986), 193.

Index